CANADA

UNITED STATES

MEXICO

Bahamas

Cuba

Puerto Rico

Jamaica   Haiti

Dominica

St Lucia

Barbados

TRAVEL

NORTH AMERICA

(AND AVOID BEING A TOURIST)

Contents

001 – 007

Brave New World

008 – 027

The Joy of Slowing Down

Sit still
Take a long walk
Get to the beach
Gardens of contemplation

028 – 047

Make It Good, Do It Right

Leave your mark
11 great ways to be a better traveler
Stay to give back
Under-tourism in the USA: keep it low profile
A word on giving
It's the little things checklist

048 – 073

The Land That Time Forgot

Remains of the days gone by
Grand Canyon's hidden waterfalls
High drama from outer space and inner Earth
Nature is their muse
Beauty is timeless
Hobbies in the wild
And then there were people
National parks on the big screen

074 – 097

Follow Nature's Lead

Spring
Summer
Autumn
Winter
Stay close to nature
Lead the way: animal migrations

098 – 159

Bright Lights, Big Cities

Shine the spotlight
Cities we love and the people who love them
Our favorite city hotels
Design on a dime
Betting on microbrands
Where millionaires share the wealth
Understanding our past to build a better future
Glorious urban ruins
The kitchen heroes
A special note about extra special meals
Find nature near American cities

160 – 189

The Company You Keep

Bring your crew
Mind your elders
Romantic interludes
Go it alone
Unconventional accommodations
How to travel in a group – without being a jerk
The stuff to bring
Tools of the trade

190 – 243

On the Road

Mini road trip itineraries
Canadian Rockies for chionophiles
American southwest for art pilgrims
California's Pacific coast for hedonists
The locals to know
The motel refurb

244 – 269

Expand Your Mind

Cult classics
Spiritual folkways
Spas and escapes for body and mind
The woo-woo ways
Retreats for self-care
This shit is bananas

270 – 283

Take Care

ESSENTIAL TRAVEL TIPS AND HACKS   274
INDEX   277
ACKNOWLEDGMENTS   282
ABOUT THE AUTHORS   283

Opposite: the horizon is calling

CHAPTER 1

BRAVE NEW WORLD

We are undergoing a massive shift in how we consider and relate to the world around us. Technology has enabled us to stay connected with an ease that would have been impossible even one generation ago.

Previous page: a new day
dawns in Virginia

Opposite: setting off on
an adventure

This connectedness, in many ways, only accelerates what feels like more and more pressing matters – human calamities, climate disasters, health crises – that cast long, dark shadows over our furiously spinning globe. Being connected gives us front row seats to all sorts of once-in-a-lifetime events, world happenings, and unthinkable realities. At the same time, the sheer scale, impact, and speed of the information deluge is impossible to navigate. The shock of a global pandemic and the immediate impact it had on our lives has raised so many questions about the future and what everything in it – our economies, our health and safety protocols, our interpersonal interactions – will look like.

And yet. If one thing has been clear throughout the pandemic, it's that the desire, the urge, the need to travel remains unwavering.

Can anything good come of such an overwhelming situation? We have to hope it can. We're working toward – and hoping for – a post-pandemic mindset less focused on travel consumption and more focused on stewardship. Where people will put more thought into choosing their destinations, spend more time in one place, and work harder to connect to the communities that welcome them. In the best-case scenario, we will all be less preoccupied with labels and checklists and Instagram likes and more interested in how we move through the world and care for it – and for each other.

A decade ago, Fathom made its internet debut. We seeded our travel website with a few personal stories – one was about checking into a low-key surf retreat in the off-season, another was about discovering the atelier of a talented leather artisan, and another recalled an encounter with an injured hawk on a bird-watching expedition. What made these stories Fathom stories? Well, they were all rooted in discovery and serendipity and offered a quirky alternative to the straightforward, envy-inducing travel writing and glossy luxury hotel coverage that dominated travel media at the time. Many of the ideas and the situations that inspired us – slow travel, wellness travel, multigenerational travel, going off-grid – never felt like trends; they just felt right. What was personal for us turned out to resonate with many others who also found that DIY, custom-made travel was a fun, cool, and thrilling way to explore near and far. It turns out your instinct and curiosity are usually better guides than Google spreadsheets and someone else's checklist.

From left: flotation therapy in the Bahamas; spare, striking pool-meets-beach scene at Cuixmala in Costalegre, Mexico

In our first book, *Travel Anywhere (and Avoid Being a Tourist)*, we established that human interactions in the world tend to fall into one of two categories: those of the tourist or those of the traveler. The tourist visits established destinations within their comfort zone, stays in hotels owned by large corporations, and expects a certain level of amenities and service. Knowledge of the local culture is limited; interactions with it, even more so. Perhaps the tourist will be waited on by locals or will buy a woven belt from an artisan who has a shop in the lobby, or will meet a drummer after a performance, but that's about it when it comes to connecting with the community. The same pattern follows with the environment: other than a note to leave your towels on the rack if you don't want them to be changed – a notice that usually gets ignored by guests and housekeeping – hotels don't post information about their energy efficiency or responsibility practices, though they'll distribute lots of pamphlets for activities like swimming with dolphins and coupons for chain restaurants.

The traveler, on the other hand, endeavors to have a more responsible visit. One that is "authentic" and "sustainable" (big buzz words!) and, in simple terms, directly benefits the people in a community as well as themselves. The traveler stays in locally owned hotels and relies on the recommendations from the staff, whose names they know by day two. Eager to engage in the community's economy, the traveler takes public transportation, spends money in small restaurants and shops, and safely ventures off the beaten path, careful to be respectful of the flowers underfoot. This person may be open to paying a little more to know that their hotel is using a reverse osmosis system or engaging in a recycling project, and is thrilled to participate in the on-site sea turtle conservation program. The visit overall is low impact or, better yet, regenerative – meaning that they left the place a little better off than they found it.

We're purposely exaggerating these portraits of the two traveler types to drive home a point and make a strong case for one mindset over the other. And we're happy to see that in recent years more people have evolved from being tourists, a model that's outdated and unsustainable, to being travelers. People are shifting from being passive receivers to active players on vacation, and this, we applaud. Because that's the ultimate goal in everything we do at Fathom: we want to encourage traveling – the kind that is conscious, thoughtful, engaged, and aware of its impact, in addition to being fulfilling, eye- and heart-opening, exciting, and fun.

Reflection perfection in the valley of the Maroon Bells in Aspen, Colorado

For many of us around the world, the pandemic has kept our wanderings closer to home. And this has made several things clear: first – what a privilege it is to have nature (any nature!) at our fingertips, be it a clear view of the sunset or a wily squirrel tightroping a telephone line. Second, when your movements are restricted, you really learn to appreciate having room, and especially wide open spaces where your imagination and spirit can feel free – gazing up into a clear night sky when you're camping in the desert or walking along a beach at dawn. Finally, we feel an unbounded respect for our personal relationships: for our loved ones and also the community at large that helps shape our interests and activities. As a result, we have a newfound appreciation for what we can find in our own backyard: the driving routes made scenic with thoughtful twists and turns; the parks, forests, and fields managed and preserved for the public; the innovative foods born from multiple cultures intertwined as neighbors.

When we consider the majesty of nature, the beauty of open spaces, and the richness of an inspiring community, we're humbled to realize how lucky we are to have it all here in North America. We may live in New York City, but we've always kept at least one eye on (and often our whole bodies in!) the rest of the world. Lately, though, we've become (re)acquainted with the vast offerings we have on our home continent, a wild and varied bounty of history, geography, nature, spirituality, culture, design – from the Atlantic to the Pacific, from the Arctic Ocean to the Caribbean.

We're feeling hopeful about how we'll travel as a post-pandemic society. Here at Fathom, we like to say that you don't have to call yourself an explorer, conservationist, pioneer, or philanthropist in order to move through the world like one. This book is for people who want to make discoveries – and for those who are unsure how to find what they are looking for. We'll help you navigate your own way by shining a light on places you thought you knew and introducing you to destinations you haven't considered before. We'll guide you toward awe-inspiring beauty, mystery, intrigue, adventure, wonder, and relaxation – some of which is hiding in plain sight. We hope to serve you by laying out a few options, clearing the path, and pointing you toward the horizon.

Happy travels.

Opposite: water in free fall in Telluride, Colorado

7

CHAPTER 2

THE JOY OF SLOWING DOWN

Giving ourselves more time to spend in a destination means giving up a little of the planning, a little of the control. But deliberately doing less while traveling is actually doing more of something else – sharpening our ability to sit still, be quiet, listen deeply, and pay attention to details. And that makes room for more to happen: accidental discoveries, serendipity, surprise – the things we hold in the highest regard, and the things that make the most lasting impressions.

Previous page: a Virginia valley seen from above

Opposite, from top: night falls at Twin Farms in Vermont; rounding up the team on the beach in Zihuatanejo

As travelers who are really into "seeing it all," we are certainly coming around to the idea of taking it easy. There's an increasing interest in the idea of reaping joy from slowing down. The hard part about actually doing it is learning to resist the things that normally hijack our time (work emails, social media updates, fretting about what to do next, ticking through a checklist of recommendations), and realizing that the place we are in and the people we are with at a particular moment are enough.

Slowing down means stopping on the side of the road to take a look around. Hiking to the higher precipice for a change in perspective. Going back to the same shave ice truck in Kauai again and again because you think the purple taro with coconut foam is one of the best things you've ever tasted – and you just want to make sure.

When you consider the bigger picture, slow travel is better for local economies, better for the environment, and better for human connection. The more time we spend somewhere, the more often the setting becomes a character on our journey. (The fewer snap judgments we'll make, too.)

The slower we go, the more we can take in, seeing a place for all its unpolished truths and idiosyncrasies, cracks, fissures, complexities, and discrepancies. When you go deep – well, that's when you really get to the good stuff.

We have plenty of recommendations for going slow. So slow, we hope, that you'll stop in your tracks.

To better get accustomed to the pace, let's start with some basic exercises.

SIT STILL

Doing nothing is really doing something when there's plenty to watch, hear, taste, and see from where you are perched.

Catskill Mountains, New York, USA

The scene: solitude and fresh mountain air. Fill up a thermos, stoke the firepit, and take a seat in an Adirondack chair outside one of the beautifully minimalist two- and four-person A-frame cabins at **Eastwind** (_eastwindny.com_) in Upstate New York. Each cabin has a firepit and lofted bed and is furnished with vintage finds, so each feels special in its own way. There's an outdoor wooden sauna (for sitting quietly in the heat) and a nearby scenic 2-mile (3.2 kilometer) chairlift called the **Skyride** (_windhammountain.com_) that takes you to the summit of Windham Mountain. When you are ready to move, you can rummage through Eastwind's closet of handsome Hunter wellies and rain gear for a long stroll in inclement weather. Or try the open-air **rail bike contraption** (_railexplorers.net_) and pedal on the tracks through maple trees and along the Esopus Creek.

Barnard, Vermont, USA

Every whim is unobtrusively catered to at the extremely splurge-y 18th-century farmhouse **Twin Farms** (_twinfarms. com_). With freestanding cottages and hundreds of acres of gorgeous fields and forest, it's a feast for the eyes and the stomach. Lavish amenities like fireplaces, screened porches, private hot tubs, and tailored menus push the place over the top. The experience truly peaks when the fall foliage does, but there is plenty of relaxing to do all year round – under the living room's wood rafters, sitting on a plush couch looking through floor-to-ceiling windows at the rolling hills; in the Japanese furo, watching the changing leaves; at the apiary, where you can hear the meditative hum of the honeybees at work; or in a four-poster bed late in the morning (without your children, as it's an adult-only hotel), watching the snow fall. "There will be apple trees and flaming lilies, and the moon over the low mountains and you and me, after dinner, sitting ... on the terrace, and inside, when it becomes chilly, the fireplace and lamplight and lots of books," Sinclair Lewis wrote of the farm, which he and journalist Dorothy Thompson owned and entertained in from the 1930s to the 1950s.

Yelapa, Mexico

You'll really feel the impact of taking things step by step after flying into Puerto Vallarta, Mexico, catching a taxi forty minutes south to the tiny fishing village of Boca de Tomatlán, then boarding a small power boat for a half-hour cruise down the Pacific coast, past dolphins playing, until you disembark at **Verana's** (_verana.boutique-homes. com_) private pier in the jungle of Yelapa. You will be greeted by staff leading mules that will carry you and your luggage to your accommodations – a thatched-roof palapa with no walls. (Other options include bungalows, enclosed studios, and light-filled casas.) Large terraces, gardens, and ocean views are included, with plenty of options for sitting still – be it in an Acapulco chair, hammock swing, plunge pool, daybed, or chaise lounger.

Opposite, from left: Catskills country flora; looking out the big picture window at Eastwind, New York

This page, from top: cozy and colorful digs at Twin Farms, Vermont; a sunny reading corridor at Verana in Yelapa, Mexico

The spectacular California coastal views at Sea Ranch in Sonoma County

Westerly, Rhode Island, USA
Weekapaug Inn (_weekapauginn.com_) wants to be your home away from home (if your home were a grand restoration of a 1939 classic New England inn), where sailboats, fishing gear, and a discreet, black-bottomed pool are all at your disposal. Throw open the windows of the very cozy bedrooms and hear the sound of the ocean. Pad down to the beach and flop onto a blanket just over the dunes, where there are 2 miles (3.2 kilometers) of sand but not another building in sight. Adirondack chairs are scattered across a huge lawn where children and dogs play, and a patio provides wooden rocking chairs and a stone fireplace where perhaps you will strike up a conversation with the inn's resident naturalist. A meal of locally caught lobster, Matunuck oysters, and native beets is as memorable as a sunset over **Quonochontaug Pond**. Massages at Relais & Châteaux sister property down the road **The Ocean House** are a Zen bonus.

Sonoma County, California, USA
The Sea Ranch (_searanchrentals.com_) is a tiny, environmentally planned private community (with plenty of vacation home rentals) stretching for 10 miles (16 kilometers) along Highway 1 at the northern end of the majestic and rugged Sonoma County coast. Walking trails offer wide-open views of the Pacific Ocean, barking sea lions, and migrating whales; terraces offer the sounds of crashing waves on the ocean bluff at sunset. Feeling contemplative? Take a seat in the **Sea Ranch Chapel**, an organic structure of cedar, shell, and copper, illuminated by incredible stained-glass windows.

Maui, Hawaii, USA

You won't be slurping mai tais at the hotel bar of **Lumeria** (*lumeriamaui.com*), but instead sampling the detox menu of fruits, veggies, and superfood-infused broths from the retreat's "liquid chef." Located on the lower slopes of **Haleakala volcano**, Lumeria is naturally secluded with a fence wall of lava rock, relatively far from Maui's popular beaches. Sparsely decorated rooms encourage guests to spend most of their time lounging in the hammock garden, slowly making their way along the labyrinth of meditation paths, and increasing their vibrations with crystal healing sessions. The only high-tech amenity here is an iPod dock alarm clock, which is presumably there to make sure you make it to your 8am yoga session. When you need even more calming surroundings, head to the saltwater swimming pool and firepit in the courtyard.

Richland Center, Wisconsin, USA

Candlewood Cabins (*candlewoodcabins.com*) has been offering couples and small groups a place to unplug and unwind in the south-western corner of the state since the mid-'90s – with a single cabin. Today, there are seven unique, modern, minimalist but cozily (tastefully!) decorated cabins that are so popular, Candlewood takes bookings twenty-four months in advance (many reservations are booked a year ahead of time). Inside, you'll find an eclectic mashup of mid-century, modern, and flea-market pieces, as well as wood-burning stoves and big picture windows – a perfect stage for reading a good book. Outside, you'll find woods, valleys, rolling hills, lots of state parks, picnic spots, snowshoe trails, and Frank Lloyd Wright's former home and studio, **Taliesin**, along with the homes in the area built by his architecture disciples.

Candlewood's modern country charms (outside and in) in the middle of the Wisconsin woods

TALK A LONG WALK

Everyday life fades into the background when it's you and the elements and a long road ahead.

California Missions Trail, California, USA

Before the TikTok baby millionaires, the Hollywood set, the yogis, the surfers, and the miners of gold, spiritual seekers, led by a Franciscan monk in 1769, traversed 800 miles (1287 kilometers) of **California wilderness** to establish small chapels and convert the Indigenous peoples into communities of Catholic faith. You can make a road trip of visiting all twenty-one missions along the west coast, since they are all on or near **Highway 101**, or you could join the **California Mission Walkers** (_missionwalk. org_) and amble very old pedestrian pathways, where you'll run into redwoods, succulents, citrus trees, grazing sheep, earthquake-damaged bell towers, bougainvillea cascading over the adobe walls of California's first cemetery, and rustic little churches with Pacific Ocean views.

Saguenay Fjord Trail, Quebec, Canada

Quebec's 146-mile-long (235-kilometer-long) **Saguenay Fjord** is an under-the-radar wildlife area of dramatic natural beauty accessible by walkers and hikers of all abilities over a variety of distances. Quaint little Canadian villages dot the fjord on either side. Seals, blue whales, and a bounty of Atlantic salmon chart the glacier waters, as black bears, beavers, and moose protect the balsam fir and birch forests. To experience this natural park from a falcon's view, a four-day excursion rambles through rocky alpine lookouts with views over the fjord some 1150 vertical feet (350 meters) down. Camping sites and huts are available for shelter.

Pointe des Châteaux Trail, Guadeloupe

A jewel of the Caribbean, the **Guadeloupe Islands** feel like tropical New Orleans – lively, colorful, and filled with music, with an emphasis on French and African cooking techniques. Since it sees relatively low traffic from visitors, Guadeloupe has a decidedly local vibe – even at one of its most visited sites, a limestone peninsula offering various hiking trails for birders, ecology buffs, and outdoor enthusiasts. A three-hour stroll on the main island of **Grande-Terre** shepherds visitors through rocky outcrops, golden beaches, salt marshes, blue lagoons, and clear vistas of the other islands in the archipelago from the top of the headlands. This is the land that the Arawak people walked for 1100 years until the 8th century, and it's home to tons of birds, like terns, noddies, sandpipers, plovers, and songbirds, who love grazing the tide pools and gliding on the Caribbean breeze.

Opposite, from top: navigating an undulating cliffside trail in Kauai; the welcoming waters off the Pointe des Châteaux Trail in Guadeloupe

Presidential Traverse, New Hampshire, USA

Above the tree line of New Hampshire's **White Mountains**, this moonscape-like route connects nine peaks named after US presidents via 9000 vertical feet (2743 meters) of climbing. European-style lodging huts dot the trail, hosting hikers in bunks along the way. Midway through the trek is the summit of **Mount Washington**, the highest peak in the north-east, where, on a clear day, the view extends across five states. From that point in the hike, the rewarding views keep on coming: a large boulder field near the **Lake of the Clouds Hut**, the deep chasm of **Oakes Gulf**, and the oldest continuously used and maintained hiking trail in the country, **Crawford Path**. The through-hike is 20 miles (32 kilometers) point to point and takes one to four days to complete.

Appalachian Trail, USA

The nation's longest marked hiking footpath – and possibly its most famous – starts at **Springer Mountain, Georgia**, crossing fourteen states, six national parks, and eight national forests on its way north to **Mount Katahdin, Maine**. Flat sections are few and far between, and, because of the constant ascents and descents, a through-hiker's total elevation gain roughly equates to hiking Mount Everest from sea level and back sixteen times. Those who walk it in its entirety, in sections over time or as a whole, are called "2000-milers" – but many more enjoy day hikes and short expeditions through the "green tunnel," a canopy of old-growth spruce forests and layers of mountain, with bursts of openness in places like **Hump Mountain**, **McAfee Knob**, and **Franconia Ridge**.

Kalalau Trail, Hawaii, USA

You can only begin to grasp the sheer magnitude and untouched beauty of the plunging green cliffs of **Kauai's Nā Pali Coast** if you have access to a helicopter or boat. There are no roads for cars on much of this part of the island, leaving the North Shore practically untouched. But stretching along the jungle cliffs between **Ke'e Beach** and **Kalalau** is a beautiful – and sometimes treacherous – 11-mile (18-kilometer) hiking path skirting the idyllic Hawaiian coast. Cascading waterfalls, tropical flowers, and views of the Pacific extend over the horizon. We repeat: this is not a walk for the faint of heart; terrain is steep and often narrow, with windy ledges, and it gets slippery when wet (which is often on the island). The bulk of hikers do just a piece of the trail – a day trip from Ke'e Beach to **Hanakāpī'ai Beach** that equals a 4-mile (6-kilometer) round trip.

The Great Divide Trail, Canada

Wandering through the vast wilderness of the **Canadian Rocky Mountains**, this 700-mile (1127-kilometer) route traverses the rugged continental divide between Alberta and British Columbia, passing through five national parks – **Waterton Lakes, Banff, Kootenay, Yoho,** and **Jasper** – and eight provincial parks, with through-hikers taking around eight to ten weeks to complete the full route. It's grander and wilder than the paths in the Lower 48 (expect a little bushwhacking along the way). But the magnificent trail-in-progress winds its way through glaciers, rocky peaks, wildflower fields, and plenty of picture-perfect wildlife-in-habitat scenes, including mountain goats, moose, wolves, and bears. Carry a map and a compass, and know how to use both.

Pacific Crest Trail

This 2650-mile (4267-kilometer) hiking and equestrian trail goes from **Mexico** to **Canada** via **California, Oregon,** and **Washington** and generally takes the entire snow-free season to walk. To experience a part of it is to see the beauty of the desert unfolding into the **Sierra Nevada**'s rolling uplands and great expanses of ice, and the jaw-dropping panoramas of deep pine forests outlining the powdered-sugared **Cascade Range**.

Coastal hikes, woodsy walks, and misty strolls are at once grounding and uplifting

GET TO THE BEACH

Perfect the art of the beach blanket hang or just get caught up in the sea breeze.

The Florida Keys, Florida, USA

A chill drive down the rocky island chain that flicks off the southern tip of the Floridian peninsula is easy, affordable, tropical, and part of a unique ecosystem. Sustainable newcomer **Baker's Cay Resort** (*bakerscay.com*), in diving paradise **Key Largo**, has the tagline: "A place where life slows down and spirits rise." The area is fresh, modern, open, and good for families (even dogs) with different needs: diving, back-country boating, sunset cruising, or chilling near the tiki bar at the pool. **Little Palm Island** (*littlepalmisland.com*) is a gorgeous, grown-ups-only retreat with vintage British West Indies vibes – cane furnishings and rich paint colors, thatched bungalow roofing, a huge seashell fireplace mantle – in **Little Torch Key**. No phones, TVs, alarm clocks, or other modern disturbances to get in the way of hammock swinging and following iguanas as they make their way along a crushed shell path. Kayak deliberately through the **Great White Heron Refuge** in **Big Pine Key**. Spend time communing with slow-moving, endangered sea turtles at **The Turtle Hospital** (*turtlehospital.org*) in **Marathon**. Or take an unhurried glass-bottomed boat through the United States' first undersea park, **John Pennekamp Coral Reef State Park** (*pennekamppark.com*).

Zihuatanejo, Mexico

"Sleepy surf town" may be the golden phrase in Mexico travel, and though Pacific Ocean towns like Todos Santos and Sayulita have been notably roused in recent years with an influx of visitors, Zihuatanejo remains delightfully in repose. You'll find just enough action at **Thompson Zihuatanejo** (*thompsonhotels.com*), the recently renovated fifty-six-room property that sits directly on the white sands of **Playa la Ropa**. Rise with the sun (speaking of sleepy ...) and accompany the hotel chef to the local fish market before returning back to base with your haul for a beachfront cooking class. Once you've perfected the art of grilling red snapper with a hibiscus cooler in hand and taken a dip off your swim-up suite, amble up the road to **Loot** (*loot.mx*), a gallery/board shop/coffee joint/bar that's the exact amount of cool you'd expect from an under-the-radar surf spot. If you're looking for barefoot beachfront luxury, head up the coast to **Troncones** and **Lo Sereno Casa de Playa** (*losereno.com*), a ten-room come-and-don't-leave spot to recharge and chill.

Opposite, clockwise from top: a colorful, hearty brunch at The Maidstone in East Hampton, New York; a breezy bedroom at Olas in Tulum connects with its natural surroundings; fire-roasting fruit at Thompson Zihuatanejo; ubiquitous – but always welcoming – palm trees at the beach in Mexico

Opposite: a stunning stairwell at the '70s-era beach house–turned–hotel Olas in Tulum, Mexico

The Hamptons, New York, USA

Hampton beaches are truly a state treasure. Eighty miles (129 kilometers) from New York City on the tip of **Long Island**, they are extremely wide, sandy, clean, and quiet. Large grassy dunes protect the beaches from erosion and give the migrating birds, endangered toads and snakes, and piping plovers privacy and protection from the elements. **A Room at the Beach** (_iwantaroomatthebeach. com_) in **Bridgehampton**, previously owned by Martha Stewart and Donna Karan, has ten eclectic bungalow rooms, a pool, bicycles, and beach passes. The yard, with its cozy seating arrangements, is the real star, particularly the table nestled under twinkling lights and a row of slender redwoods. It's only a ten- or fifteen-minute walk from the Jitney or train, making it a nice option for those without a car. **The Maidstone** (_themaidstone.com_) in **East Hampton** has sixteen Scandinavian-designed rooms and three cottages that bring a bright, fresh, thoughtful esthetic to the land of shingle-style houses bordered by hedgerows. Take a morning and evening swim or beach walk, then spend the middle of the day admiring the Danish modern furnishings, fabulous art collection, and designer odds-and-ends.

Harbour Island, Bahamas

Expect understated chic at **Pink Sands** (_pinksandsresort. com_), a kind of open-secret retreat for Caribbean beach enthusiasts. Check into a quaint oceanfront cottage, immediately put on a swimsuit, and head to the blushing beach (truly light pink!), where you'll want to remain for the length of your stay. Maybe there's a break to dine on lobster quesadillas at **Sip Sip** (_sipsiprestaurant.com_), everyone's favorite casual eatery, or float for a while in the **Queen's Bath**, a collection of craggy scooped-out rocks on the Atlantic Ocean side of **Eleuthera** that become sun-warmed pools at low tide. Shuffle over to sweet boutique hotel **The Landing** (_harbourislandlanding. com_) for a few days of superb and simple eating. India Hicks designed the rooms, so it's a feast for the eyes too. If you need to bring a crew, rent the eleven-room **Bahama House** (_elevenexperience.com/bahama-house-harbour-island_) in **Dunmore Town**, a stylish and cozy home away from home that comes with its own tiki bar and a 35-foot (11-meter) Scorpion RIB boat for afternoon sails.

An invitation for a dip in Sea Island, Georgia

The Golden Isles, Georgia, USA

Midway between Savannah and Jacksonville, on Georgia's Atlantic coast, are the barrier islands of **St. Simons Island, Sea Island, Little St. Simons Island,** and **Jekyll Island**, known for their mash-up of old-world formality and Southern ease. It's about a twenty-minute drive (or boat ride) between the islands, and it's easy to hop around, though it's even easier to settle onto a veranda, taking in the marshy grasses and red sunsets, mint julep in hand. **The Cloister at Sea Island** (*seaisland.com*), **The Lodge**, and other grand hotels and clubs were made for the Rockefellers, Morgans, Pulitzers, and Astors, who arrived by yacht or locomotive to hunt and swim and golf and picnic (until World War II made such activities seem frivolous, and the millionaires abandoned the vacation spot). Today, guests in need of a recharge can take daily dips in the refreshing waters, laps at the beautiful club pools, paddleboard in the salt marshes, horseback ride on the beach, and (randomly!) participate in an infamous bingo night.

Tulum, Mexico

Over the years, this laidback and low-key seaside enclave has become a hotspot for the festival-going set looking to try on a boho lifestyle (and fringe bikini). There are certainly more visitors than ever before, and much of the beach road is fringed with mezcal cocktails, dance parties, and boutiques promoting consumption to the max. But if you are looking to take it easy and keep your eyes on the prize – swimming in the clear, warm waters of the Caribbean Sea – you'll find it a little more off the beaten path at **Olas Tulum** (*olastulum.com*), a once-private, '70s-era beach house built by Austrian engineer Carlos Schober, who designed it to work in synthesis with the natural environment. To this day, the palapa provides shade, the curved walls promote cool air flow, and the underwater streams feed into the showers and sinks. You'll feel even more connected to the surrounding waters when you see how close proximity to **Sian Ka'an Biosphere Reserve** (a UNESCO World Heritage Site) provides a serene and secluded beach experience. It's just a few feet from your room to the sand, where beach towels, shade palapas, and lounge chairs are waiting for you at **Habitas Tulum** (*habitastulum.com*), the preferred spot for the digital nomads who are actually getting work done between dips and fresh juices. If you'd rather avoid the go-go scene (and all those Millennial wannabes) on the main drag but still want the best Tulum has to offer – daily yoga, beach-facing open-air massage pavilions, and easy access to the Maya ruins – stay at **Jashita Hotel** (*jashitahotel.com*), which comes with a few bonuses, like high style in beautifully furnished rooms and a protected cove that makes swimming easy and algae-free.

Ideal vacation pose found on a hammock at the beach or on a freshly made bed with a nice sea breeze at Olas in Mexico

GARDENS OF CONTEMPLATION

Botanical landscapes are best when dreamed up by poets, artists, and eccentrics.

LongHouse Reserve, East Hampton, New York, USA Tucked away on a 16-acre (6-hectare) reserve at the end of Long Island, textile designer, author, and collector Jack Lenor Larsen built his home and sculpture gardens "as a case study to exemplify a creative approach to contemporary life." Visitors may take their time roaming the grounds to experience landscaping and architecture as an art form (flowering ornamental borders, a canopy of deciduous trees, a 7th century Shinto shrine–inspired home). Sculptural installations (by Buckminster Fuller, Yoko Ono, Kara Walker, and Willem de Kooning, among others) surprise and delight when juxtaposed with nature. It's intimate and innovative, a veritable playground for those seeking creative inspiration. *longhouse.org*

Jardin Escultórico Edward James (a.k.a. Las Pozas), Xilitla, Mexico A group of surreal fantasy structures more than 2000 feet (610 meters) above sea level were created by artist, poet, and surrealist supporter Edward James in a subtropical rainforest in the mountains. A labyrinth of paths and living walls leads to pools, waterfalls, nonsensical doors that open to nothing, and towering staircase structures that lead nowhere. *laspozasxilitla.org.mx/en*

Hunte's Gardens, St. Joseph Parish, Barbados An antidote to the meticulously manicured resorts on the island, this place is lush and overgrown, with an ancient sinkhole that is now a wonderful home for royal palms. There are plenty of hideaways and antique stone benches for taking in the trees, birds, wind, and classical music wafting from the horticulturalist's home, which you are invited into, and is filled with wildlife, old furniture, and a tuned piano for guests to play. *huntesgardens-barbados.com*

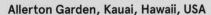

Allerton Garden, Kauai, Hawaii, USA
Tropical paradise with a raucous backstory. Do not skip the two-hour guided tour of the outrageously creative garden, which served as a living theater for the architect-and-artist couple who built outdoor "rooms" to host wild, hedonistic parties for notable visitors to their particularly stunning slice of oceanfront. There are exotic water features, sculptures, and unbelievably giant plants – like the Moreton Bay fig trees with their humongous roots (made famous by a *Jurassic Park* cameo).
ntbg.org/gardens/allerton

Forestiere Underground Gardens, Fresno, California, USA In the early 1900s, a Sicilian immigrant and citrus grower, following the beat of his own drum and trying to escape the oppressive Central Valley summer heat, turned farmland into catacombs: a vast network of subterranean tunnels, Romanesque arches, courtyards, and rooms. The excavation – all done by hand with shovels and picks – lasted forty years, spanning 10 acres (4 hectares) and going 25 feet (8 meters) deep, planted with fruit trees, shrubs, and grapevines.
undergroundgardens.com

Museo Dolores Olmedo, Mexico City, Mexico Olmedo was a fabulously successful businesswoman who hoarded a treasure trove of folk art, pre-Hispanic artifacts, and one of the world's best collections of work from Frida Kahlo and Diego Riviera (scandalous backstories included) in a rambling 16th-century hacienda at the southern edge of the city. The grounds are inhabited by a wild mix of colossal agave plants, colorful dahlias, tons of strutting peacocks, gnarled cypress trees, and a pack of rare hairless xoloitzcuintli dogs, one of the most ancient breeds on the continent (highly regarded by the Mesoamericans 3500 years ago).
museodoloresolmedo.org.mx

Longwood Gardens, Kennett Square, Pennsylvania, USA When a 1000-plus-acre (400-plus-hectare), 18th-century Quaker farm became a private residence circa 1906, it also became a canvas of sorts for owner and industrialist Pierre S. du Pont, who drew inspiration from the world fairs he attended across the country. One such brainstorm yielded an enormous pipe organ (it took fourteen railway freight cars to transport), which, when played, can be heard throughout the conservatory greenhouse. There are surprising vistas at every turn, plus native wildflower fields, a water garden, elaborate fountains (du Pont loved water features), and a 60-foot-tall (18-meter-tall) carillon, a musical instrument normally found in bell towers, that plays its sixty-two bells in concert for visitors in the summer and fall.
longwoodgardens.org

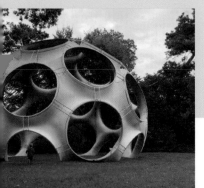

Opposite: garden details in summer and winter at Longwood Gardens, Pennsylvania

This page: little art spectators run wild at LongHouse Reserve in East Hampton, New York

CHAPTER 3

MAKE IT GOOD, DO IT RIGHT

Even the most expert adventurers can evolve their travel practices.

Previous page: butterflies do their part in nature's cycle

This page: a lake in Montana's Glacier National Park

A better travel path looks like this:

·   Explore more mindfully. Tread more carefully. Give more than take.

·   Choose greener, smarter, and less crowded destinations.

·   Reduce the number of flights booked (one of the highest-impact decisions a traveler can make) and spend more time in one place.

·   Support businesses that are acting responsibly toward their local community and the planet at large.

"Green travel" and "sustainability" are big, loaded words that travelers and industry players have been throwing around for years. But a post-pandemic world brings to light a newer challenge: can we move beyond green (doing less damage), beyond sustainable (recycling and reusing), and into regeneration (making the place better)? Regeneration demands a level of consciousness that many of us haven't considered before. It's not leaving a place as we found it – it's leaving it better off.

Whether you're a millennial or boomer, and you regard travel as a rite of passage, a reward, or a privilege, we can all appreciate the challenges of preservation and the opportunities for growth. We want to have fun, meaningful, transformative experiences we can treasure and share. So let's figure out how we can do that in a more thoughtful way than ever before.

This chapter lays out recommendations for becoming a more active participant in the communities we visit – engaging in conservation, contributing to local economies, building cultural connections, bringing about positive change, and having a great time while doing it all.

LEAVE YOUR MARK

Ready to move beyond those little signs asking you to reuse your hotel towels?

Build Tropical Forest Health

Roll up your sleeves to adopt and plant endemic Hawaiian trees through the **Hawaiian Legacy Reforestation Initiative**, an environmental program resulting in over 400,000 new plantings so far. On Hawaii's Big Island, a tour starts by hopping into a carbon-neutral vehicle as a guide educates you about the reforestation of rare, native trees like the māmane and ko'oko'olau. The work you put in becomes part of a larger ecosystem to ensure overall forest health. On the island of Oahu, ride horseback through a forest to plant your seedling among the endangered wildlife that thrive in these protected grounds. A tree-tracking program allows you to follow your tree's growth into the future. *legacyforest.org*

Make Your Art an Homage

Ever since the Hudson River School painters committed the parks to canvas in the 19th century, the **National Park Service** has encouraged artists to develop their work in the great outdoors – today through more than fifty residencies across the country for writers, sculptors, painters, musicians, and other creatives. Projects, programs, and locations range from wilderness cabin stays in Alaska's Denali National Park to working in a contemporary studio overlooking Weir Farm National Historic Site in Connecticut. Each park has its own application process and timeline, but residencies typically last two to four weeks and include lodging and an invitation to share work with the public. *nps.gov*

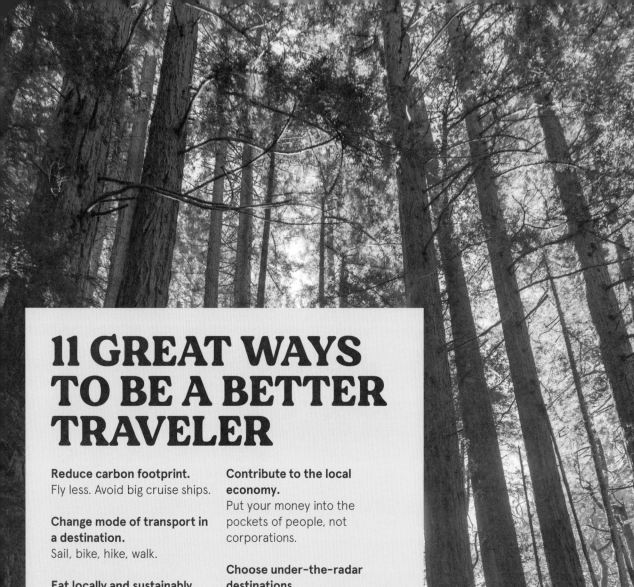

11 GREAT WAYS TO BE A BETTER TRAVELER

Reduce carbon footprint.
Fly less. Avoid big cruise ships.

Change mode of transport in a destination.
Sail, bike, hike, walk.

Eat locally and sustainably.
Practice the Slow Food philosophy.

Avoid bottled water unless absolutely necessary.
If everyone asks for filtered water, businesses will convert to it.

Protect natural resources.
And donate to environmental causes.

Cut down on single-use plastics.
Pack reusables for the plane and the hotel.

Contribute to the local economy.
Put your money into the pockets of people, not corporations.

Choose under-the-radar destinations.
Correct for over-tourism and visit places that need support.

Show respect to those who serve you.
Tips, kindness, consideration, gratitude.

Share with friends and family.
Pass along creative travel solutions and sustainable hacks.

Engage in direct giving after your trip.
Build and support local connections.

Dig Into Conservation

The **Sierra Club**, founded in 1892 by John Muir (geologist, zoologist, botanist, glaciologist, and environmental philosopher), is now the largest and most influential environmental organization in the United States. Volunteers build and maintain trails, parks, and wildlife areas throughout the United States, Canada, and the Caribbean. Several service adventures, such as trail building California's Laguna Mountain (an LGBTQ+ trip) and trail repair in Eagle Cap Wilderness, Oregon, will get you up and working in the great outdoors. _sierraclub.org_

Protect the Ocean

Ensure ecological integrity and help achieve strong, long-term protection of native Hawaiian areas, like **Papahānaumokuākea Marine National Monument**, which encompasses 582,578 square miles (1,508,870 square kilometers) of the Pacific Ocean, an area larger than all of the US's national parks combined. Long-term volunteers are relied upon to assist in various projects in the continuing effort to "bring the place to the people." Currently, volunteering is one of the only ways to see the site, and it's good for those who care deeply about marine ecosystems and environmental issues (and are strong swimmers). Help looks like a variety of activities: assisting field research for monk seals, helping with native plant propagation, and removing marine debris. _papahanaumokuakea.gov_

Opposite: towering redwoods on the Pomo Canyon Trail, California

This page, from left: Sierra Club service along the Idaho–Montana border; blooming magnolias greet spring like an old friend

Clockwise from top: classic street
scene in Havana, Cuba; snacking on
tortilla chips in Playa del Carmen,
Mexico; cycling with G Adventures

Opposite: Sian Ka'an Biosphere
Reserve in Tulum

Cultivate a Creative Mind
At **Chalk Hill Artist Residency**, emerging and established
artists can work in a sun-drenched farmhouse on a 265-
acre (107-hectare) ranch/think tank created by architect
John Carl Warnecke in California's Russian River Valley.
(He's known for developing Logan International Airport,
the American Hospital in Paris, and buildings at Stanford
and Georgetown universities.) Residencies are generally
solitary experiences that allow for long, quiet days. The
program lasts between two and six weeks, and artists
can roam the property's oak woodlands, hiking trails, and
bucolic vineyards for inspiration. *chalkhillresidency.com*

Support Local Artisans

For tour operator **G Adventures**, giving back and being a force for good are fundamental corporate principles. How legit are they? For starters, founder Bruce Poon Tip, a member of the Social Venture Network Hall of Fame, wrote the only business book to have ever been endorsed by the Dalai Lama. Almost all of G Adventure's 700-plus small group tours, which typically target the eighteen-to-thirty market, have a G for Good component, often developed through the company's non-profit arm, Planeterra Foundation. For example, on an eight-day biking tour around Cuba with stops in Havana, Cueva de los Portales (Che Guevara's headquarters during the Cuban Missile Crisis), and Playa Ancón beach, the cross-cultural exchange brings travelers to a women's collective that practices traditional embroidery techniques in the rural Manaca Iznaga community and would normally not have access to the tourist market. On itineraries through the Yucatán Peninsula, in addition to exploring colonial towns and Maya ruins and swimming in underground caves, travelers spend time at a volunteer-run restaurant that helps support a youth art program in Playa del Carmen. _gadventures.com_

Opposite, clockwise from top: wandering through the vines at Chalk Hill in California; sunset contemplation at Playa Viva in Mexico; explorations with the English in Mind Institute in Haiti; Chalk Hill Artist Residency's stunning property in Sonoma County

Develop Skills for Meaningful Employment

English in Mind Institute, a non-profit, adult English program in Port-au-Prince, Haiti, was launched by an NGO after a devastating earthquake. It is now a Haitian-led, Haitian-taught, and Haitian-administered operation that offers biweekly English language classes that follow a Cambridge University syllabus (with advanced levels and the premiere TOEFL exam). Why English? Haitians who speak the language can find work in restaurants and hotels, corporate offices and schools, and attain university scholarships. The organization offers ten-day volunteer opportunities that incorporate teaching, service with partner organizations, and guided tours that showcase the beauty and promise of an island nation often misrepresented in the media. *englishinmindinstitute.org*

Monitor Coral Reef Health and Marine Life

Oceanic Society's volunteer and family vacations offer hands-on opportunities for travelers to participate in conservation-focused research efforts that study a range of threatened species and habitats. Learn reef monitoring techniques and how to identify tropical fish from local biologists in Puerto Rico. Assist researchers in studying behavioral ecology of spotted and bottlenose dolphins in the Bahamas. Four-day family expeditions in the San Francisco Bay Area and ten-day small boat trips along coastal Alaska provide intimate and in-depth explorations of exciting marine environments. *oceanicsociety.org*

Farm(stay) on the Land

The only certified organic farm in the Virgin Islands is run by a thoughtful long-distance hiker–turned–farmer dedicated to cultivating peace among communities of nature and people. **Ridge to Reef**, in the north-west mountains of Saint Croix, United States Virgin Islands, stresses respecting locals as much as its agricultural practices. Beyond self-guided tours and Community Supported Agriculture, anyone can camp on the jungle farm or stay overnight in an off-grid treehouse cabana. Volunteers can get their hands dirty in the fields and rainforest. The farm also hosts interns and apprentices for two- and six-month stints, teaching all aspects of organic farm production and maintenance. *ridge2reef.org*

STAY TO GIVE BACK

Embrace hotels making smart, sustainable choices that contribute positively to the local community.

Playa Viva, Juluchuca, Mexico

South of Zihuatanejo, in a small agricultural town nestled between the Pacific Ocean and the Sierra Madre Mountains, this pristine eco-retreat was conceived on a Regenerative Development model built around environmental and community awareness. After recognizing that the property is surrounded by beautiful beaches, an estuary, and ancient ruins, but also poor schools and a poaching problem, the Playa Viva team got to work. They built an organic agricultural system to benefit both the local residents and the hotel, lead a volunteer-run sea turtle conservation project (you can apply to volunteer there if you can speak conversational Spanish), operate completely off-grid, and have a trust that funnels investment into local education, health, and economic development. It's no small thing that Playa Viva is also extremely good-looking and nice to be part of. Farm-to-table meals and daily yoga sessions are included in the stay, and the airy organic structures that serve as rooms and communal spaces blend seamlessly into the environment. *playaviva.com*

Flat Creek Ranch, Jackson Hole, Wyoming, USA
A dude ranch for low-impact dudes. The experience
starts with a rigorous 15-mile (24-kilometer) drive across
the National Elk Refuge with crazy Grand Teton views
before arriving for your secluded stay in one of five
historic (and luxuriously refurbished) cabins in the pine
woods. The former homestead (circa 1921) is on the
National Register of Historic Places and has a hard-earned
BEST certification, a program with serious criteria for
environmental, community, and economic sustainability.
The place stays up to date with sustainability measures –
solar energy, recycling, non-intrusive wilderness activities,
and a general commitment to a greener future – while
providing guests with incredible back-country access,
a dining philosophy centered around the seasons, and
a wood-fired hot tub for easing post-hike aches and
marveling at the stars. *flatcreekranch.com*

Stanford Inn, Mendocino, California, USA
Environmental stewardship is at the helm of this family-
run inn on the Big River on California's northern coast.
Invigorated by the energy and vitality of the area, the
Stanfords pledged to create and maintain a peaceful
escape centered around their organic farm, beloved
plant-based restaurant, wellness center, and a slew of
nature activities, workshops, and classes. They have a
rigorous recycling and composting program, biodiesel fuel
trucks, and the Environmental Leadership Field School to
mobilize future leaders of the sustainability movement.
stanfordinn.com

Montage Palmetto Bluff, Bluffton, South Carolina, USA
The Palmetto Bluff Conservancy was created to ensure the
preservation of the thousands upon thousands of verdant
maritime forests and winding rivers that define the
spectacular Lowcountry geography. Wildlife educational
classes, workshops, tours, and research programs use
the vast outdoor classroom as a learning tool. Artists'
residencies and community events ensure intentional
interactions with each other and the land. There are suites
and village homes full of southern charm, but we love the
cottages with their fireplaces and furnished screened-in
porches. *palmettobluff.com*

Opposite: Playa Viva's ecologically
harmonious bungalows in Mexico

This page: prime seating at
Playa Viva

Hix Island House, Vieques, Puerto Rico

This Zen-like compound on a quiet island east of Puerto Rico took a decade to build with intention, low-impact elements, and wabi-sabi design features that conserve energy, reduce repair and maintenance, and minimize the use of chemicals. The all-solar guesthouse (the first in the Caribbean) is completely removed from the electrical grid. Gray water from the shower and basin flow to the papaya and lemon trees on the property. Spacious, self-contained lofts have sea views, private terraces, and outdoor showers. Kitchens are stocked with homemade bread, local coffee, eggs, and milk for making healthy, hearty breakfasts after outdoor yoga. The 50-foot (15-meter) ionized pool (a thing of beauty!) runs on the power of the sun. _hixislandhouse.com_

Inn by the Sea, Cape Elizabeth, Maine, USA

This elegant oceanfront resort has a serious eco streak, with solar panels, rubber and cork flooring, green cleaning products, and biofuel for heating. There's a Silver LEED-certified spa and nectar gardens to support butterflies. Service is sweet without being obsequious – a knock on the hotel room door may be a toasted marshmallow delivery. The hotel evokes Portland's attitude in a nutshell: thoughtful, cozy, and community minded. Clean, bright, modern loft cottages and beach suites are great for families, big groups, and pets. There's a fantastically forward-thinking, seasonally driven restaurant, and a wooden walking path through the resort's "rabbitat," a woodsy briar patch for cottontail rabbits (they're endangered!) separating the inn from the ocean beach. As part of the hotel's advocacy work with the Gulf of Maine Research Institute, they arrange educational jaunts for guests on Portland's lobstering boats. _innbythesea.com_

Volcano House Cabins and Campsites, Big Island, Hawaii, USA

Just a few miles from the original 1846 Volcano House are a group of ten rustic, one-room camper cabins nestled in a fragrant eucalyptus forest within Hawaii Volcanoes National Park. The always-in-demand accommodations are low-key and low-impact – no running water, no bathrooms, one electric outlet – but there is a refurbished community bathroom (hot showers!) and a front desk courtesy phone. The hotel, which maintains its own sustainability initiatives (recycling, sourcing local foods), can also arrange to set up (and take down) a tent for two inside the National Park. _hawaiivolcanohouse.com_

Rockhouse, Negril, Jamaica

Forty studios, bungalows, and villas weave along a dramatic cluster of rocky cliffs set on sparkling blue-on-blue Caribbean waters. The food is as fresh as can be, often sourced from Rockhouse Organic Farm across the street. The staff is professional and cool – and will remember how you like your rum. The hip crowd is decidedly unhurried and fantastically laid back, and the vibes are uniformly harmonious. Bold guests try the local sport – cliff diving – by leaping off a bridge into the sea below. (It's a thrill!) In short, Rockhouse offers a postcard-perfect Jamaican idyll, but one with heart and soul, actively giving back to the community through its non-profit Rockhouse Foundation, which is also supported by its sister outposts, Skylark Hotel on Seven Mile Beach in Negril and Miss Lily's restaurant in New York City. The foundation has invested millions in seven schools in Jamaica and in Negril Library – and fed families during the pandemic. Hotel guests are encouraged to visit the schools and meet the spirited, smart, and well-rounded students. Owner Paul Salmon is a model of what a foreign owner in a developing country can do to act responsibly; he invests in the staff, the guest experience, the environment, and the community. *rockhouse.com*

Opposite: down the beach path in Cape Elizabeth, Maine

This page, clockwise from top left: cozy en-suite fireplace at Inn by the Sea, Maine; local bluefin tuna from the Inn's Sea Glass restaurant; Rockhouse in Jamaica embraces nature in its design

The spacious, sunlit lobby at The Breakers in Palm Beach, Florida

Spirit Bear Lodge, Klemtu, British Columbia, Canada

A stay at this remote, one-of-a-kind, Indigenous-owned wildlife viewing lodge in the heart of the Great Bear Rainforest is a commitment to become part of the cycle of stewardship of the land, its culture, and its legacy of knowledge. Monitored closely by the governing body of the Kitasoo/Xai'xais First Nation, Spirit Bear's impact tourism program allows the people of the tribal territories to grow economically and provides a sustainable path for future generations. Every single aspect of the lodge is created and maintained with the intention of sustainability, regeneration, and revitalization of the Kitasoo/Xai'xais culture. For guests, this means access to spectacular wilderness, rare animal species, and real interactions with the local community who help make the lodge possible; Spirit Bear employs nearly 10 percent of the population. *spiritbear.com*

Hotel El Ganzo, Los Cabos, Mexico

It's nice to see a hotel that's built on sustainability practices and is still continually doing more. Stylish and beachy with a rock-and-roll attitude, you could spend an indulgent weekend at this hotel (just twenty minutes from San Jose International Airport) without ever thinking about the pool running on solar power, the water bottles being reusable, or the cactus-based laundry detergent cutting down water usage by 80 percent. You could drink margaritas, eat guac and chips, and listen to live music without learning about how the hotel uses permaculture as the main framework for its mission or noticing what flourishing sustainable agriculture looks like: learning gardens for children, organic farmers' markets, recycling programs, and free arts education in the permanent community center they built across from the hotel. But once you catch that vibe, your whole stay will be even cooler. *elganzo.com*

The Breakers, Palm Beach, Florida, USA

They say you can't teach an old dog new tricks, but this grand dame resort with century-old bones now regularly implements ecologically friendly practices to protect its oceanfront environment and enhance the quality of life for future generations. These days, the Green Team oversees water conservation (reverse osmosis irrigation for the golf course) and waste and energy reduction. The resort's do-gooder philosophy extends to developing a culture of wellbeing for employees (all two thousand–plus of them), who participate in education, fitness, and impact projects and give back regularly to local causes. *thebreakers.com*

Cosmos Saint Lucia, Saint Lucia

High on a ridge, just north of Saint Lucia's old French capital and just south of Anse Chastanet Beach and marine reserve, is a modernist open-air eco-lodge with big ideals and a light touch. Rendered in white coral, polished concrete, and teak, the sophisticated hillside villa is powered by solar energy, harvests rainwater, discourages single-use plastics, prioritizes locally sourced food (including the harvest from their fruit garden), and supports the local economy through employment and guest activities. The infinity pool, where you will surely want to spend a lot of time, is hemmed in by colorful bougainvillea and relies on a saltwater ozone system that uses ultraviolet light (not chemicals) for a truly refreshing swim. *cosmosstlucia.com*

Clockwise from left: a performance in the Big House at Spirit Bear Lodge; close encounters of the bear kind in British Columbia's Great Bear Rainforest; animal totems at Spirit Bear Lodge

UNDER-TOURISM IN THE USA: KEEP IT LOW PROFILE

Expand your list of places of interest – and give some breathing room to over-touristed spots.

Under-the-radar states with small-town charms, awesome food scenes, gorgeous scenery.

Alabama
This way: Montgomery – Huntsville – Birmingham – Talladega National Forest

Signs you've made it: deep veins of American history, Legacy Museum, Scott and Zelda, biscuits, upland pine woodlands

Maine
This way: Portland – Freeport – Camden – Bar Harbor – Acadia National Park

Signs you've made it: dramatic ocean views, lobster rolls, knit sweaters, antiques, LL Bean outlet, and the highest point on the eastern seaboard

Montana
This way: Helena – Philipsburg – Glacier National Park

Signs you've made it: sifting for sapphires, journals of Lewis and Clark, horseback riding, bison steak, taxidermy, huckleberry shakes, big skies

South Dakota
This way: Rapid City – Custer State Park – Badlands – Wall

Signs you've made it: Black Hills, Badlands, buffalo, wildlife loops, Crazy Horse, Mount Rushmore

These American islands may take a little more work to get to, but that's what makes them so great.

Orcas Island, Washington
This way: Moran State Park – Obstruction Pass State Park – Mount Constitution – Twin Lakes – Eastsound

Signs you've made it: waterfalls, evergreen trails, apple barns, artist studios, oysters, innovative farm-to-table fare

Cumberland Island, Georgia
This way: St. Marys – Greyfield Inn – Dungeness – First African Baptist Church – Brickhill Bluff Campsite

Signs you've made it: fishing, horses, Carnegies, empty beach, oaks dripping with Spanish moss, wood-fired clams

Islands of Lake Champlain, Vermont
This way: Isle La Motte – South Hero – White's Beach – Island Line Bike Trail – North Hero – town of Grand Isle

Signs you've made it: cyclists, farm stands, eagles, Queen Anne's Lace, Champ (the local Loch Ness Monster), homemade ice cream

The Apostle Islands, Wisconsin
This way: Lake Superior – Madeline Island – Devils Island – Raspberry Island

Signs you've made it: bears, birds, sea caves, sandstone cliffs, kayaks, 19th-century lighthouses

Opposite: canoes and rocks in the water in Glacier National Park

This page, from left: breakfast is served at Greyfield Inn in Georgia; the mighty South Dakota Badlands

A WORD ON GIVING

A straightforward guide to ensuring give-back efforts have positive impacts.

Opposite: keeping it light along the beach in Haiti

Travelers have a lot of good intentions ... which can have some adverse effects. As Indian poet and travel writer Vikram Seth said, "God save us from people who mean well." Following the guidelines of the Center for Responsible Travel (CREST, *responsibletravel.org*), travelers can maximize their contributions by empowering local and Indigenous communities in attaining jobs, making lasting healthcare improvements, and providing education. Before offloading second-hand clothes, donating computer equipment, building a well, treating kids to candy, or generally imposing your will on a place or group of people, consider the following:

Misguided contributions can burden recipients by perpetuating cycles of dependency, corruption, and pollution. It can be a lot of work for a community to handle "gifts" they never requested and cannot use. It's a smart policy to check with them beforehand about what would be most useful to them.

Empower communities by funding projects they have already identified and decided on.

Work with local institutions and agencies to identify product needs, then make purchases locally if you can.

Indiscriminately giving out candy or toys to kids risks encouraging them to skip school and flock to tourists. It may seem harmless, but arbitrary gifts of trinkets or money may ultimately lead to a loss of dignity and begging.

Support is most effective and sustainable when you contribute through an established non-government organization with expertise and effective results in the area.

Support initiatives that are getting kids off the streets and into school.

IT'S THE LITTLE THINGS CHECKLIST

It only takes a bit of practice to develop good travel habits.

Before You Go
Bring your own toiletries
Pack reef-safe sunscreen
Drop a few pounds from your luggage
Carry a reusable water bottle

While You're There
Opt for sustainable activities
Skip a few rounds of housekeeping
Don't haggle too much
Minimize waste

Once You're Back
Give solutions-oriented feedback
Donate to a cause
Share your finds (and souvenirs) with friends
Plan another visit to go deeper

CHAPTER 4

THE LAND THAT TIME FORGOT

One of the most common myths of North America is that there wasn't much going on here until it was "discovered" by Christopher Columbus in 1492. But Columbus wasn't even looking for a "new world;" he just got lost on the way to India, where he had hoped to find his fortune in an even older world.

In fact, and pretty obviously, North America is as old as the rest of the continents, part of the original mega continent that covered part of the Earth until continental drift and tectonic movements created fissures and rifts that eventually separated the giant landmass into smaller portions, resulting in the continents, seas, and mountain ranges we know today.

AGE OF GIANTS

Many of these ancient geological forms have been given what sound to modern ears like awesome, mythic names. Presenting the supercontinents: Rodinia! Pannotia! Pangaea! The oceans could be gods: Tethys, Khanty, Rheic. Other names are more familiar, like the continents of Siberia, Kazakhstania, and Baltica. Laurentia was the continent that eventually became North America – or at least the portion that spans roughly from Canada's Northern Territories down to Texas and east to the Atlantic Ocean. When the area in much of what is now the middle of the continent flooded with a vast inland sea, Laurentia split into two new continents: Laramidia in the west and Appalachia in the east.

But despite being an old and shifting rock, North America's earliest human life (that we've found so far) is fairly recent (30,000 years) when compared to the earliest Homo sapiens remains discovered (so far): 315,000-year-old fossils in Morocco. It's a matter of heated debate where the first North American settlers came from (Asia or Europe or Africa?) and how (on foot or by boat?) and when they got here, but we'll get to that later.

Why the archaeology lesson in a book on travel? Because it reframes our adventures to know that the pebbles underfoot, the stripes in the hillside, and the scratchings on a rock face may have been formed thousands or millions of years ago. And it helps explain why you might see fish fossils embedded in the canyon rocks you're climbing in Utah.

Traveling with a sense of a timeline enriches our understanding of what was here before us. It's also a humbling reminder that nothing is constant – and this endless evolution will continue after we're long gone. Humans are leaving an indelible mark on Earth, but while our impact (and, ahem, irresponsible behavior) might accelerate certain events, the natural world was never fixed to begin with.

Previous page: a volcano comes to life

This page, from top: swimming in a Mexican cenote; cruising into Arches National Park in Utah

REMAINS OF THE DAYS GONE BY

Looking down into Zion
National Park, Utah

Opposite: along the beach
at Joggins Fossil Cliffs in
Nova Scotia, Canada

When we think of ancient natural sites, we tend to think of Giant's Causeway in Ireland or Victoria Falls on the Zambia–Zimbabwe border (which already had an awesome name from the Kololo-Lozi people – Mosi-oa-Tunya, "the smoke that thunders" – before it was "discovered" by Scotsman David Livingstone). But North America is rich with its own natural geological wonders that have shifted and formed over the eons. Here's a brief timeline of where to see the land as it once was.

Time Flies

310 million years ago

Joggins Fossil Cliffs, Nova Scotia, Canada
The Bay of Fundy may be famous for having the highest tides in the world, but those high-pressure waters pounding against the sandstone cliffs are doing something even more impressive: revealing fossils that date back to the Coal Age, when the area was blanketed by swamp forests. The fossils unearthed at this UNESCO World Heritage Site span the entire ecological food chain of the time, from plants to predators, including *Hylonomus lyelli*, the first reptile. One hundred million years later, her descendants would become dinosaurs, modern reptiles, and birds and long after that, the rest of Earth's vertebrates, including mammals. (She's a grandmother of us all!) No wonder Darwin name-checked Joggins in his *Origin of the Species*. *jogginsfossilcliffs.net*

270 million years ago

Zion National Park, Utah, USA
The Western Interior Seaway was formed when the Pacific and North American tectonic plates crashed into each other, creating a shallow sea that ran from the Arctic Ocean to the Gulf of Mexico and from the Rockies to the Appalachian Mountains, splitting North America in half and entirely covering what's now Montana, Colorado, Texas, and the eastern half of Mexico. When the waters drained over millions of years, sand became sandstone, clay became shale, and layers of incredible rock formations were left behind. All those arches and canyons and valleys and layers you see in this part of the world? They were once the bottom of an ocean floor.

This is why the sedimentary layers that formed at Zion between 270 and 110 million years ago include the fossils of ancient clams, coral, sea lilies, and countless other fish and marine life. See what you can spot in the cliffs as you climb 1488 feet (454 meters) up to Angels Landing, a hike that revs the heart rate, as there's nothing between you and that drop but a chain bolted into the rock (and your steady footing). Other trail paths, like Emerald Pools, Canyon Overlook, and Hidden Canyon, are easier and no less dramatic or beautiful. From March to October, the park shuttle is the only way to get around, which keeps traffic to a blessed minimum. *nps.gov/zion*

Opposite: searching for relics of
the past at Joggins Fossil Cliffs in
Nova Scotia, Canada

200 million years ago

Ghost Ranch, New Mexico, USA

Let's talk about dinosaurs, because you can't talk about the land that time forgot without talking about the reptiles that have captured our imaginations since they were first discovered. The Mesozoic Era, the Age of Reptiles, spanned from 252 to 66 million years ago and was divided into three periods: the Triassic (252–201 million years ago), the Jurassic (201–145 million years ago) and the Cretaceous (145–66 million years ago, at which point they were wiped out by an asteroid or meteor that landed in the Yucatán).

Among the first dinosaurs during the Triassic were *Coelophysis bauri*, small, 100-pound (45-kilogram) reptiles. The remains of hundreds of them can be seen on a tour of the colorful Coelophysis quarry here. Fun fact #1 to tell your travel pals: paleontologists estimate the age of dinosaurs based on the age of the rocks that preserved the fossils, as the fossils themselves are too old for carbon dating. Fun fact #2: you might recognize the landscape from the Georgia O'Keeffe paintings. She lived and worked at Ghost Ranch. Fun fact #3: O'Keeffe wasn't the only one drawn the setting. *No Country for Old Men, All the Pretty Horses,* and *The Ballad of Buster Scruggs* are just a few of the movies that have been filmed here.

But seeing the ruins is but one of many reasons to visit. Ghost Ranch also offers trail rides on horseback at sunset; archery lessons for small groups; guided hiking expeditions; week-long retreats for mind and body; workshops for photography, calligraphy, silversmithing, and pottery; as well as special programs dedicated to youth and seniors. You can stay overnight at the on-site lodge or DIY at the campground. *ghostranch.org*

190 million years ago

Antelope Canyon, Navajo Nation, Arizona, USA

Legions of tourists come here to marvel at – and Instagram – the stunning slot canyons formed by rainwater carving its way through 190-million-year-old red sandstone – both slowly over hundreds of years and more aggressively through more recent flash flooding. Upper Antelope Canyon is the most famous, and therefore the most crowded, though not the only option. Located on Navajo Tribal Lands, it cannot be accessed except on a guided tour by a licensed operator. *antelopecanyon.az*

110 million years ago

Dinosaur Park, Laurel, Maryland, USA

Would you like to have a dinosaur fossil named for you
and displayed at the Smithsonian Museum in Washington,
D.C.? If you are eagle of eye and careful of step, you
might find one underfoot at the open-air site in suburban
Maryland, where budding paleontologists are allowed to
look alongside the pros. No digging, though, just looking:
digging might damage what's underground. The west
coast may get more credit as former dinosaur stomping
grounds, but Maryland is home to one of the most
important dinosaur fossil sites east of the Mississippi
River. The first discovery, in 1858, were teeth of *Astrodon
johnstoni*, Maryland's herbivorous state dinosaur.
Hundreds more fossils of dinosaur eggs and bones have
been found there since, along with those of the crocodiles
and plants that lived alongside them.
pgparks.com/3293

80 million years ago

Monument Rocks and Castle Rock, Gove County, Kansas, USA

The next time you're driving across the United States and
find yourself in the western end of the Kansas prairie,
follow the signs that point a few miles off I70 and US83
down rough dirt roads. Here you'll find, where you
might least expect them, tall limestone, chalk, and shale
formations, the sedimentary relics of what was once the
floor of the Western Interior Seaway. Monument Rocks,
which are also known as Chalk Pyramids, are a series
of 70-foot-tall (20-meter-tall) towers that rise out of
nowhere like big, ancient mushrooms on the flat and
barren landscape. Forty-odd miles (60-odd kilometers)
away in the Castle Rock Badlands, a cluster of limestone
pillars make Castle Rock look like a medieval castle with
towers of varying heights. If you're envisioning a dragon
circling overhead, you're not far off: in the 19th century,
explorers found complete fossils of ancient reptiles
and birds here. Today, both sites are on private land, so
you won't find tourist information centers or gift shops
anywhere. Just the rocks, and maybe, if you're lucky, a
fish fossil underfoot. *travelks.com*

75 million years ago

Dinosaur Provincial Park, Alberta, Canada

More dinosaurs! Right before they were wiped out by a giant meteor event, dinosaurs were in their heyday – stronger, more varied, and more pervasive than ever. (There's a reason they called this period "The Age of Dinosaurs.") The world's best trove of fossils – 150 full skeletons from forty-four species – have been found at this UNESCO World Heritage Site in the Alberta badlands. The whole park is beautiful, with streams and such rock formations as column-shaped hoodoos. If you want to DIY, head for the Trail of the Fossil Hunters, a half-mile (1-kilometer), forty-minute walk to the 1913 quarry. But for better insight into what you're seeing, sign up for a park tour, especially if you want to explore a bonebed (former dig site). *albertaparks.ca*

Former dinosaur stomping grounds at Ghost Ranch, New Mexico

GRAND CANYON'S HIDDEN WATERFALLS

Deep in the Grand Canyon, the five waterfalls of Havasu Falls are a true and stunning oasis – turquoise waters tumbling over orange rock. Little wonder the Havasupai Tribe, the People of the Blue-Green Waters, have guarded them for centuries and protected them fiercely. You have to really want it to get here: first you need a permit, then you have to score one of the limited number of reservations. You have to spend at least one night at the campground or the lodge and carry most of your supplies with you. And you have to be fit enough to hike 8 miles (13 kilometers) – in very little shade, in possibly very high temperatures – down to the valley floor to reach Supai Village, the most isolated town in the continental United States, then another 2.5 miles (4 kilometers) to reach Mooney Falls. But, oh, the reward when you make it. As soon as you get over the sheer awe (warning: you won't), you get to bask in one of the most beautiful places you'll ever be.

70 million years ago

Grand Canyon, Arizona, USA

The Grand Canyon, one of the Seven Natural Wonders of the World, is easily the most famous and stunning natural landmark in the United States, notable for its overwhelming majesty and scale. At 277 miles (446 kilometers) long, up to 18 miles (29 kilometers) wide, and more than a mile (1.6 kilometers) deep, it's bigger than Rhode Island. Theodore Roosevelt, on beseeching the American people to protect the Grand Canyon and not commercialize it, once said, "Leave it as it is. You cannot improve on it. The ages have been at work on it, and man can only mar it."

How *many* ages have been at work remains a matter of considerable debate, with theories placing the age of the canyon from 6 to 70 million years old. At risk of confusing things, the oldest rocks at the bottom of the canyon are about 2 billion years old. (Geology: so contentious!) The theories, however, only underline the larger point that the land we walk on is ever changing and evolving. Thermochronology testing has revealed that the different sections of the canyon were formed at different times. The Hurricane segment was first, carved by ancient rivers 50–70 million years ago. Things then dried up for a few million years, until waters carved the Eastern Grand Canyon segment 15–25 million years ago. Finally, melting Rocky Mountain snows (or groundwater? more raging debates!) looking for a path to the Pacific Ocean dug the majority of the last canyons – Westernmost, Muav, and Marble – 6 million years ago, forming what became the Colorado River, which still runs through the canyon and continues to shape it. Confused? The Trail of Time exhibit will help clarify things. The interactive, 3-mile (5-kilometer) walking trail helps visitors understand the passage of geological time: along the path, one step equals one million years. Visitors can explore the park so many ways: on foot, by helicopter, on a mule, on solo expeditions, or on guided tours. For a trip that combines railroad history, architecture, and heritage, climb aboard the Grand Canyon Railway to the South Rim and stay at the bottom of the canyon at Phantom Ranch.

Many different people and cultures who have lived in the Grand Canyon for 12,000 years have left their mark, from First Peoples to explorers to miners. Eleven tribes still have ties to the Grand Canyon, and five call it home. Visitors can spend time with the Havasupai on the bottom of the canyon on the South Rim; with the Hualapai, who operate the Skywalk and a luxury hotel on the West Rim; with the Navajo and the Kaibab Paiute in the north; and the Hopi in the Four Corners. *nps.gov/grca*

Opposite: the magnificent Havasu Falls in the Grand Canyon, Arizona

66 million years ago

Cenotes, Yucatán Peninsula, Mexico

Few natural ruins are better experienced in a bathing suit. (Sadly.) Cenotes, the thousands of sinkholes scattered throughout the Yucatán Peninsula, are a notable exception. The ancient Maya people, who worshipped them as holy sites and relied on them for fresh drinking water, might have mixed feelings about the tourist attractions they have become. But you can't blame modern humans: cenotes are incredibly fun – and beautiful! – to swim and snorkel and scuba dive in, especially when the sinkholes connect to vast underwater rivers and cave systems filled with stalactites, stalagmites, and friendly little fishies. While the best cenote may be the deserted and unmarked one a generous local leads you to, among the most picturesque are Gran Cenote and Tak Be Ha near Tulum, Suytun near Valladolid, Yaxbacaltun near Mérida, and Cenote Yokdzonot near Chichén Itzá.

Cenotes continue to evolve over time as rainwater seeps through the region's porous limestone, but scientists believe they originated 66 million years ago when the asteroid that killed the dinosaurs landed just off the north-west coast of the Yucatán. The impact caused all kinds of geological havoc, including fissures that rippled out from the center of the Chicxulub crater (now buried underground), resulting in the tidy Ring of Cenotes around Mérida and all the other cenotes, out to the Caribbean Sea.

60 million years ago

Bryce Canyon, Utah, USA

This national park packs quite a punch: it's small and compact (read: you can visit in a day if that's all the time you have) but staggeringly beautiful. Bryce was once a freshwater lake, which explains its amphitheater-like shape today. (The trail that runs along the perimeter at the top, leading to trails down into the canyon, would have been the edge of the lake.) The canyon is filled with thousands of picturesque, spire-like limestone hoodoos that built up over time and were revealed as the lake drained, and were then further formed by rain, snow, and ice carving away at them. Must-see stops at Bryce include Inspiration Point, Sunrise Point, and the 38-mile (61-kilometer) scenic drive loop. If you have time, Fairyland Canyon is a mildly strenuous 8-mile (13-kilometer) trail that more than pays off in views and picture-perfect selfie moments. *nps.gov/brca*

The vast Grand Canyon, Arizona

10 million years ago

Mammoth Cave National Park, Mammoth Cave, Kentucky, USA

The National Park Service estimates this cave to be 10 million years old, the result of rainwater slooooowly seeping through 350-million-year-old limestone, forming the extensive network of stalactites, stalagmites, and underground rivers, lakes, and caverns that is still expanding today. The result is the world's longest cave system, 400 miles (640 kilometers) of which have been explored so far. Humans have been finding their way into the caves for some 6000 years, as evidenced by the artifacts that have been unearthed by archaeologists – including gourds, drawings, grass moccasins, and mummies. A recent discovery is adding a few years to the story: the preserved teeth, jaw, and cartilage of a 330-million-year-old *Saivodus striatus*, a prehistoric shark that would rival a modern great white in size, dating from the Late Mississippian geological period, when the area was covered by a shallow sea. Visitors have been exploring the cave for centuries, first led by enslaved people like Stephen Bishop, who was brought to the caves as a teenager in 1838 and remains one of the caves' best explorers. Today, the most atmospheric (and maybe scary!) underground tours are those lit by torches. Mammoth Cave, the second oldest tourist attraction in the United States, is also a UNESCO World Heritage Site and an International Biosphere Reserve. The 130 wildlife species that call the caves home have adapted to the unique environment, notably the Kentucky cave shrimp (they're endangered, translucent, and albino) and the Eyeless Cave Fish (they "see" with no eyes). *nps.gov/maca*

5.5 million years ago

2.1 million years ago

Opposite: standing at the edge of Meteor Crater, Arizona

Makauwahi Cave Reserve, Kauai, Hawaii, USA

Hawaii's eight islands were formed as magma from Earth's core erupted and piled up on itself until it built into land masses – beginning with Kauai 5.5 million years ago and ending in Hawaii (a.k.a. the Big Island) 700,000 years ago – as the Pacific Tectonic plate slowly moved along a north-westerly path. In many ways, each island reveals its own take on geological time, progress, and decay. Secrets from the Earth abound everywhere, but one of the most interesting is inconspicuously nestled between stables and a beach on the south side of the island. You'll have to crouch down to get into the triangular hole in the rock face to access the Makauwahi Cave Reserve, and you'll probably need someone to point it out to you, but the payoff is great. The vast limestone cave and sinkhole is Hawaii's richest and best preserved fossil site, and it definitely feels like a find. _cavereserve.org_

Yellowstone Caldera, Yellowstone National Park, Wyoming, USA

Volcanoes happen deep beneath the Earth, when bubbling, brewing layers of hot magma and molten rock shoot to the surface and burst through. Dramatic and destructive. Yet also beautiful, when they leave behind natural phenomena like calderas, landforms created by the inward collapse of a volcano's peak. Most of Yellowstone National Park – all those geysers and hot springs – was formed by three massive volcanoes. The first, 2.1 million years ago, was the biggest in history, spewing ash as far away as Missouri and forming Island Park Caldera. Number two, 1.3 million years ago, was much smaller in comparison, but large enough to create Henry's Fork Caldera. The most recent one, Lava Creek, erupted 640,000 years ago, creating a 35-mile-wide, 45-mile-long (56-kilometer-wide, 72-kilometer-long) Yellowstone Caldera. If you find yourself particularly captivated by dramatic rainbow colors, from blue at the center to red at the edges, don't miss Grand Prismatic Spring 12 miles (19 kilometers) away. If you're keeping a checklist of sites, Old Faithful is about the midway point between the two. _nps.gov/yell_

HIGH DRAMA FROM OUTER SPACE AND INNER EARTH

50,000 years ago

Meteor Crater, Winslow, Arizona, USA

About 50,000 years ago during an asteroid collision in space, a 150-foot-wide (46-meter-wide) meteor of iron and nickel came crashing down to Earth. The impact – equal to 20 megatons of TNT – made a crater that is today a size equivalent to twenty football fields. In the 1960s and '70s, Apollo Mission astronauts trained here to practice for moon landings. This wasn't the meteor that killed off the dinosaurs, but it will still give you a humbling sense of how much more intense that one must have been.

40,000 years ago

La Brea Tar Pits, Los Angeles, California, USA

Los Angeles may be the land that worships the young, but smack in the center of the city are bubbling tar pits that hold the secrets to the Pleistocene Epoch. It turns out tar was an excellent material for trapping the Ice Age flora and fauna that got stuck in it, preserving them in near-perfect states for future study. More than one million fossils have been removed since 1906, including bones belonging to mammoths, sloths, dire wolves, saber-toothed cats, and coyotes, along with countless insects and plants, some of which are on display at the museum. Ongoing excavations at two active sites, which the public can visit, are expected to double the total haul. "Tar" is a slight misnomer, as the goo is actually asphalt, the lowest grade of crude oil, which rises to the surface from an underground petroleum reservoir that itself is between 5 and 25 million years old. *tarpits.org*

NATURE IS THEIR MUSE

Follow the work of the painters, sculptors, and light-and-space artists inspired by these very lands.

Ansel Adams	Nancy Holt
Lita Albuquerque	Winslow Homer
Alice Aycock	Patricia Johanson
John Baeder	Maya Lin
Edward Burtynsky	Ana Mendieta
Emily Carr	Mary Miss
Frederic Church	Isamu Noguchi
Agnes Denes	Georgia O'Keeffe
Arthur Dove	Clifford Ross
Richard Estes	Richard Serra
Walter De Maria	Robert Smithson
Marsden Hartley	Michelle Stuart
Michael Heizer	James Turrell
Joan Hill	Kay WalkingStick

BEAUTY IS TIMELESS

Go ahead: take a selfie. These spots are gorgeous. Mother Nature is a master maker.

Nā Pali Coast, Kauai, Hawaii, USA It's tough to play nature favorites in Hawaii, but this 17-mile (27-kilometer) coastal stretch of cliffs, coves, and waterfalls – best seen by water – is a stunner.

Pando Aspen Grove, Richfield, Utah, USA The single biggest living organism in the world, known as the Trembling Giant, has been around for at least 80,000 years and consists of 40,000 genetically identical aspen trees that share one root system across 106 acres (43 hectares) in Fishlake National Forest. The grove, named for the Latin word meaning "to spread," is a symbol of sustainability and interconnectedness – nature's own internet.

Keahiakawelo, Lanai, Hawaii, USA Known as the Garden of the Gods, this rock garden outside Lanai City is another geologist's dream: a red dirt desert strewn about with boulders and rock towers formed by centuries of erosion.

Arches National Park, Utah, USA A rock paradise with more than 2000 arches and a host of other geological wonders that continue to evolve over millions of years. They form immense bridges, windows, sandstone walls, and statues reflecting the orange and red glow of the sun.

Iceberg Alley, Newfoundland and Labrador, Canada Every spring and summer, hundreds of icebergs of varying shapes and sizes break off the western coast of Greenland and slowly make their way south. A beautiful parade.

El Yunque National Forest, Puerto Rico, USA In the only tropical rainforest in the United States, you can jump into a natural pool and walk under waterfalls at the end of your scenic hike.

Agua Azul, Palenque, Chiapas, Mexico The southern tip of Mexico is rich with waterfalls, but few are more dramatic than this collection of turquoise-blue cascades where rivers converge in the Lacandon Jungle.

Opposite: a bird's eye view of Nā Pali Coast, Kauai, Hawaii

Opposite: hiking Arches National Park, Utah

Cannon Beach, Oregon, USA
The entire Pacific Coast is a knockout, but the imposing, 235-foot (72-meter) Haystack Rock just off the expansive beach makes this an especially dramatic spot.

Banff National Park, Alberta, Canada It's a toss-up what's more striking up here, the jagged mountains or the glacial lakes. Either way, you're the winner.

The Piton Mountains, St. Lucia Two lush green volcanoes, Gros and Petit, are beacons of beauty on the Caribbean island's west coast.

Hierve el Agua, Oaxaca, Mexico The two natural phenomena may look like waterfalls but are instead petrified mineral deposits that built up over time, as calcium-rich spring water tumbled down the mountainside (like stalactites in caves, only outside). Bring a bathing suit; although the name means "the water boils," visitors can bathe in the cool waters of the small pools overlooking the mountains.

Underwater Coral Reefs, Bonaire This Dutch Antilles island is a scuba paradise, with excellent year-round conditions for divers and underwater photographers of all levels. Among the best sites are 1000 Steps, Karpata, Salt Pier, and Hilma Hooker.

Wrangell-St. Elias, Alaska, USA It's remote, rugged, icy Alaska to striking extremes in size (equal to six Yellowstones, making it the biggest US National Park), scale (home to nine of the sixteen highest peaks in the USA), and magnitude (four mountain ranges meet here). And glaciers, so many glaciers in all their states – flowing, receding, or simply being gorgeous.

Pictured Rocks National Lakeshore, Michigan, USA Incredible rock colors and blue waters on Lake Superior. The shore is lined with gorgeous pebbles, and at the right time of year, you might catch sight of the Northern Lights.

Armstrong Redwoods State Natural Reserve, Sonoma County, California, USA The California redwoods are towering, humbling beauties. Along the paths here are Colonel Armstrong Tree (the oldest, at 1400 years) and Parson Jones Tree (the tallest, at 310 feet/94 meters).

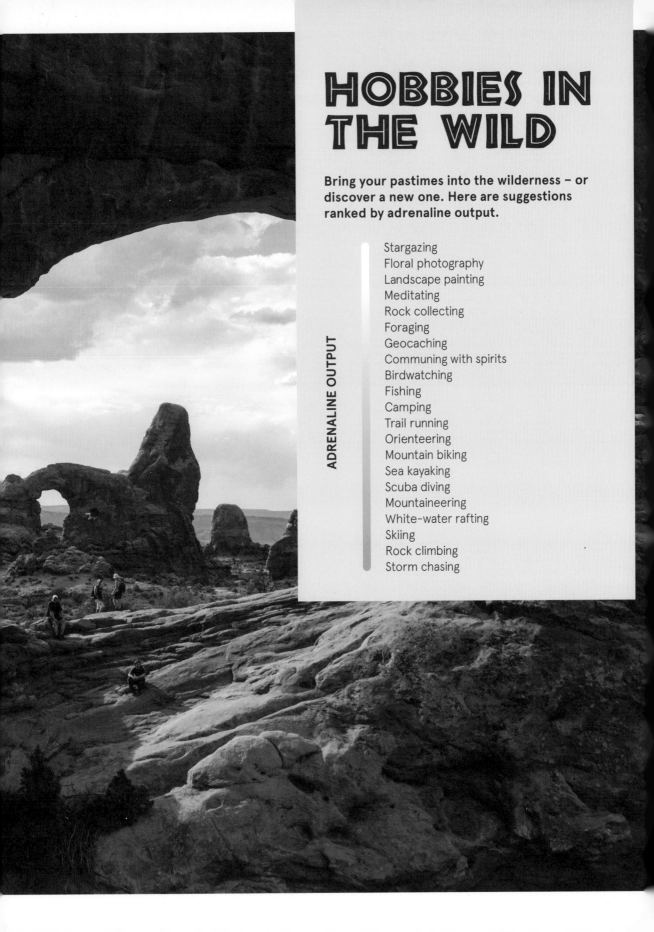

HOBBIES IN THE WILD

Bring your pastimes into the wilderness – or discover a new one. Here are suggestions ranked by adrenaline output.

ADRENALINE OUTPUT

Stargazing
Floral photography
Landscape painting
Meditating
Rock collecting
Foraging
Geocaching
Communing with spirits
Birdwatching
Fishing
Camping
Trail running
Orienteering
Mountain biking
Sea kayaking
Scuba diving
Mountaineering
White-water rafting
Skiing
Rock climbing
Storm chasing

AND THEN THERE WERE PEOPLE

So where did the first North American people come from? That's a good question. For a long time, the most popular theory held that the Clovis people arrived first, 13,000–15,000 years ago, marching from Siberia to Alaska across the Bering land bridge (which is now covered by the Bering Strait), hunting and gathering bison and wooly mammoth as they made their way to all points south.

Newer discoveries make competing theories: that proto-settlers arrived on boats from Japan by hopscotching across the Pacific 16,000 years ago, surviving on marine-rich kelp forests and seafood on the journey. Other archaeologists believe that 19,000-year-old tools that have been attributed to the Clovis actually have more in common with those used by the Solutrean people from Spain and France, who would have gotten to the New World on boats, following the seals they hunted across the north Atlantic.

But the latest evidence could blow all these theories away: a trove of more than 1900 tools found in the Chiquihuite Cave in the Astillero Mountains in Zacatecas, Mexico, are, according to radiocarbon dating, between 25,000 and 33,000 years old. Scientists don't yet know who made them or where they came from. But if these people came from Asia across Beringia and down to Mexico, they would have endured incredible hardship doing so, as the northern reaches of Earth were covered by large ice sheets at the time. Still, if it turns out to be true, North Americans will have more birthdays to celebrate than they previously thought – some 15,000 more.

The following sites are a window to the civilizations and the people with the oldest ties to this land.

Meadowcroft Rockshelter and Historic Village, Avella, Pennsylvania, USA

The site that claims to be the oldest human settlement in North America – 19,000 years old – was discovered accidentally by a farmer in 1955. Since then, archaeologists have found more than 2 million artifacts and ecofacts – tools, pottery, food remains – used by the early hunter-gatherers who took shelter under the rocky overhang. Visitors can take tours of the still-active archaeological site with Dr. James M. Adovasio, the scientist who first excavated the Rockshelter. The outdoor museum complex claims to be the oldest site of continuous habitation in North America, and other exhibits let visitors tour wigwams in a re-created 16th-century Monongahela village, sit in desks in an 1834 schoolhouse, and watch 19th-century blacksmithing in action. *heinzhistorycenter.org/meadowcroft*

Murray Springs Clovis Site, Sierra Vista, Arizona, USA

The San Pedro Riparian National Conservation Area near the Mexico border is one of the best documented sites of early humans in North America. Archaeologists have unearthed a trove of Clovis tools, which were used to hunt the animals whose remains have been found: a mammoth, a dozen bison, horses, and even, shocking as it may sound, camels. Another fantastic find here are extraterrestrial nanodiamonds somewhat controversially believed to be from a comet that crashed into the southern Canada/Great Lakes area, leading to a mass extinction of animals. From Canada to Arizona: that was one big impact. Other nearby Clovis sites are Lehner Mammoth Kill Site, Escapule Clovis Site, and Naco Mammoth Kill Site. *blm.gov/visit/murray-springs-clovis-site*

From left: an iceberg floats through the Labrador Sea; a 16th-century Monongahela Village at Meadowcroft Rockshelter and Historic Village, Pennsylvania

Opposite, from top: Chaco Canyon's ruins and Dark Sky stars in New Mexico

Teotihuacán, Teotihuacán, Mexico

In the centuries when B.C.E. turned into C.E., Teotihuacán, the City of the Gods, was home to 200,000 people, making it one of the first great cities of the Western Hemisphere. It was rich in architecture, urban planning, and trade in the luxury goods of the time, like ceramics, cacao, and exotic feathers. Very little is known about the Teotihuacanos – not where they came from, nor why their dominant culture ultimately collapsed – though we know that a spider goddess was their premier deity and that remains have been found there of the Maya, Mixtec, and Zapotec peoples. It's worth a day trip from nearby Mexico City to see the ruins that remain along Calzada de los Muertos (Avenue of the Dead), such as the Citadel, the Temple of the Plumed Serpent, and the Pyramid of the Sun, one of the largest pyramids in the world. You can climb it, though one of the best vantage points might be from above in a hot-air balloon.

Chaco Canyon, Nageezi, New Mexico, USA

The Chacoan people thrived in the harsh high desert environment here for centuries, developing sophisticated architectural and engineering systems, as evidenced by the remains still visible today. They built Great Houses, stone buildings aligned to lunar and solar paths, with multiple floors and hundreds of rooms, and also roads to connect the surrounding communities that converged here for economic and social exchanges. The Chaco civilization waned by the 12th century as people moved away, but these ancient Puebloans are the ancestors of contemporary Southwestern tribes. Camping overnight in Chaco Canyon is an excellent way for visitors to experience the petroglyphs, cliff dwellings, and ruins of the canyon, which has been designated an International Dark Sky Park. *nps.gov/chcu*

NATIONAL PARKS ON THE BIG SCREEN

Film directors and location scouts know Mother Nature is an excellent set designer. Grab the popcorn and watch US parks shine in their supporting roles.

Arches National Park, Utah
Indiana Jones and the Last Crusade

Badlands National Park, South Dakota
Dances with Wolves

Canyonlands National Park, Utah
127 Hours
Thelma & Louise

Crater Lake National Park, Oregon
Wild

Death Valley National Park, California
Star Wars, A New Hope

Denali National Park and Preserve, Alaska
Into the Wild

Glacier National Park, Montana
The River Wild
Continental Divide

Glen Canyon National Recreation Area, Arizona/Utah
Planet of the Apes (the 1968 original)

Redwood National Park and State Parks, California
E.T., The Extra-terrestrial
Return of the Jedi
The Lost World, Jurassic Park

Zion National Park, Utah
Butch Cassidy and the Sundance Kid

Cahokia Mounds, Collinsville, Illinois, USA

Very little is known about Cahokia, the prominent community at the fertile intersection of the Mississippi, Illinois, and Missouri rivers. One of the biggest cities in the world at the turn of the first millennium and the most influential pre-Columbian Native American city north of Mexico, it was home to the Mississippians, accomplished builders whose structures ranged from practical homes to monumental public works like Woodhenge, a circle of wooden poles used as a solar calendar aligned to the stars. Today, Cahokia is notable for the eighty earthen mounds around the complex, which visitors can climb and learn about in the museum center. Built by people diligently moving one woven basket of dirt at a time, the tallest, at 100 feet (30 meters), is Monks Mound, the largest earthwork in the Americas. *cahokiamounds.org*

Cobá, Yucatán Peninsula, Mexico

At its peak between 600 and 900 A.D., the ancient Maya city of Cobá was home to 50,000 people. Today it is one of the best preserved of Mexico's Maya ruins. Cobá, which means "waters stirred by the wind," is surrounded by two large lagoons in the dense jungle between Tulum and Valladolid. Archeologists first learned about the site in the mid 1800s, and it remains largely unexcavated. But visitors can explore the shaded walkways that were once a network of white roads called sacbeob, three settlements, and climb 120 steps to Ixmoja, the highest Maya temple in the Yucatán. That's one more reason to pick Cobá over its former rival, the more touristy Chichén Itzá, where climbing is forbidden.

L'Anse aux Meadows, Great Northern Peninsula, Newfoundland, Canada

Columbus was hardly the first European to make it to North America: the Vikings beat him by four centuries, charting a course along northern seas and landing in Newfoundland around 1000 A.D. The excavated settlement at this UNESCO World Heritage Site in Newfoundland is the only authenticated evidence of Vikings in North America. It includes eight structures – one forge, three homes, and four workshops for iron production and woodworking, along with 800 artifacts like knitting needles and oil lamps. (Industrious, those Vikings!) The ruins here closely resemble those from a similar time period that have been found in Greenland and Iceland, and also correspond with stories about Leif Erikson in the Vinland Sagas and other Norse tales.

Lake Powell meanders in Glen Canyon National Recreation Area in Utah

CHAPTER 5

FOLLOW NATURE'S LEAD

Maps are amended, trade routes change course, borders are redrawn. Yet we pay more attention to these artificial boundaries – our endeavors to control the world – than we do to the slow growth of the giant sequoia or the dependable, age-old migratory path of the shaggy bison.

Previous page: fishing at The Lodge
at Blue Sky in Utah

Opposite: a carefree romp at
Nimmo Bay in British Columbia

As we have read, heard, and even witnessed with our
own eyes, when human economies are on hold, nature
flourishes. The rivers run, the winds blow, the trees
continue their steady climb upward. A very lucky thing
for us humans, indeed, as we benefit greatly from this
separate performance schedule.

Over a thousand studies regarding humans in
nature conducted over the last several years point to
the same outcome again and again: the more time we
spend in natural settings, the better we feel emotionally,
psychologically, energetically. Getting to know an outdoor
place really well is the best way to start. Whether it is
observing nature from your backyard, a fire escape, or
a bench in your local park, finding a place where you
can sit for a long time and notice what's going on with
the creatures and plants at different times of day and in
various weather conditions and throughout the seasons
reduces feelings of isolation and loneliness, creates a
meditative practice, and cultivates connection with the
little worlds all around you.

No wonder people are increasingly drawn to the
great outdoors. If you are privileged to have access to
a beach or woods, your mental and physical health is in
for a treat – in the form of stress reduction, increased
vitamin D, and improved immunity.

When it comes to building a trip in the wilderness
of North America, the sheer multitude of options can be
dizzying. The continent is vast and outrageous in terms of
geographical offerings and environments, from the Great
Plains to the Canadian Shield to the Caribbean islands.
All the major biomes of the world can be found here –
desert, grassland, rainforest, tundra, coral reef – with
massive mountain ranges, active volcanoes, monolithic
glaciers, the planet's largest freshwater area, and the
world's most active geysers.

Experiencing nature is a beautiful thing whenever and
wherever you can get it. If you want to take it to a new
level, why not build a trip around an event like a wildflower
superbloom, a lunar eclipse, or a frozen forest waterfall?
If you're worried you'll miss the crowds, link up with an
animal or insect migration.

Consult Mother Nature's calendar and map out fresh
ideas for mingling with nature across the continent.

SPRING

Maple sugar shacks, superblooms, and severe and humbling landscapes will have you bowing to the cactus crown.

Buckets catching sap from taps in maple trees is a harbinger of spring in the northern latitudes. Centuries ago, European settlers in Canada observed First Nations peoples boiling sap into sugar to use as a high-caloric food at the end of a long, harsh winter. Today, Canada produces 80 percent of the world's maple syrup, and the tradition is still rooted in ritual. Visiting a **cabane à sucre (sugar shack) in Eastern Canada** during sugar season is as delicious as it sounds. The festive springtime activity begins with a bike, hike, snow shoe, sleigh ride, or cross-country ski to a family-run cabin surrounded by maple trees. Inside the wooden house warmed by a roaring fire, diners dig into an indulgent feast honoring the sweet amber stuff. Traditionally, the menu begins with split pea soup and maple-cured ham and ends with taffy made from hot syrup poured onto snow.

In California, **Antelope Valley**'s poppy reserve does a costume change every spring, when an **annual bloom of fiery orange flowers** blankets the entire 8-mile (13-kilometer) **Mojave Desert** grassland tract, generally from March through May. After particularly significant rains one season, NASA captured the burst of color from outer space.

Opposite: an explosion of wildflowers in Texas

This page: enjoying the big sky at The Lodge at Blue Sky

From left: a desert superbloom in California; the skies put on a sunset show for Appalachian Trail walkers in North Carolina

A combination of sun, wind, and a very wet rainy season sets the stage for the **rare botanical desert phenomenon known as the springtime superbloom**, when an unusually high proportion of wildflowers reveal themselves at once. When the specific conditions are just right (often around the second week of March), **California's Anza-Borrego Desert State Park** reveals thick carpets of desert lilies, evening primrose, ghost flowers, sunflowers, and purple sand verbena.

Saguaro National Park, in **Arizona**, is the prime spot for meeting the statuesque saguaro: tree-like cacti that can grow to 40 feet (12 meters) tall over 175 years or so, delivering quite the emotional punch with their anthropomorphic arm gestures silhouetted against the sunset. **May and June evenings bring out huge white flower crowns on the giant plants**; in summer, cacti bear a red flowering fruit topper (a feast for long-nose bats, coyotes, and cactus wrens). To this day, the Tohono O'odham Nation collects the fruit to eat fresh and preserve in jams. You'll find the densest population of cacti in the western district, but don't overlook the agave, Indian paintbrushes, and prairie clovers that also burst through the sand each spring. Cruise along Bajada Loop Drive or Picture Rocks Road for an eyeful of golden poppies.

Big Bend National Park's Chihuahuan Desert, the largest desert on the continent, stretching along Mexico, Texas, New Mexico, and Arizona, can be a pretty inhospitable place for people (see: over 115°F/46°C weather). But incredible desert scenery – volcanoes, curiously eroded rocks, old mines, hot springs, archeological sites, and a high and dry wilderness ecosystem – are among the park's incredible offerings. Some hardy plant species persist; unlike in other places across the United States, **spring does not frolic in like a lamb, but explodes with color** and life and high winds and a bloom of prickly poppies, enormous trumpet-shaped jimson weed (a hallucinogen used by Indigenous peoples), desert willows, rock nettles, and marigolds.

Every spring, **The Texas Hill Country Wildflower Trail** plays host to a particularly lovely assortment of wildflowers due to a convergence of several environmental and geographic characteristics. Thanks to Texas icon Lady Bird Johnson's devotion to preserving and restoring native species, landscape architects to this day work 800,000 acres (323,749 hectares) of highway median blossoms, sowing new seeds and pruning existing buds into vistas of bluebonnets, mountain laurel, Indian paintbrushes, violet horsemint, Mexican plums, and prairie verbena, from Austin to San Antonio to Fredericksburg to San Marcos. A real treat is taking the 4.5-hour driving loop through Vanderpool, Mountain Home, and Ingram. Known as the **Western Kerr, Bandera and Real County Scenic Drive**, it covers some of the Hill Country's prettiest countryside.

Yellow bird flowers stand out against a bright California sky

SUMMER

Firefly sanctuaries, u-picks, hatch chiles, and hot-weather grapes.

Every July and August in the **Mexican state of Tlaxcala** – about two hours outside Mexico City – hundreds of thousands of **fireflies begin their mating dance in the forests of pines, oaks, and oyamel**, resulting in a nocturnal light show that spans 35 miles (56 kilometers), from the ridgeline at the northern tip of the woods to the volcano of Popocatépetl. High elevation means the air is thin and fresh and wet, an ideal climate for Nanacamilpa lightning bugs. Piedra Canteada (*piedracanteada.com.mx*), a local eco-lodge and tourism company, escorts guests to the firefly sanctuary for a unique spectating experience. Be prepared to walk in total darkness with no flashlight, bug repellent, or cellphones to keep light pollution (and people pollution) to a minimum. (You wouldn't want to ruin the amorous mood.)

Come May and June, it's total **mango madness on the Eastern Caribbean island of Saint Lucia**, a mountainous volcanic spit of land with verdant rainforests and silky beaches. Trees laden with the heavy tropical fruits line the roads and bend into yards, dropping bright and juicy orbs onto the sand. It's easy to collect an armful on your way to the beach, and you can sample as many as forty varieties – from European imports like the Julie and Graham to the Asian Woz to the local Palwee – each with their own texture, flavor, and color.

Honeysuckle, iris, marigolds, and other gorgeous blooms burst onto the scene every summer in **Crested Butte, Colorado's wildflower capital** (with an annual flower festival dedicated to the blooms to prove it). The high alpine valleys surrounding the town are suited for a variety of native species.

Berry u-picks (strawberries, raspberries, blueberries) are a beloved summer tradition all across the continent. But unlike those ubiquitous and domesticated berries, **the lesser-known huckleberry cannot be tamed, growing wildly in the forests of north-western Montana, mainly in Flathead and Kootenai National Forests and Glacier National Park.** Day hikers and road trippers – along with black bears, deer, and coyotes – can be found passionately picking the juicy little berries, tongues purple, throughout July and August. The towns of Whitefish, Seeley Lake, and Trout Creek (population: 300, and declared "Huckleberry Capital of Montana" by the state's legislature) honor the deep-purple gems with annual festivals showcasing "fresh hucks" in all their glory – in ice creams, pies, cobblers, jams, sodas, and barbecue sauces.

From July to September, recreational scallopers don snorkel masks and **ply the seagrass beds of Florida's panhandle in search of tasty bay scallops** they must pluck by hand (commercial scalloping is not permitted here, nor are the bivalves sold in stores or served in restaurants). Shellfish lovers can link up with boat charters in Homosassa and Crystal Rivers run by crew who know the best place to drop anchor and hunt for mollusks – and bump into those huge Floridian sea cows – a.k.a. gentle manatees.

Opposite: cruising the waters that surround Nimmo Bay in British Columbia

This page, from left: pondering the Adirondack Mountains at The Point in New York; a flower child in a superbloom in Agoura Hills, California

83

The celebrated Hatch chile

Opposite: out for a ride around The Lodge at Blue Sky in Utah

An under-the-radar wine culture is extending its hearty tendrils in the **Valle de Guadalupe region of western Mexico**, where Pacific coastal plains and a Mediterranean-type microclimate provide **ideal conditions for harvesting red grapes**. Add to that the serious local chefs providing inventive fine-dining options, and it's no wonder seasoned oenophiles and gourmands alike refer to this area of Baja as the Napa Valley of Mexico (only better, we'd argue, as it lacks pretension, exorbitant pricing, hefty crowds, and a silly wine train). The spirit of innovation is particularly apparent along the Wine Trail during the **summer harvest celebration, Fiestas de la Vendimia**, when parties, pressings, picnics, and more show off the best the region has to offer.

The **Perseids peak in August**, when night owls can catch a show of zippy, long-tailed meteors sailing across the sky – twenty to fifty per hour throughout the nights and early mornings of the two-to-three-day event. **Nevada's Massacre Rim International Dark Sky Sanctuary is one of the best viewing spots** for the naked eye (NASA recommends giving yourself forty-five minutes to adjust to the darkness). If you really count your lucky stars, you may even catch an "earthgrazer," a very long, slow, and memorable meteor that travels horizontally across the evening sky.

August and September is **Hatch chile season in New Mexico.** The super-hyped peppers are limited in availability, typically only attainable during these months, when a rampant fan base orders fresh, dried, and frozen shipments for delivery to all ends of the country, and when the smell of the sweet-spicy chile, grown in the Hatch Valley and irrigated by the Rio Grande, is literally in the air across the state. Chile-roasting operations pop up at roadside stands, in supermarket parking lots, and in backyard fire pits, and braided dried pepper garlands decorate nearly every door. The prized crop is part of New Mexico's identity, but years of climate change mean the future is uncertain for the delicate cultivar.

AUTUMN

Fiery leaf colors, jewel-like persimmons, low-level aurora borealis, and cranberry bogs as far as the eye can see.

The grapes are hanging heavy on the vine throughout **southern Ontario**, which sits along the same latitude as Tuscany and Oregon. The modern winemaking tradition around here may be less than fifty years old, but the hundred-plus wineries in the handful of wine regions didn't take long to make their mark. Prince Edward County, the island on Lake Ontario two hours east of Toronto that's drawing growers with an edgy sensibility, is **known for its pinot noirs (at Keint-He Winery) and chardonnays (at Closson Chase)**. Ward off any hangovers with a wood-fired pizza while overlooking the vineyard at Norman Hardie Winery. Self-direct your visit by following the Taste Trail, stopping at farm stands, cideries, and eateries, or the Millennium Trail, a 30-mile (48-kilometer) former railway that makes for a nice bike ride. Late September brings the TASTE festival, where local producers showcase their best. And while you're taking in the gorgeous changing leaves, don't forget to walk along the beach: **Sandbanks Provincial Park has some of the most beautiful shoreline in Canada** and is home to the Sandbanks Music Festival in September. If you come later in the season, you might see wine growers "hill up" – bury their vines to insulate them from the oncoming winter chill.

What a sight! The **flooding of ruby-red cranberry beds** (originally cultivated by the Narragansett people of the Algonquin Nation) **coincides with fall foliage season throughout New England and Wisconsin** (the nation's leading producer of the crop), so finding your way to a cranberry bog delivers a double dose of colorful grandeur. Workers harvest cranberries during Cranberry Time by flooding the fruit beds and wading into waist-high waters to collect the floating berries. Those who want a closer look can book a marsh walk or boat ride at many of the family-run bogs.

New England charm without the crowds can be found in **Michigan's Upper Peninsula**, a remote but idyllic region of the Midwest that feels like a great secret – particularly during prime **leaf-peeping season** every autumn. The UP – as locals call it, pronouncing each letter – is pristine and untouched. You can hike the Porcupine Mountains, careen down a mountain slope on a bike, and check out Isle Royale, one of the least-visited national parks in the United States. You'll come for the nature but you'll stay for the Yoopers (as the locals are called) who run cozy and unpretentious inns, microbreweries, adventure companies, and a bakery selling house-roasted coffee, fruitcakes, and preserves made by the monks of Poorrock Abbey (_poorrockabbey.com_).

Michigan's **Headlands Dark Sky Park** is a 550-acre (223-hectare) expanse on the shores of Lake Michigan, made up of undeveloped beaches and an **ideal low-latitude location to spot the aurora borealis** – a mecca for stargazers. Due to the low pollution levels, at night the park offers unobstructed views showcasing more of the universe above. Technically, there's no camping allowed, however the park is open 365 days a year and you can stay as long as you'd like. If you're not up for an all-nighter, plan ahead and rent a room in The Guest House (_midarkskypark.org_), a large home on the property that accommodates twenty people with private bedrooms and bathrooms.

November brings the **persimmon harvest in Indiana**. The autumnal-hued fruit can be found throughout Hoosier woodlands and on the occasional city street. The most important use for the pulp is to produce a warm persimmon pudding for dessert on Thanksgiving Day. This grand treat requires freshly whipped cream on top.

Opposite: trees doing what they do best around Ontario as leaves change in the fall

WINTER

Time slows down with frozen waterfalls and desert meteor showers.

A snow-dipped forest hike through **Multnomah Falls, Oregon**, requires a pair of sturdy boots or (even better!) ice cleats, tire chains for your car, and definitely a hot thermos. A little extra work goes a long way – you will be rewarded with temple-like solitude and **massive ice sculptures in the form of frozen waterfalls**.

California's Death Valley, the hottest place on Earth, also has one of the darkest night skies in the United States. (The International Dark-Sky Association has given it the Gold Tier designation.) The darkest part is in the north-west of the park, around Ubehebe Crater, where, with the naked eye, one can see the Milky Way's shadows as well as the Andromeda and Triangulum galaxies. Consult a night sky atlas and time your visit with the **annual Geminid meteor shower** in December (bonus points if you can coordinate with a new moon) for a showstopping, neck-craning experience that involves witnessing tons of giant fireballs radiating from the constellation Gemini.

Long dark nights make winter an excellent time to **spot the elusive Northern Lights** that dance in the sky from September to April but are at their best from January to March. The closer to the North Pole you get, the better your chances of seeing them and the more dazzling the spectacle. Two excellent spots are **Fairbanks, Alaska**, which sits under the Auroral Oval, a celestial area of concentrated aurora light activity, and the forests around the **Athabasca University Geophysical Observatory near Edmonton, Alberta**, where they study the aurora borealis.

The **Fang, in Vail, Colorado**, has long been popular with ice climbers drawn to the 100-foot-high (30-meter-high) **ice column that forms in extreme temperatures** and is notable because it freezes entirely, from top to bottom. (A waterfall's base doesn't always freeze.) The safest route for spectating, though, is a lovely, moderate forty-minute hike to the base.

In **Alaska's Chugach State Park**, just outside Anchorage, a roaring **200-foot (61-meter) waterfall** dazzles as it turns to ice while water continually flows into a blue pool at its base. You can follow the trail there or witness the moving sculpture from the viewing deck, a fairly easy, round-trip hike that's less than 2 miles (3 kilometers).

The icicle-laden **Mainland Ice Caves** of the **Apostle Islands National Lakeshore in Wisconsin** form each winter when Lake Superior's caverns freeze over. The ice needs to be at least 10 inches (25 centimeters) thick before the National Park Service allows visitors to take the 2-mile (3-kilometer) hike to the caves.

The milky-blue waters of Alberta's largest reservoir, **Lake Abraham, surrounded by the snow-capped Canadian Rockies**, are filled with naturally occurring methane – not necessarily something to celebrate due to its dangerous (and flammable!) designation as a greenhouse gas. But come winter, when the waters freeze, big **methane bubbles form and get trapped just under the surface**, a beautifully strange phenomenon that draws photographers and outdoor enthusiasts alike.

Opposite: frozen methane bubbles in Abraham Lake in Alberta

This page, from left: the Northern Lights; paddle boarding in Nimmo Bay, British Columbia

Earthship Biotecture, Taos, New Mexico, USA This eco-construction company builds totally off-grid homes for self-sufficient living that take care of the six things humans need to live a "harmonious life on Earth" (everything from clean water to fresh food to waste management). You can find their autonomous houses all over the world, but you can spend a night or a week at one of their WiFi and Netflix-enabled Earthship rentals at headquarters – funky jungle greenhouses with fountains, fish ponds, and banana trees – on a beautiful mesa overlooking the Sangre de Cristo mountains. *earthshipglobal.com*

Nimmo Bay Wilderness Resort, British Columbia, Canada Once upon a time, a young family who wanted a life immersed in nature set out to build an off-grid lodge on Canada's wild west coast in the Great Bear Rainforest. Forty years later, the nine-cabin resort (with a floating dock, sauna, wildlife excursions, and seasonally driven meals) continues its ethical, climate-friendly, thoughtful approach to hospitality, reviving weary spirits and encouraging adventure and organic connection with nature. *nimmobay.com*

STAY CLOSE TO NATURE

Where to rewild yourself.

Primland, Meadows of Dan, Virginia, USA Planted on 12,000 acres (4865 hectares) among the spectacular Blue Ridge Mountains, Primland's tree houses are cozy, French-designed cabins built around solid treetop branches, with decks that give way to panoramic views of the valley. Guests get around on 4x4s, throw tomahawks, shoot sporting clays, hook fish, climb big trees (with harnesses), exercise at the outdoor gym in the woods, and, come evening, explore the night sky over cocktails with the resort's Director of Astronomy. *primland.com*

Opposite, from top: a bowl of soup at Nimmo Bay; dockside action at The Point, New York

This page, from top: a cozy fireplace at The Point; a bedroom treehouse at Primland in Virginia

Mustang Monument, Nevada, USA Activist and philanthropist Madeleine Pickens rescued 650 mustangs heading to the slaughterhouse; they now run like the wind at her wild horse sanctuary in Wells, a few hours west of Salt Lake City. The guest accommodations include ten beautifully appointed and hand-painted teepees, as well as a lavish ten-room cabin and a cozy saloon. Resident Native Americans share their history and stories in the evenings, a lovely end to adrenaline-fueled days spent riding, four-wheeling, and dining under the stars. It gets even better: 100 percent of the profits benefit Saving America's Mustangs. *mustangmonument.com*

Azulik, Tulum, Mexico This hotel is compelling for what it does not offer: WiFi, cell service, AC, or television. The adults-only, off-grid, wellness-minded treehouse villas won't contribute to artificial light pollution, either. Instead, an Azulik staffer comes over with candles at dusk. Most villas only have bathtubs, because "the shower is an invention of rushed men." Spend time swinging on a hanging bed, chilling out on the clothing-optional beach, or trying out rejuvenating spa experiences like Mayan steam treatments, hot stone massages, and shaman-led rebirth rituals. *azulik.com*

The Point Resort, Saranac Lake, New York, USA An adults-only getaway for those who like roughing it Rockefeller style. The whimsically decorated stone and timber mansion is one of the Adirondack Great Camps built by Gilded Age magnates along Upstate New York's lakeshores. Then and now, the house delivers nature in luxurious trappings – rock climbing in the High Peaks and boat rides in the resort's mahogany Budsin during summer and, in winter, skating, ice fishing, and curling on the frozen lake or cross-country skiing and snowshoeing on miles of paths that stretch through the Adirondacks. *thepointresort.com*

Fogo Island Inn, Nova Scotia, Canada

This award-winning retreat caters to adventure seekers, nature enthusiasts, design lovers, and experiential travelers who like the idea of taking planes, trains, and ferries to an extremely isolated location on the edge of the North Atlantic across the sea from Greenland. The striking hotel, an all-inclusive run as a nonprofit that reinvests all funds in the island, is sparking a new form of cultural tourism in an environment where guests feel at home and in total harmony with the surrounding seas and landscape. *fogoislandinn.ca*

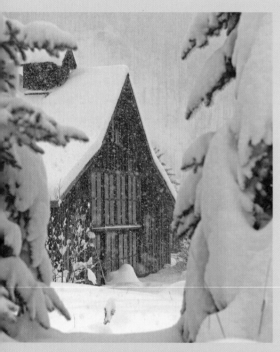

From top: the setting at The Lodge at Blue Sky; the library at Fogo Island Inn in Nova Scotia; the bathhouse at Dunton Hot Springs in Colorado

Opposite, from top: Dunton Hot Springs at dusk; the outdoor pool at The Lodge at Blue Sky; the indoor pool at Dunton Hot Springs

Jungle Bay, Soufrière, Dominica

On a school trip to Saint John's Cinnamon Bay in 1972, young Samuel Raphael was so inspired by the environmental lessons he learned that years later he returned to his native Dominica – which remains one of the least-visited Caribbean islands – to put those principles into practice. After the decade-old boutique resort was destroyed in a 2015 tropical storm, the hotel committed to following international geotourism and ecotourism guidelines in building sixty eco-villas overlooking Soufrière-Scotts Head Marine Reserve. Dominica has its sights set on becoming one of the world's first climate resilient nations, a mission that has fueled the resort's focus on environmental and socio-economic preservation, along with efforts at preserving the Amerindian (Kalinago) culture and providing meaningful employment to islanders. Immersive guest experiences run the gamut from snorkeling to hiking the cloud forest to hands-on cooking and drumming lessons. But you could also just hang at the beach. *junglebaydominica.com*

The Lodge at Blue Sky, Park City, Utah, USA California couple Mike and Barb Phillips took a sustainable approach to designing their love letter to the pristine outdoors, choosing to build their resort in a spot that would require virtually no tree removal. This remote beauty in the foothills of the Uinta Mountains consists of luxurious creekside cabins, local limestone–and–pine suites built into the hillside, an infinity pool, a restaurant (serving "modern mountain" cuisine based on the confluence of the Chinese, Spanish, and Native American cultures that worked the western railroad expansion), and an adventure outpost for a ridiculous number of outdoor activities on a 3500-acre (1416-hectare) parcel of land near Park City and Salt Lake. Much of the produce is sourced on the farm (everything else comes from neighboring suppliers), which also serves as a refuge for outcasts, like the injured livestock and abused horses who make up the Saving Gracie Equine Healing Foundation. _aubergeresorts.com/bluesky_

Dunton Hot Springs, Colorado, USA You'll be staying in a reincarnated ghost town buried in the San Juan Mountains. There's an old saloon and dance hall, adorable hand-hewn log cabin suites, and gorgeous indoor-outdoor mineral springs. Horses are at the ready for rugged mountain rides. Technical hikes are equipped with fixed cables, ladders, and bridges. Sleigh rides, ice climbing, and Nordic skiing are on offer in winter. Western comfort foods come from the farm, the river, and the local vineyard. To get even closer to nature, guests can opt to spend the night in one of the kitted-out teepees dotting the property or book one of the eight luxurious tents at Dunton River Camp, just steps from the Dolores River. _duntondestinations.com/hot-springs_

LEAD THE WAY: ANIMAL MIGRATIONS

As social creatures, we humans are now all too familiar with exercises in isolation and quarantine – which may give us a better appreciation for species who make an art of moving around together. The ultimate travelers, these birds, bugs, and mammals traverse large swaths of land or water – or both! – despite changing environmental conditions. All in the name of species survival.

King of the North: Polar Bears

The small, unassuming Canadian town of Churchill stands at an ecotone – a juncture of ecologically and geographically defined areas: the western coast of central Canada's Hudson Bay, the Arctic tundra, and the boreal forest. Accessible only by Hudson Bay Railway or airplane, those who make the trek to the tundra at the shores of the Hudson Bay will find it to be a stopover for more than one thousand bears on their annual migration to the pack ice. Since they are normally solitary creatures, there's no other place on earth where humans can witness so many bears at once (safely, and from a distance). But they are not alone. There are also bearded seals, gray wolves, caribou, Arctic foxes, and the emerald Northern Lights, making the region a veritable jewel in the country's wildlife crown.

Queen Baleen: Pacific Gray Whales

These magnificent creatures undertake what is considered the longest mammal migration in the animal kingdom, beginning in the Bering and Chukchi seas and making their way 12,500 miles (20,117 kilometers) south to the warm waters of the Baja Peninsula: Scammon's and San Ignacio lagoons and Magdalena Bay. There are some serious feminine vibes in this protected area, as hundreds of whales give birth in the back reaches of the lagoons and newly pregnant females act as midwives, helping with delivery and care of the young. Once they've given birth, new moms may look for "friendlies" – small tour boats of peaceful humans – to interact with and show off their calves. The most curious of all "spyhop," vertically poking their heads out of the water. Over the first few months of life in the lagoons, babies will learn how to dive, breathe, monitor currents, and socialize.

Regal Resting Place: Monarch Butterflies

From November to March in Michoacán's Santuario de la Mariposa Monarca el Rosario, in Angangueo, when 100 million monarchs gather, the fir forests are ablaze with orange flutters, a sensory experience completely unique to interior Mexico. In some places, the ground is so deep with resting butterflies, it looks like a bed of fall flowers. Fly into Mexico City and rent a car for the two-hour journey west through dusty mountain roads, past strange ruins and mysterious monasteries, and eventually into the fragrant transvolcanic pine forests hidden well in the central highlands. Pay close attention to road signs and directions and arrive at the butterfly sanctuary by noon, when activity peaks.

Opposite: it's a toss-up who wins the prize for cuteness – sea lions or bears

Monarch butterflies converge every year in Michoacán, Mexico

Beachy and Free: Wild Horses

The undeveloped sands and salt marshes of the windswept barrier islands of Assateague and Chincoteague, between Ocean City, Maryland, and the Virginia coast, is an area known for its unique band of wild horses who have been roaming miles of the pristine area for hundreds of years. (Legend has it they are descendants of shipwrecked equine survivors.) Every July, at slack tide (a roughly thirty-minute period between tides when there is little to no current), herders on horseback called the Saltwater Cowboys round up a large group of feral horses to help them find their way across the Assateague Channel to the east side of Chincoteague Island. The pony swim attracts lots of hippophiles, so your best bet, if you want to see equine swimming action, is to charter a boat (plan a few months in advance) or catch the horses coming to shore in the marshlands at Pony Swim Lane. Make a few days of it, enjoying the low-key towns, small B&Bs, local restaurants, and beach walks with wild horses in the distance.

Pit-Stop Partiers: Sandhill Cranes

For thousands of years, sandhill cranes have been migrating along an hourglass-shaped route called the Central Flyway, stretching from Siberia to Mexico. The path cinches into an 80-mile-wide path in Nebraska's Central Platte River Valley, where 600,000 of the leggy creatures fuel up on corn and have their fill of the invertebrates found in the Platte's sandbar-filled channels. During the springtime bacchanal, the cranes exhibit behaviors (like dancing!) that can only be found at this prairie stopover, thus attracting thousands of "craniacs" and their binoculars, keen to catch sight of elaborate mating rituals and hear impressive whooping sounds. Birdwatching during sunrises and sunsets in March are particularly epic, and The National Audubon Society organizes crane-viewing trips (and even overnight photography blinds) within the 2400-acre (971-hectare) Rowe Sanctuary they operate along the river.

Tons of Idle Fun: Alaskan Walruses

Alaska in the summer is prime time for spotting walruses. Every July and August, thousands of male walruses leave the waters of Western Alaska to bask in the midnight sun and rest their thousand-pound bodies – brown and wrinkly, and lazily piled up so their heads are resting on others' backs with their ivory tusks gleaming. It's quite a sight. These "haulouts" (land areas where walruses congregate when not swimming) typically happen two weeks after the sea ice recedes, and tours along the Alaska Peninsula are available to view this sea-to-beach event. You have to fly from Anchorage to small fishing communities near Bristol Bay, then travel by bush plane or boat to remote lodges or camping outposts. It's remote and rugged and expensive and wild.

A Buzzy Light Show: Synchronized Fireflies

Each year, from late May to mid June, a unique species of lightning bugs flashes their bioluminescent bodies in synchronized patterns. The elaborate mating display makes the woods look absolutely magical to those lucky enough to see it in action. Travelers can pay a visit to the Elkmont Viewing Area of the Great Smoky Mountains National Park in Gatlinburg, Tennessee, during the peak flashing season (an eight-day event), but only if they have entered – and won – the lottery for a coveted ticket. (The lottery opens in April.)

Flying South for the Winter: Shorebirds on the Go

In the northern hemisphere, birds fly south for the winter. This is not news. If you live along their path, you might see them stopping in fields to rest along the journey. Not so the sandpipers, short-billed dowitchers, semipalmated plovers, and black-bellied plovers who make a pit stop in the mudflats at Mary's Point in New Brunswick in late summer and early fall to eat as much as they can before beginning their nonstop flight to South America.

Wild horses roam free on Assateague Island in Maryland and Virginia

CHAPTER 6

BRIGHT LIGHTS, BIG CITIES

So far, we've spent the majority of this book extolling the virtues of open spaces, wide vistas, and blissful emptiness as far as the eye can see. Time to turn to something a little closer to home: the rambunctious, jam-packed, head-turning, and often noisy glory that is the big, bad city.

We say all this with love, by the way, because the metropolis is the place we call home. In fact, New York City, where we both live (Jeralyn in Brooklyn and Pavia in Manhattan), may be the most rambunctious, head-turning-est, and damn-noisiest of them all. (Bueno, si, we see you, Mexico City.)

Cities aren't easy places to navigate. At their worst, they're too dense, too claustrophobic, too intense, too invasive, and just too much. There's never enough room, green space, or resources to go around. Cities are corrupt, full of big businesses that abuse the system and politicians who let them get away with it. Cities are crowded: about 83 percent of Americans live in urban areas, and 22.6 million people live in greater Mexico City alone.

And yet. At their best, cities are a marvel of unparalleled electricity – hotbeds of creativity, magnets for new ideas, centers of commerce and exchange. Cities force different peoples and cultures to learn to live together, an intermingling that has given rise time and again to exciting and dynamic fusions in music, food, language, literature, politics, and style. If things are always moving in the city, it's because its citizens push for it, zooming in new directions light years ahead – and taking the rest of us along for the ride. The leaders and visionaries who challenge norms, fighting for justice and inspiring others to join the cause, are often the products of cities. Fulcrums of passion and catalysts for change, cities are where dreamers and strivers go to turn their visions into realities.

Let's hear it for the noise.

Previous page: an elegant perch at Maison de la Luz in New Orleans

Opposite, clockwise from top: the neon lights of Edmonton; the dining room at Frasca Food and Wine in Denver; the welcoming Woodlark Hotel in Portland; the Museum of Human Rights in Winnipeg

SHINE THE SPOTLIGHT

The checklist of North America's top urban areas – the best known, most populous, and most visited – would include Mexico City, New York, Toronto, Los Angeles, Washington, D.C., San Francisco, Miami, Chicago, and Dallas. And while these cities deserve their many accolades, they're increasingly sharing the spotlight, which is easy to understand when you see what these so-called second- and third-tier cities have to offer.

Portland, Maine, USA

The no-fuss and unpretentious spirit makes life Downeast wicked good.

Low-key and understated with just the right amount of quirky charm, Portland embodies the classic Maine virtues – including an unwillingness to show off.

The Old Port neighborhood is a charmer, all cobblestone streets and salty ocean breezes. Low brick buildings are home to specialty independent boutiques where the merchandise – toys, housewares, clothes, books – was clearly selected by a smart and knowing proprietor who's probably on hand to help you out. Visit Treehouse Toys (*treehousetoys.us*) for games, puzzles, and books; Portland Trading Co. (*portlandtradingco. com*) for men's and women's fashion, along with home and apothecary products with a vintage vibe; Sherman's (*shermans.com*) for books and paper products; and Fitz & Bennett (*fitzandbennetthome.com*) for super chic housewares, both old and new. When you're ready for a snack, try the local favorites: potato doughnuts at The Holy Donut (*theholydonut.com*), lobster roll at Eventide Oyster Co. (*eventideoysterco.com*), fries at Duckfat (*duckfat.com*), flavored fudge at Old Port Candy Co. (*oldportcandyco.com*), and cocktails at Blyth & Burrows (*blythandburrows.com*). The Press Hotel (*thepresshotel. com*) was once home to the printing plant and offices of the Portland Press Herald (the state's largest newspaper). Its library is decorated with newspaper-print wallpaper and there's even a typewriter station where you can write letters and have them mailed for free, courtesy of the hotel.

Get out to one of many paths along the rugged coast for a walk that's relaxing in the happy sunshine and dramatic and invigorating when it's wet and chilly. Make arrangements through the Portland Museum of Art (*portlandmuseum.org*), another local treasure, to visit the Winslow Homer Studio at the tip of Scarborough Beach State Park, then wind your way along the nearby rocks and cliffs, passing homes you'll wish you could live in.

Farther up the coast at Cape Elizabeth Light (one of more than sixty lighthouses in Maine), an excellent lobster roll awaits at The Lobster Shack at Two Lights (*lobstershacktwolights.com*) – one to rival the lobster roll at the Bite Into Maine food truck (*biteintomaine.com*) at scenic Portland Head Light at Fort Williams Park. Ah-yup, you'll eat a lot of lobstah rolls. Maine is nothing if not consistent.

For a few more reminders of why the best things are timeless, stop for an espresso and a scone at Tandem Coffee and Bakery (*tandemcoffee.com*), a contemporary cafe in a former 1960s gas station, and, for a hearty breakfast fry-up, grab a seat in the old-fashioned diner car at Miss Portland Diner (*missportlanddiner.com*).

Clockwise from top left: Portland Head Light at Fort Williams Park; typewriters on the wall in the lobby at The Press Hotel; a lobster roll at The Lobster Shack

New Orleans, Louisiana, USA
Follow that beautiful ragtag gang of party people.

Every time we hear that old, bluesy standard "Do You Know What It Means to Miss New Orleans," recorded by NOLA's singular Satchmo and swinging Lady Day, Louis Armstrong and Billie Holiday, we're immediately put into a (much welcome) Crescent City trance. New Orleans isn't a big city, but it's a famous one – with its own sounds and songs and foods and rituals and way of life.

It's the one place in America where it's always time to eat a great meal, join a band, booze on the street, start a parade, and wear a feather boa. (Incidentally, it's also the one place in America where you can do all of those things at the same time.) Our favorite districts are Marigny/Bywater for bohemian vibes, a vibrant art scene, and live music on Frenchmen Street; Tremé for Creole cottages, small mom-and-pops, cool music joints, and multicultural landmarks (it's the oldest African-American neighborhood in the city); French Quarter for all that life (music, food, cocktails, history, voodoo, architecture) packed into a charming neighborhood grid; the Garden District for old-school imbibing, oyster slurping, po'-boy slamming, and lunching with ladies; and Uptown for eye candy in the form of mossy vines, palms, white-tablecloth bistros, blooming magnolias, and architectural beauties.

Cocktails for everyone at Bar Marilu at Maison de la Luz Hotel in New Orleans

Okay, okay, it's not all about 'round-the-clock dancing, drinking, and dining (though it's certainly a big selling point). Make room in your days to seek out several beloved, state-of-the-art museum institutions like the verdant Besthoff Sculpture Garden at NOMA (*noma.org*), the beautifully designed and wonderfully contemporary Louisiana Children's Museum (*lcm.org*), the comprehensive Ogden Museum of Southern Art (*ogdenmuseum.org*), the bold Contemporary Arts Center New Orleans (*cacno.org*), and the wildly thorough exhibitions at The National WWII Museum (*nationalww2museum.org*).

Boise, Idaho, USA
There's more to the Gem State capital than potatoes.

That the tallest building in town is a mere eighteen stories – and towers over everything else – is but one reason why Boise (it's "boy-SEE," please, not "boy-ZEE") is a city without the typical things you'd expect of a city.

For one thing, it's located in a high desert and surrounded by very welcoming natural environments. Boise River runs through the city and makes for a lovely and leisurely float on a raft or a tube, starting at Barber Park down to Ann Morrison Park. Greenbelt is a Boise treasure, a 25-mile (40-kilometer), traffic-free and tree-lined path that runs along the river, providing ample opportunities for biking, birding, fishing, and snacking on tacos along the way. Greenbelt winds around the Ribbon of Jewels, ten parks named for women who were civic leaders and philanthropists. Head to Lucky Peak for boating, fishing, and watersports on the reservoir.

To really get your heart pumping, make your way north to the Boise Foothills for even more mountain biking, hiking, and horseback riding all the way up to the local ski resort, Bogus Basin (*bogusbasin.org*). If you're a serious athlete, Sun Valley (*sunvalley.com*) ski resort is only a few hours away in Ketchum, and world-class rafting is even closer on the Snake River.

A performance with a view at the Idaho Shakespeare Festival

You'll hear that Boise has the largest Basque population outside Spain, which explains why you'll see so many Xs in names around here, but the best way to experience the culture is by visiting during Jaialdi (*jaialdi.com*), the Basque festival held every five years.

Turning to the arts, Boise is home to the largest open-air street art gallery in the north-west, Freak Alley Gallery (*freakalleyboise.com*), between 8th and 9th Street and Bannock and Idaho. What began with a drawing on a door in an alley in 2002 is now a living work by many artists that is always evolving and changing. Somewhat more timeless are the outdoor performances of classics, plays, and musicals produced every summer by the Idaho Shakespeare Festival (*idahoshakespeare.org*). Another literary lion with a strong claim to the area is Ernest Hemingway, who spent his last years in Ketchum and is buried in an inconspicuous grave in the cemetery. People leave behind bottles of booze and coins for good luck. If you're looking for a good read from someone who has not yet achieved literary stardom, head to Rediscovered Books (*rdbooks.org*), the beloved independent bookstore and literary events space where the staff takes special pride in making excellent recommendations.

The garden mural at El Cortez in Edmonton

Opposite, clockwise from top left: pondering at the Eiteljorg Museum and grooving at Fountain Square in Indianapolis; on the table and in the restaurant at Bündok in Edmonton

Edmonton, Alberta, Canada
No longer just a stopover on the way to Jasper and Banff.

This humble, blue-collar town, known as the Oil Capital of Canada due to its proximity to Alberta's massive tar sands, keeps a relatively low profile. But a recent infusion of young creatives is helping the city bloom.

82nd Avenue NW, otherwise known as Whyte Avenue, is packed with bars, restaurants, and shops of all kinds, and deserves a walkthrough on your first time in town. Make stops at Poppy Barley (*poppybarley.com*) for a cute new pair of shoes, Maven and Grace (*mavenandgrace.com*) for home goods, Kent of Inglewood (*kentofinglewood.com*) for beard products and a haircut, Black Dog Freehouse (*blackdog. ca*) for a drink or two, and Yelo'd Ice Cream & Bake Shoppe (*yelod.ca*) for Filipino-inspired soft serve. On Saturday, pop into Old Strathcona Farmers' Market (*osfm.ca*) to sample green onion cake (a scallion pancake) if you haven't already on a night out (it's an Edmonton post-drinking favorite). Also note the colorful mural across the street by big-time Spanish street artist Okuda San Miguel. Whyte Avenue is long: biking it is a good idea, but biking on it isn't. Avoid the crowds by cycling along 83rd Avenue NW if you're heading east or 81st Avenue NW if you're heading west.

This one is especially great for families: Fort Edmonton Park (*fortedmontonpark.ca*) is a living history museum with interactive exhibitions and original and reconstructed buildings designed to take you back in time to an 1846 fort and streets from 1885, 1905, and 1920. The past comes alive through horse-drawn wagon, pony, and streetcar rides; boat-building and bead-trading demos; and traditional Aboriginal games.

Edmonton's food scene may be the best reason to visit. Experimenting – with local ingredients, with beverage pairings, with the look of the dining room – is the name of the game. Woodwork (*woodworkyeg.com*) helped kick off the city's culinary craze when it opened in 2013 and is still going strong. The Mexican fare is inventive at El Cortez (*elcortezcantina.com*), where tacos come in wild forms, like filled with bulgogi. A hip-hop-inspired Asian cocktail bar and restaurant in the historic Mercer Warehouse, Baijiu (*baijiuyeg.com*) delivers on the unexpected, through drinks made with exotic ingredients like toffee-infused Japanese whiskey and a sixteen-seat speakeasy tucked away somewhere inside. Cozy Bündok (*bundokyeg.com*) may be one of Canada's best restaurants, for food that's eye-catching, highly shareable, and bursting with flavor. Clementine (*barclementine.ca*) is a beautiful, tiny, Art Nouveau–inspired cocktail bar that will transport you to 1920s Paris.

Indianapolis, Indiana, USA
It's going places. Come along for the ride.

It may be the birthplace of Wonder Bread, but there's nothing boring about this up-and-coming indie haven in the Midwest.

The nature-meets-culture campus at Newfields (*discovernewfields.org*) includes an impressive collection of Asian, African, and Oceanic arts (and much more!) at Indianapolis Art Museum; the 1930s Lilly House (a National Historic Landmark); and 100 acres (40 hectares) of woodlands and wetlands and a really big lake at The Virginia B. Fairbanks Art & Nature Park, along with nature parks, gardens, and a greenhouse, with sculptures scattered throughout.

See just about everything by following the Indianapolis Culture Trail (*indyculturaltrail.org*) on foot or by bike along 8 miles (13 kilometers) through six cultural neighborhoods downtown. The city replaced a lane of traffic with a smooth bike path to make room for it. Follow Canal Walk (or, better, kayak it) through a smaller stretch of downtown along Indiana Central Canal (built in the 1930s) to see old and new Native American art at Eiteljorg Museum (*eiteljorg.org*), the best of two dozen sports at N.C.A.A. Hall of Champions (*ncaahallofchampions.org*), and the writing of a beloved native son at Kurt Vonnegut Museum and Library (*vonnegutlibrary.org*).

After sunset, head to the lively Fountain Square neighborhood for a meal at Bluebeard (*bluebeardindy.com*), Iaria's (*iariasrestaurant.com*), or Three Carrots (*threecarrotsfountainsquare.com*), then catch the musical acts performing at HI-FI (*hifiindy.com*), White Rabbit Cabaret (*whiterabbitcabaret.com*), and Pioneer (*pioneerindy.com*).

Opposite, clockwise from top:
Matt's in the Market overlooking
Pike Place Market; a strong retail
aesthetic at Flora and Henri in
Pioneer Square; Matt Fortner
of Matt's tossing pasta; Pioneer
Square; a mural at The State Hotel

Seattle, Washington, USA
The town that tech built is doing a lot more than coding.

In the last decades, the city on the Sound has grown from a sleepy Pacific Northwest town characterized by grunge music and Boeing airplanes into a global metropolis transformed by Microsoft, Starbucks, and Amazon. It's the mixture of the classic mainstays with the innovative disruptors that makes Seattle thrive.

Founded by Microsoftie Paul Allen and designed by starchitect Frank Gehry, Museum of Pop Culture (*mopop. org*) practices "radical hospitality and equitable access," with exhibits and programs dedicated to pop culture (Minecraft, sci-fi movies, book clubs) and the rich musical history of Seattle (with artifacts from Quincy Jones, Jimi Hendrix, Pearl Jam, and Nirvana).

The food in this town is no joke. Assemble a picnic from the vendors at Pike Place Market (*pikeplacemarket. org*) – including savory Chinese pastries from Mee Sum (*meesum.com*) across the street – and make your way to Gas Works Park in the Wallingford neighborhood on Lake Union for great city and water views. The quirky park, built on the site of an old coal gasification plant, repurposed old factory buildings into children's play barns and picnic shelters. If you get too hungry at the Market to take it to go, sit down to some of the best Pacific Northwest fare in town at Matt's in the Market (*mattsinthemarket. com*), overlooking both Elliott Bay and the hustle and bustle of the market vendors below. For Spanish-style tapas, cocktails, and vino, grab one of the very few seats at intimate Jarr Bar (*jarrbar.com*), and to carbo-load on handmade pastas and authentic sauces, hit Pasta Casalinga (*pastacasalingaseattle.com*), also in the market.

Locally owned boutique hotel The State (*statehotel. com*) occupies a historic 1904 landmark brick building with old-meets-new design that captures the essence of the Pacific Northwest. The artwork is by emerging local artists, with portraits featuring noteworthy Seattleites, and the wallpaper on each of the eight floors is different. Hotel junkies might rather stay at Ace Hotel Seattle (*acehotel.com/seattle*), the hotel group's original location, which opened in 1999 and kicked off the 21st century industrial-chic hotel-cum-hostel craze that's made its way around the world.

The striking Denver Art Museum

Opposite, clockwise from top left; tacos at Wynkoop; a food truck at Civic Center EATS; the Capitol Building; serenity at the Clyfford Still Museum

Denver, Colorado, USA
Flying high for so many good reasons.

The Mile High City is a compelling mix of old cow-town charm (cue the National Western Stock Show and Rodeo) and global influences (thanks to an influx of Vietnamese, Ethiopian, Russian, and Central and Latin American folks). There's a good chance you can catch a direct flight to its airport, a massive hub for many airlines, and here are a few reasons to stay a while.

The Capitol Hill neighborhood packs a cultural punch. The minimalist Clyfford Still Museum (*clyffordstillmuseum. org*), tucked behind the far flashier Denver Art Museum (*denverartmuseum.org*), is a fitting showcase – that is to say, peaceful and restorative – for its modern art renegade namesake, with a thoughtful permanent collection and rotating shows. Within a few blocks are the Denver Library (*denverlibrary.org*), the Center for Colorado Women's History (*historycolorado.org/center-colorado-womens-history*), and Molly Brown House Museum (*mollybrown. org*), the Victorian former home of the "unsinkable" Titanic survivor. Walk up the western-facing steps of the beautiful Capitol Building to take a photo on the step that marks Denver's 1-mile-high mark. Don't miss the public art interspersed between the museums and library, and grab lunch from one of the food trucks at Civic Center EATS (*civiccentereats.com*) from May to October.

There are many great live music venues in Denver (like Mission Ballroom, Bluebird, Ogden, the Gothic, Paramount Theatre, and the Fillmore), but Red Rocks (*redrocksonline. com*) is one of the greatest venues in the USA to see live music, catch a movie, or experience sunrise mass on Easter Sunday. The amphitheater is carved into the side of a mountain, ensuring pristine acoustics, an unparalleled experience, and no bad seats in the house, especially on a warm summer night when the city lights twinkle in the distance and the sky is filled with heat lightning. Sporty types can access the park on special days and run up and down the nearly 400 stairs at an elevation of nearly 6500 feet (2 kilometers) above sea level.

Denver has no shortage of breweries in just about every area of town, from the massive Coors Brewery (*coorsbrewerytour.com*) in Golden to a more intimate taproom experience at Crooked Stave (*crookedstave.com*). Most breweries offer tours, tasting rooms, and a restaurant or brewpub. Star Bar (*thestarbardenver.com*), a great (if bro-y) dive on Larimer, is a standout not only for its selection of brews but for the Skee-Ball and karaoke on offer. This craft beer obsession was born at Denver's first brewpub, Wynkoop Brewing Co. (*wynkoop.com*), whose co-founder, John Hickenlooper, then became mayor and Colorado's governor. If you prefer your buzz to be of the vino variety, Frasca Food and Wine (*frascafoodandwine.com*) has one of the best wine programs in the country and a top-notch Italian kitchen to match.

If you would rather achieve your altered state by inhaling instead of imbibing, you'll be delighted to know that Colorado was the first US state to legalize marijuana. If you're looking to get high in the Mile High, LivWell (*livwell.com*) is one of the most trusted dispensaries, with fun and perky packaging and products. Lightshade (*lightshade.com*) offers a higher-end experience, with bespoke lines of cannabis body care, tinctures, edibles, and drinks. Both have several locations around town. Just be mindful of the law: while it may be legal to purchase marijuana, it's illegal to smoke it in public – and you should definitely not try to bring it back home.

Nashville, Tennessee, USA

A laidback, unpretentious, deep-fried, honky-tonk of a good time.

There's a reason why the biggest names in country music have called this Southern city home: it's a hotbed and a launchpad for live music – and the whiskey and BBQ that accompany it so well.

Where would country music be without the Honky Tonk Highway, a four-block stretch along Broadway that runs down to the river, an area that's been launching musicians since the 1930s? Today the historic buildings are packed with bars and clubs where a steady stream of performers are putting on their best shows all day. The scene is informal, inexpensive, and fun, and you never know which big-name act might jump on stage for an impromptu set. The spots to know are Robert's Western World (*robertswesternworld.com*), for live music every night; Ernest Tubb Record Shop (*etrecordshop.com*), for the Midnite Jamboree on Saturdays; and Station Inn (*stationinn.com*), an old stone hut that hosts bluegrass and American roots music.

Nashville has good reason to be mighty proud of its culinary scene, thanks in no small part to chefs who both preserve Southern culinary traditions and push it in new directions, like award-winning chef Sean Brock, who oversees both Husk (*husknashville.com*), located in a Victorian mansion in Rutledge Hill (it's an outpost of his original Charleston location), and Joyland (*eatjoyland. com*), a burger and biscuit joint in East Nashville. Rolf & Daughters (*rolfanddaughters.com*) features chef Philip Krajeck's inventive take on small plates (and is a tough reservation to score, so plan accordingly). Peg Leg Porker (*peglegporker.com*) may serve the best pulled-pork sandwich you'll ever eat. Ever.

The ten rooms at Germantown Inn (*germantowninn. com*), a homey, off-the-radar boutique hotel in a Civil War-era home, are dedicated to different US presidents and historical female figures like Rosa Parks, Thomas Jefferson, and Susan B. Anthony. The decor, a mix of new and vintage, includes patriotic pops of red, white, and blue alongside funky portraits commissioned for the hotel by local designer Caitlin Mello.

San Miguel de Allende, Guanajuato, Mexico
Colonial charm for the chic set.

A jetset crowd and vibrant expat community gives this colonial Central Mexican hilltop city a great jolt of energy, even as it moves at a luxuriously slow pace that makes it easy to savor the sunny desert climate, the art galleries, and the artisanal handicrafts.

Walking is the best way to soak up the city's physical beauty – its cobblestone streets, yellow and orange buildings, magical hidden courtyards, magnificent churches, whimsical shops, and architectural details – and is an excellent way to get to know the small town. The central plaza El Jardín is always bustling: perch on a bench under the trees and watch street performers in action and little kids having fun. At the end of the plaza is Parroquia de San Miguel Arcángel, the 17th-century cathedral with the striking pink turrets and towers. Another terrific colonial-era church to visit is Oratorio de San Felipe Neri. You'll recognize it from the pink facade. Inside is the ornate 1735 chapel Santa Casa de Loreto, a copy of the structure in the Basilica in Loreto, Italy, that some Catholics believe was the home of the Virgin Mary. Moving on to the secular, Biblioteca Pública (*facebook. com/BibliotecaPublicaSMA*) is a cultural center that includes a library, a bookstore, a sweet garden cafe, the headquarters to the local English newspaper (there are *a lot* of expats here), and a performance space.

San Miguel has a fantastic craft tradition, so definitely leave room in your suitcase for souvenirs. The city's oldest market, Mercado Ignacio Ramírez, is a covered market that leads down into Mercado de Artesanias (Artisans Alley), a pedestrian stretch lined with stalls where you'll find beautiful handmade artisanal crafts and gifts like hand-painted ceramics, whimsical metal light fixtures, embroidered dresses, table runners, textiles, and silver jewelry.

Drive out to El Charco del Ingenio (*elcharco.org.mx*), a succulent-filled botanical garden and nature preserve, to walk, hike, or run the trails around the canyons. Spend another fun afternoon just outside SMA in the hot springs and pools at La Gruta ("The Grotto," *spalagruta.com*). Feast at the end of the day on a steak dinner at Bovine (*bovinerestaurant.com.mx*), a high-design brasserie that's also home to Mesa Dragones, a private Casa Dragones bar. If you're getting the impression that Casa Dragones is San Miguel's hometown tequila, you're not wrong, and the best place to learn the proper way to sip it is at their beautiful six-seat tasting room (*casadragones. com/tasting-room*) in the historic Dôce 18 Concept House (*doce-18.com*).

Opposite, from left: the Station Inn; a feast at Husk

This page: La Casa Dragones

Houston, Texas, USA
Meet the Lone Star State's rising weekend destination.

Time to reconsider what you thought you knew about a town that delivers more culture than cowboys.

Yes, everything is bigger in Texas. The Houston metro area, home to 6 million people, is known for its energy industry and vastly sprawled urban areas connected by highways and byways. Expect to spend a lot of time driving – and for your car time to be handsomely rewarded. The destination barrios you'll want to visit are bustling Downtown, the quaint Montrose, the upscale River Oaks, the creative clusters of West University–Rice Village, the walkable Museum District, the revamped Upper Kirby, the business and retail Memorial, and the massive shopping and food stretch of Galleria/Uptown.

While the Contemporary Arts Museum (*camh.org*), Museum of Fine Arts (*mfah.org*), The Menil Collection (*menil.org*), and the Menil-commissioned, non-denominational Rothko Chapel (*rothkochapel.org*) still reign as an art lover's dream, check out nearby Art of the World Gallery (*artoftheworldgallery.com*) for a bevy of contemporary works by many South American artists, stroll the grounds of Cullen Sculpture Garden (*mfah.org*) to see pieces by Calder and Bourgeois, or drop by the lesser-known-but-just-as-lovely Bayou Bend (*mfah.org*) for decorative arts, paintings, and formal manicured gardens. The new-ish Menil Drawing Institute (*menil.org/drawing-institute*) is an impressive addition to the many Menil offerings. Isabella Court is an architectural marvel from the 1920s that is now home to Inman Gallery (*inmangallery.com*), among others. James Turrell's Twilight Epiphany Skyspace (*moody.rice.edu/james-turrell-twilight-epiphany-skyspace*) on the Rice University campus hosts musical performances and is made with LED lights that react to sunrise and sunset. It's free to visit.

If you're here for retail therapy, start in River Oaks, where the side-by-side shops of Sid Mashburn (*sidmashburn.com*) and Ann Mashburn (*annmashburn.com*) stock both casual and dressy pieces, while Kick Pleat (*kickpleat.com*) provides edgier contemporary brands. Elegant Gordy & Sons Outfitters (*gordyandsons.com*) carries finery not often seen in hunting and fishing shops. For hipster flair, the town has a sprinkling of LP stores, including Sig's Lagoon (*sigslagoon.com*). And for furniture treasures, drop by Reeves Art + Design (*reevesantiqueshouston.com*) for mid-century pieces and Kuhl-Linscomb (*kuhl-linscomb.com*) for more contemporary interior options.

Opposite, clockwise from top: city-proud street art; trains zip through fountains on Main Street Square; sculptures at the Menil Collection; retail therapy at Kuhl-Linscomb

CITIES WE LOVE AND THE PEOPLE WHO LOVE THEM

What makes a city special? Because no one knows that answer better than the creative spirits that help define them, we asked a few people we admire to share the best of their hometowns (and then asked ourselves the same questions).

MIAMI, FLORIDA, USA
Guerdy Abraira
Destination wedding planner

Best thing about Miami: The culture fusion.

Best people-watching: Prime 112 restaurant. You won't be disappointed.

Favorite neighborhood: The Seven Villages hidden amongst the predominantly Spanish Mediterranean-style neighborhood of Coral Gables. You will find clusters of themed architectural homes: Pioneer Village, French Normandy Village, Chinese Village, Italian Village, French Country, French City, Dutch South African. Truly remarkable.

I don't want tourists to know about: Let's just say, stay away from the highways. The lane markings seem to have no meaning. They keep me on my toes every time.

Most underrated: The cultural and arts communities.

Most overrated: The beach scene on Ocean Drive in South Beach.

Dream meal: Byblos, a Turkish restaurant in Miami Beach. And the black truffle pide appetizer.

Favorite local institution: Little Haiti Cultural Complex.

Best movie based in Miami: *The Birdcage*.

In the city escape: Le Bouchon Du Grove in Coconut Grove.

Nearby escape: Wat Buddharangsi Buddhist Temple in the Redlands in Homestead.

No trip to Miami is complete without a mojito.

MEXICO CITY, MEXICO
Gabriela Cámara
Chef/restaurateur of Contramar, Entremar, Cala, Itacate del Mar, and Tata Begò

Best thing about Mexico City: It's lively and vibrant.

Best people-watching: La Lagunilla antique/flea market on Sundays.

Favorite neighborhood: Roma/Condesa.

I don't want tourists to know about: I'm not telling!

Most underrated: The parks.

Most overrated: The street tacos.

Dream meal: El Hidalguense.

Favorite local institution: Bar El Sella.

Best movie based in Mexico City: *Amores Perros*.

In the city escape: Xochimilco, a neighborhood with canals and gondolas.

Nearby escape: Tepoztlán in Morelos.

No trip to Mexico City is complete without a long lunch at Contramar. (Tell them Fathom sent you!)

From left: lunch at Contramar; shopping in Mexico City

CHICAGO, ILLINOIS, USA
Wesley Taylor
Photographer, musician, and creative soul

Best thing about Chicago: All the different neighborhoods. You can always find your people.

Best people-watching: Coffee shops. My favorites are Intelligentsia in Logan Square and Sawada Coffee in the West Loop, where the seats by the window are a great spot for portraits or selfies. Also, the lake on North Avenue Beach.

Favorite neighborhood: Wicker Park/Bucktown. It's where I first lived when I moved to the city, and the mix of shops, restaurants, and fun street art will always feel like home.

I don't want tourists to know about: the beaches and parks further north, like Foster Beach and Horner Park. So many hidden gems.

Most underrated: Non-deep dish pizza. My favorites are the thin crust from Lou Malnati's, thin rustic crust from Nancy's Pizza, and Detroit Style from Paulie Gee's in Logan Square.

Most overrated: The Bean. It's definitely a must, but when you've seen it once, you've seen it 100 times.

Dream meal: Tonkotsu ramen at Wasabi Ramen in Logan Square. Heaven in a bowl.

Favorite local institution: The Art Institute of Chicago.

Best movie based in Chicago: *While You Were Sleeping*. I love that the train plays such a big role in the storytelling. Another favorite is the Netflix show *Easy*. It's so cool to see familiar street corners and bars.

In the city escape: Coffee shops or cafes nestled under the train tracks – my favorite is La Colombe in Wicker Park, under the Damen Blue Line stop. Watching the snow fall under the tracks during the winter is a magical experience. I also love Dorian's, a cozy cocktail bar around the corner. The walls are lined with hundreds of vinyl records and the design is great, so stepping inside feels like stepping back in time.

Nearby escape: Antique stores in the suburbs of Elgin or Bourbonnais for vintage goodies.

No trip to Chicago is complete without an espresso from Metric Coffee, a walk or bike ride on the lakefront, and a six-piece wing meal from Harold's Chicken, with mild sauce and extra mild sauce on the side for the fries.

LOS ANGELES, CALIFORNIA, USA
Maurice Harris
Artist, florist, and owner of Bloom & Plume and Bloom & Plume Coffee

Best thing about Los Angeles: It's the most amazing backdrop for beautiful relationships.

Best people-watching: Through the window of my floral studio, Bloom & Plume, and Porridge and Puffs – no one should leave LA without eating there.

Favorite neighborhood: Hancock Park.

I don't want tourists to know about: The Underground Museum.

Most underrated: My coffee shop, Bloom & Plume Coffee.

Most overrated: Hollywood.

Dream meal: My Two Cents and Jon & Vinny's.

Favorite local institution: Union.

Best movie based in Los Angeles: *Chinatown* and *Clueless*.

In the city escape: A small park in Echo Park near my house.

Nearby escape: Angeles National Forest.

No trip to Los Angeles is complete without going up to the Griffith Observatory and experiencing a pollution sunset.

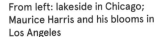
From left: lakeside in Chicago; Maurice Harris and his blooms in Los Angeles

The library at Commodore
Perry Estate

Opposite, from left: the dining room
at The Grey and The Grey Market

AUSTIN, TEXAS, USA
Kelly Krause
Writer, community-builder, brand strategist

Best thing about Austin: The amount of green space, trails, and water activities at your fingertips.

Best people-watching: Lady Bird Lake Hike & Bike Trail.

Favorite neighborhood: Bouldin Creek.

I don't want tourists to know about: River Place Nature Trail Canyon Trailhead.

Most underrated in Austin: Donn's Depot.

Most overrated: The heat.

Dream meal: The Suadero tacos at Suerte, two to three plates from the dim sum cart at Emmer & Rye, and biscuits from Olamaie.

Favorite local institution: Austin City Limits Live at The Moody Theater.

Best movie based in Austin: I'm going the obvious route with this: *Office Space* and *Dazed and Confused*.

In the city escape: If I want to chill, Commodore Perry Estate. If I want to move my body, Mount Bonnell stairs, with a peaceful and mindful moment at the top of the hill.

Nearby escape: Balcones Canyonlands National Wildlife Refuge.

No trip to Austin is complete without a morning sunrise dip in Barton Springs Pool, followed by breakfast tacos at Veracruz All Natural or Pueblo Viejo. Definitely make room to squeeze in Ellsworth Kelly's Austin installation at Blanton Museum of Art, and follow it up with a great meal and music.

SAVANNAH, GEORGIA, USA
Mashama Bailey
Chef/partner of The Grey & The Grey Market

Best thing about Savannah: Being on the water.

Best people-watching: Tybee Island, for a cast of characters different from any other beach town I've ever seen, and Forsyth Park to see tourists and locals intermingle.

Favorite neighborhood: Baldwin Park.

I don't want tourists to know about: Picker Joe's, the antique mall that has basically furnished my entire house.

Dream meal: Narobia's Grits and Gravy.

Favorite local institution: SCAD. To have the campus spread through downtown adds so much youthful and artistic energy to this often-sleepy town.

Best movie based in Savannah: *Midnight in the Garden of Good and Evil*. Classic.

In the city escape: I take a walk through the neighborhoods downtown. It's easy to find space while admiring the architecture and greenery.

Nearby escape: Beauford, South Carolina, a beautiful city with good food and loads of Geechee Gullah culture.

No trip to Savannah is complete without a trip to Mrs. Wilkes' Dining Room for the food and atmosphere.

VANCOUVER, BRITISH COLUMBIA, CANADA
Christina Luo
Calligraphy and lettering artist; owner of Fox and Flourish

Best thing about Vancouver: Breathing that fresh Vancouver air the moment you step out of the YVR airport.

Best people-watching: Trout Lake duck pond. With bonus points for the ducks and dogs!

Favorite neighborhood: East Vancouver. To be more specific and potentially cliché, I've always wanted to live in Mount Pleasant/Riley Park.

I don't want tourists to know about: The deliciousness that is the Aberdeen mall food court in Richmond.

Most underrated in Vancouver: The Cinematheque, my go-to theater for festival releases and the most influential and classic films.

Most overrated: The Gastown "Steam Clock," brought to you by two electric motors and built in the late 1970s to resemble an antique.

Dream meal: The Ramen Butcher. And when I want something akin to ramen but lighter and veg, squash ramen at Harvest Union.

Favorite local institution: SORT, a hidden stationery and design shop in Kitsilano (full disclosure: I also work here) and Paper-Ya stationery store on Granville Island.

Best book based in Vancouver: *Mistakes to Run With: A Memoir* by Yasuko Thanh, a frank and devastating retrospective of the author's turbulent life as a runaway teenage sex worker in Vancouver.

In the city escape: Any art gallery, such as Centre A, Vancouver Art Gallery, Museum of Anthropology at UBC, and The Polygon.

Nearby escape: Day trip to Harrison Hot Springs or a weekend in gorgeous Victoria, BC, a short ferry ride away.

No trip to Vancouver is complete without ordering a plate of our famous fried chicken from Phnom Penh in Chinatown.

TUCSON, ARIZONA, USA
Don Guerra
Community-supported baker and owner of Barrio Bread

Best thing about Tucson: The weather, especially from October to May.

Best people-watching: Cup Cafe patio at Hotel Congress.

Favorite neighborhood: Old Fort Lowell.

I don't want tourists to know about: The taquerias on South 12th. We want to keep them a secret so the lines don't get too long.

Most underrated in Tucson: The arts. Tucson is home to many great artists and art museums like MOCA: Museum of Contemporary Art and Tucson Museum of Art.

Most overrated: Complaining about the heat.

Dream meal: Brunch at Loews Ventana Canyon.

Favorite local institution: Ben's Bells, a community project that promotes kindness.

Best movie based in Tucson: *Can't Buy Me Love*.

In the city escape: The trails on The Loop.

Nearby escape: Madera Canyon.

No trip to Tucson is complete without a stop at a local brewery like Ten55 Brewing Company.

Opposite: Lion's Gate Bridge

This page, from left: the patio at Hotel Congress; iconic local cacti

MEMPHIS, TENNESSEE, USA
Rachel Knox
Senior program officer, Hyde Family Foundation; Memphis ambassador

Best thing about Memphis: The people! Memphians work so hard every day to solve our most pressing issues and inspire change. Over the past few years, there has definitely been a shift with more people working across sectors to create the systems-level change we need to create a thriving city.

Best people-watching: The riverfront parks – from little kids on play equipment to sixty-somethings on roller skates.

Favorite neighborhood: Binghampton, one of Memphis' most diverse neighborhoods. Broad Avenue is home to incredible restaurants, breweries, and spaces with locally made goods.

I don't want tourists to know about: The secret "beach" in Shelby Farms.

Most underrated: Our hip-hop scene. It's varied in sound and subject matter. Some of my favorite alt rappers are Don Lifted and Preuxx.

Most overrated: Graceland. Every city has a landmark the locals are not interested in.

Shelby Farms

Dream meal: Felicia Suzanne's. Her Sunday sugo (creamy risotto topped with a delicious gravy cooked down with beef & pork) with an old fashioned is by far one of my favorite dishes in the city. A close second would be coffee-rubbed lamb chops at Mahogany Memphis. You can't get a bad meal in Memphis.

Favorite local institution: CLTV The Collective, one of my favorite art galleries, is dedicated to supporting local Black artists.

Best movie based in Memphis: TV show *Uncorked* did a great job showcasing the city, and I would be a lousy Memphian if I didn't mention *Hustle and Flow*. But the best movies based on a book set in Memphis would be John Grisham's *The Firm*. These movies are so different from one another, but there's no one Memphis experience.

In the city escape: Shelby Farms Park or Overton Park.

No trip to Memphis is complete without barbeque. Stop at Payne's on your way out of town. It'll change your life, just like Memphis.

SAN FRANCISCO, CALIFORNIA, USA
Anna Weinberg
Owner, Big Night Restaurant Group

Best thing about San Francisco: The people.

Favorite place to people-watch: Zuni Café.

Favorite neighborhood: North Beach.

I don't want tourists to know about: The Bar at The Big 4 in the Huntington Hotel, one of the oldest bars in town.

Most underrated: The design.

Most overrated: The pizza.

Dream meal: Cotogna.

Favorite local institution: Swan Oyster Depot.

Best movie based in San Francisco: *The Parent Trap*.

In the city escape: Grace Cathedral.

Nearby escape: Sonoma.

No trip to San Francisco is complete without brunch at Park Tavern.

First chefs cook in the wood-fired oven at Cotogna, then dinner is served

Opposite, clockwise from top: provisions from Marlow & Sons; the dining room at The Odeon; downtown Manhattan; a Morgenstern's sundae

NEW YORK CITY, NEW YORK, USA
Jeralyn Gerba and Pavia Rosati
Co-founders of Fathom (and your authors)

Best thing about NYC: Its stylish citizens.

Place to people-watch: Central Park (skate circle).

Favorite neighborhood: The West Village, Fort Greene, Greenpoint, Harlem.

We don't want tourists to know about: The new parks along the Hudson and East rivers.

Most underrated: How kind New Yorkers are.

Most overrated: Why are people on double-decker buses? Get out and walk!

Dream meal: Breakfast at Balthazar, lunch at Marlow & Sons, ice cream at Morgenstern's, midnight fries at The Odeon, nightcap at Smith & Mills.

Favorite local institution: Brooklyn Academy of Music and St. Ann's Warehouse.

Best movie based in NYC: *On the Town*, *Breakfast at Tiffany's*, and *West Side Story* are the classics; *Birdman* and *If Beale Street Could Talk* are the contemporaries.

In the city escape: Rose Reading Room at the 42nd Street branch of New York Public Library.

Nearby escape: Jacob Riis Park, and Beacon to see the art at Storm King and Dia Beacon.

No trip to NYC is complete without going to bed amazed at the spontaneous, unexpected turn the day took.

OUR FAVORITE CITY HOTELS

We have a soft spot for boutique hotels with an independent streak that could only be found in the cities they call home.

USA

ARIZONA
Hermosa Inn, Scottsdale
The former hacienda of artist Lon Megargee is a cowboy-chic boutique hotel. (His original artwork can be found on the walls.) The forty-three cozy guest rooms and casitas have fireplaces, patios, and vaulted ceilings. Have a cocktail or dinner at LON's on the firepit-dotted patio. What's that aroma in the air? Alligator juniper. *hermosainn.com*

CALIFORNIA
The Charlie, Los Angeles
Just off Sunset Strip is a hidden cluster of charming bungalows once owned by Charlie Chaplin himself. Each English-style cottage is named after his famous friends who stayed here back in the day – Marilyn, Betty, Marlene. With its discreet service and refurbished Tudor details, it feels like a Tinseltown fairytale come true. *thecharliehotel.com*

Petit Ermitage, Los Angeles
Residential vibes here give you a sense of what it would be like if you lived (it up) in West Hollywood. The owner's personal collection of art – Rauschenberg, de Kooning, Miró – hangs on the walls, and the rooftop garden, with its saltwater pool, striped couches, and candelabras at night, truly feels like a private refuge – perfect for a romantic tryst. *petitermitage.com*

Cavallo Point Lodge, San Francisco
Set in the beautiful Marin Headlands park, near the Golden Gate Bridge, the hotel's views are fantastic. The Healing Arts Center & Spa offers outdoor fitness activities, chakra readings, soul-balancing sessions, and other woo-woo treatments to remind you that you are in the hippie California quadrant. *cavallopoint.com*

COLORADO
The Crawford Hotel, Denver

When Union Station was lovingly restored from a janky train station into a bona fide destination with restaurants, shops, bars, stores, and, yes, access to trains, the developers crafted The Crawford Hotel. Its three floors each represent a different era of the station's history, and no two rooms are alike. *thecrawfordhotel.com*

The Little Nell, Aspen

The best address in town is located at the foot of the Aspen Gondola, which makes for immediate ski-in, ski-out (or hike-in, hike-out) mountain access. The vibe is comfortable and rich but never fussy, and the rooms have interesting layouts, gas log fireplaces, and private balconies. The slopeside cafeteria (you have to take a gondola to get there) offers a huge fireplace and incredible views of Elk Mountains, while elegant Element 47 restaurant has one of the best wine cellars in North America. The Little Nell is known for exceptional service, from the attentive ski concierges to the sommeliers, as well as for its après-ski scene. *thelittlenell.com*

Clockwise from left: outside at Hermosa Inn, Arizona; the Golden Gate Bridge seen from Cavallo Point Lodge, San Francisco; slopeside at The Little Nell in Aspen

The private pool and the punchy lobby at The Betsy in Miami

FLORIDA
Casa Faena, Miami

The glitzy Faena Hotel may get all the attention – for the show-stopping theater, the celebrity chef restaurants, the sumptuous hammam, the oceanfront rooms, the dramatic floor-to-ceiling murals in the entrance, and the 25-karat-gold wooly mammoth skeleton sculpture – but the smaller inn across the street is the real (and more affordable) charmer. A Spanish-style villa with Art Deco touches, its fifty rooms, decorated with four-poster beds and artisanal accents like embroidered Argentine blankets, are spread on three floors overlooking an atrium that's reliably filled with a striking sculpture. The cozy ground floor living room is surrounded by book- and object-filled alcoves and stained-glass windows. Guests have access to select Faena Hotel amenities but benefit from an unpretentious, residential option in the surrounding upscale Faena District, which includes an arts center, shopping bazaar, and residential tower. *faena.com/casa-faena*

The Betsy, Miami

With its Georgian architecture and elegant, contemporary interiors, The Betsy feels refreshingly low-key compared to its glitzier Ocean Drive neighbors. The lack of a nightclub means this place is perfect for families, and a carefully curated events program makes it great for culture aficionados. Get up early to secure prime sunbathing spots on the rooftop deck, or take a dip in the tiny, but very private, courtyard pool. The Wellness Garden & Spa are a great in-the-city escape. *thebetsyhotel.com*

GEORGIA
The Alida, Savannah

An excellent home base if you're young, traveling in groups (rooms and common areas are spacious, and the penthouse is a great place to throw a party), or just love new, cool, millennial-friendly hotels. The design is handsome, with very current interiors – exposed brick, beautiful tiles, brass light fixtures, oversized windows with views of the river, and leisurely reading benches. No two rooms are alike, thanks to artful additions from students at the nearby Savannah College of Art and Design. _thealidahotel.com_

HAWAII
The Surfjack Hotel + Swim Club, Honolulu

Oozing 1960s Hawaiian-beach-culture charm, with no shortage of swanky cocktails and swankified guests and locals sipping them in the lobby or in the suites upstairs, this soulful little boutique hotel has mid-century modern furniture, local artwork, and organic Hawaiian home cooking. _surfjack.com_

Clockwise from left: the atrium at Casa Faena, Miami; The Trade Room bar at The Alida, Savannah; the pool says it all at The Surfjack Hotel + Swim Club in Honolulu

Clockwise from top left: everything is striking at Maison de la Luz in New Orleans – the bar, the concierge desk, and the lounge

ILLINOIS
Chicago Athletic Association, Chicago

The Venetian Gothic landmark opposite Millennium Park received a Roman and Williams facelift, resulting in playfully reimagined vintage furnishings (like a pommel horse-turned-bench), Carrara marble bathrooms, and boxing-style robes. If you ever find yourself in Chicago in winter (why would you do that to yourself?), cozy up in the library by 19th-century fireplaces and end the night with drinks at the historic Cherry Circle Room. *chicagoathletichotel.com*

Longman & Eagle, Chicago

It doesn't get cooler than this six-room Logan Square inn, a favorite of musicians and interesting wanderers. The style is vintage and the prices are unbeatable. The bar pours stiff cocktails and the kitchen turns out incredible, meat-heavy dishes. The vibe is easy, loud, and, on most days, plaid. *longmanandeagle.com*

LOUISIANA
Maison de la Luz, New Orleans

The latest project from Atelier Ace (Ace Hotel, American Trade Hotel) is a delightfully whimsical retreat in NOLA's slightly industrial Warehouse District. With just sixty-seven keys, a private, guest-only sitting room with an adjacent breakfast nook, and a curated concierge service, travelers can expect an intimate experience. Everything has an element of theater to it, from the dramatic red walls and zebra print rug in the library parlor to the Frenchy Bar Marilou (accessed via special entrance) and the swashbuckling Seaworthy, a cocktail and raw bar situated in what feels like the belly of an old ship (think rickety wooden plank floors, metal baskets displaying shellfish, and candle holders made sculptural from long nights of dripping wax). *maisondelaluz.com*

Hôtel Peter & Paul, New Orleans

Set in a historic 19th-century church, rectory, schoolhouse, and convent in the funky Faubourg Marigny, this very special, seventy-one-room compound has a refreshingly elegant (but cool!) vibe, with rooms decorated with gingham patterns in rich hues of red, blue, green, and yellow (a palette derived from medieval religious paintings), Baroque-style wood furnishings, and simple white linens. Unique design elements can be found around nearly every corner (a corridor with a trompe l'oeil schoolhouse theater; dainty writing desks tucked under the eaves; large fringe tassels hanging from canopy beds). A lovely salon and sunny eatery in the old rectory is run by the team behind local favorite Bacchanal (*bacchanalwine.com*), so you know the drinks are good. The decommissioned Catholic church, with its soaring domed ceiling and enormous stained-glass windows, is a serene and breathtaking spot for inventive community events and performances, and the adorable sliver of an ice cream parlor, Sundae Best, is a subtle nod to families with children that all are welcome here. *hotelpeterandpaul.com*

From left: the handsome Chicago Athletic Association; the funky Hotel Peter & Paul in New Orleans

From top: an angelic display at
Hotel St. Francis, Santa Fe; Beauty
& Essex bar at The Cosmopolitan,
Las Vegas

Opposite, from left: a lounge
at Shinola Hotel, Detroit; a
drawing room at The Greenwich,
NYC; vintage is timeless at TWA
Hotel, Queens

MICHIGAN
Shinola Hotel, Detroit

A collaboration between local real estate firm Bedrock
and the now-iconic local luxury watchmaker has resulted
in a buzzy hotel symbolic of the growing Motor City
economy. Located in downtown Detroit, the 129-room
spot showcases collaborative efforts with the local
artisan community; exclusive and highly covetable Shinola
products, including a desk clock, custom blanket, and a
signature candle (naturally); and a handsome living room
awash in blue that caters very much to locals as well as
locals-for-just-a-weekend. Midwest native and NYC-
based chef Andrew Carmellini (Locanda Verde, The Dutch)
oversees the food and beverage offerings, while a curated
retail space features global brands. A lively collection of
art from near and far was curated by the Detroit gallery
Library Street Collective. *shinolahotel.com*

NEVADA
The Cosmopolitan, Las Vegas

This is the Vegas resort for people who don't think
they're Vegas people but secretly are because they love
the fun scene, energized nightlife, striking design, and
stylish rooms, many of which have terraces overlooking
the Bellagio's dancing fountains. The impressive
restaurants, spas, shops, and bars are located in a
multilevel central area that links the East and West towers.
cosmopolitanlasvegas.com

NEW MEXICO
Hotel St. Francis, Santa Fe

The city's oldest hotel is beautiful and simple, very
much like its patron saint. Filled with handcrafted wood
furniture inspired by New Mexico's centuries-old seat
of government, wrought iron details, big pillar candles
evocative of old Spanish churches, and archival black-and-
white photos of Santa Fe, it's a culturally distinct place
that will make you feel serene. Ditto the handcrafted
cocktails made with fresh herbs and local spirits.
hotelstfrancis.com

NEW YORK
The Greenwich Hotel, New York City

Located on a quiet street in Tribeca, this is as close as you can get to a sophisticated European country house in the city. Like most good country houses, there are sitting rooms aplenty, some reserved for hotel guests. Unlike most good country houses, the old-fashioned decor is counterbalanced by the modern amenities sophisticated hotel guests demand. The basement level is home to the Japanese-inspired Shibuya spa and beautiful swimming pool, and the consistently excellent Locanda Verde is the onsite restaurant. Robert DeNiro may be an owner, but this is a hijinks-free zone.
thegreenwichhotel.com

The Mark, NYC

This sophisticated and discreet hotel is a stone's throw from Central Park and Museum Mile. A handsome black-and-white lobby makes for quite an entrance. Art Deco-inspired rooms designed by Jacques Grange are filled with luxurious details (Italian linen by Quagliotti, marble bathrooms, polished nickel fittings by Lefroy Brooks, designer kitchen appliances). *themarkhotel.com*

TWA Hotel, Queens

The iconic Eero Saarinen terminal at John F. Kennedy International Airport in New York City has been transformed into a striking, 512-room hotel that feels like a time capsule dedicated to 1960s-era travel. In keeping with the building's design, the decor has a mid-century modern feel, with custom-made details like a split-flap departures board and a font inspired by Saarinen's own sketches. The world's biggest hotel gym is here (10,000 square feet, or 930 square meters), as are a rooftop infinity pool and observation deck. Collaborations include a 200-seat Jean-Georges Vongerichten restaurant, an Intelligentsia coffee bar, a Shinola custom watch bar and leather goods store, and a Warby Parker Pencil Room where visitors can write postcards to friends and family.
twahotel.com

From left: strolling The Hotel
Carpenter in Austin; cocktails at
Abigail Hall at Woodlark in Portland

Opposite: keeping it clean
at Woodlark

OREGON
Woodlark, Portland

This ridiculously adorable hotel began as a tale of two
dilapidated buildings downtown – the 1907 Cornelius
Hotel, listed in the National Register of Historic Places and
nicknamed "The House of Welcome," and the Woodlark
Building, one of Portland's first skyscrapers. The French
Renaissance and Beaux-Arts architectural details have
been reappointed and restored, and the two adjacent
buildings have merged. With the addition of large
windows, skylights, black-and-white tiles, hand-blown-
glass light fixtures, velvet furnishings, and photogenic
plants, it's now one modern hotel that is wildly warm
and welcoming. _woodlarkhotel.com_

SOUTH CAROLINA
The Restoration, Charleston

A sophisticated urban boutique hotel with Southern
charm, elegant and modern decor, and a pleasantly lived-
in feel. The hotel is built into a series of historic buildings,
and offers two options: a traditional hotel and one, two,
or three bedrooms at the Residences. The ties to the
community are deep: blue accents in the public spaces
recall Charleston's history as a center for indigo dyeing,
the hotel boutique stocks a great selection of locally
produced wares, and the menu at The Watch Rooftop
Kitchen & Spirits features the best in farm-to-table from
local purveyors. _therestorationhotel.com_

TEXAS
The Hotel Carpenter, Austin

This sunny, spacious, great-looking, and communal boutique hotel has big, minimalist rooms, a courtyard swimming pool, charming restaurant (the kind you could easily work into weekly rotation as a local), and a very nice little to-go coffee counter serving cinnamon buns and migas and other things that will destroy any hope of eating healthily for the day by about, oh, nine in the morning. While the hotel's aesthetic is super design-forward, the prices are super affordable, making this hotel a great home base for anyone eager to explore the red-hot Texas capital. _carpenterhotel.com_

HALL Arts Hotel, Dallas

This newcomer arrived in grand Texas style at the hands of owners and local philanthropists Craig and Kathryn Hall, who bought the land decades ago and spent years perfecting the plan and developing the surrounding Arts District, the largest contiguous arts district in the US. The rooms and public spaces here are at once high-tech and art-filled, with room furnishings and fixtures in many shades of white, the better to let the art stand out. Two in-house curators (one of whom Kathryn met when she served as President Clinton's ambassador to Austria) oversee a rotating collection from emerging and established artists. Ellie's, one of four in-house restaurants, was named for Craig's mother and serves Napa cuisine, including their HALL Winery wines. _hallartshotel.com_

Hotel Alessandra, Houston

A 223-room stunner all about height and volume in downtown's GreenStreet development. Local design firm Rottet Studio drummed up a story about a European sophisticate who falls hard for an oil tycoon during Houston's freewheeling days. What does that mood board look like, in design terms? Brazilian marble, French-stained-glass doors, bronze handrails, and a high, vaulted ceiling that pulls guests from the street-level entrance up a showy staircase to the second-floor lobby. A metallic color scheme and laminated glass panels give the place a warm, old-fashioned glow. The retro-futuristic ribcage architecture at restaurant Lucienne is a standout. Cozy loveseats and chairs upholstered in mohair invite canoodling in the corner after a few coupes at classy in-house cocktail spot Bardot. _hotelalessandra-houston.com_

VIRGINIA
Quirk Hotel, Richmond

Housed in a 1916 former luxury department store with care taken to preserve original features, like the 13-foot (4-meter) floor-to-ceiling windows, maple floors, and Italian Renaissance–style arches. Original local artwork hangs throughout the suites, and pastel throw pillows and room accents make the spaces feel extra dreamy. The Quirk Gallery – part art gallery, part gift shop – features artwork by emerging local Richmond artists and hand-selected stylish home goods and gifts, many evocative of the hotel's millennial pink–themed spaces. Bike rentals are available to explore Richmond to Broad Street and beyond. *destinationhotels.com/quirk-hotel*

WASHINGTON
Hotel Sorrento, Seattle

The oldest boutique hotel in town (opened in 1909) still shines at the top of its class with original wood details, vintage-modern trimmings, and handsome fabrics that harken back to a time when bow ties weren't worn ironically. The hotel has seventy-six unique guest rooms, a robust cultural program, and an elegant cider-serving lounge with a fireplace and handsome speakeasy-style bar. *hotelsorrento.com*

WASHINGTON, D.C.
Tabard Inn

The opposite of a hipster hotel, this unpretentious inn has been a pocket of warmth in an otherwise tough-as-nails town for more than a century. The thirty-five rooms are quirky and personal, filled with vintage finds from many eras. Nothing matches, and everything's perfect. Located on a quiet Dupont Circle street, the hotel occupies three Victorian townhouses and, during World War II, was home to the Navy Women Accepted Volunteer Services known as WAVES. Today, guests and visitors can have a drink by two fireplaces in three lounges or have dinner at the Michelin-noted restaurant that has specialized in local ingredients since before it was trendy. Here's another trend we'd like to see them inspire: the hotel is almost totally employee-owned. *tabardinn.com*

Whimsy at Quirk Hotel, Richmond

Opposite, clockwise from top left: charm at Tabard Inn, Washington, D.C.; in the room at Hotel Sorrento, Seattle; the lounge at Woodlark, Portland; the legendary Eero Saarinen lounge at TWA Hotel, Queens; seating at The Hotel Carpenter, Austin

CANADA

BRITISH COLUMBIA
Skwachàys Lodge Hotel & Gallery, Vancouver

Canada's first aboriginal boutique arts hotel is one part visitor accommodation and one part social housing for local Aboriginal artists on the verge of homelessness, making it a unique cultural experience in the Gastown district. Aboriginal artists helped design each of the eighteen unique guest suites, and many residents sell their work through the small onsite gallery and offer studio visits. Book well in advance to participate in a Northwest Indigenous smudging ritual or a First Nations purification ceremony in the rooftop garden sweat lodge.
skwachays.com

ONTARIO
The Drake Hotel, Toronto

This playful nineteen-room crash pad serves as an anchor to the lively, artsy West Queen West neighborhood. The Drake General Store sources some of the best souvenirs in town. Happenings (hosted by artists, DJs, and scene-makers) are scheduled almost every night of the week.
thedrake.ca

QUEBEC
Hotel Le St-James, Montréal

Opulent antique decor and European style with modern amenities like Bang & Olufsen sound systems and flat-screen LCDs. Le Spa, which offers a full menu of services for face and body, is located in the Merchant's Bank vault. For all this grandeur, the hotel is infamously known for the time it was totally booked by The Rolling Stones and their crew. _hotellestjames.com_

Hôtel Gault, Montréal

A luxurious avant-garde hotel in a former 19th-century textile warehouse with thirty light-filled loft-style rooms that have classic 20th-century furnishings and heated bathroom floors. Six different spaces are designed for chic work occasions, for groups of six to 150 people. _hotelgault.com_

Auberge du Vieux-Port, Montréal

A charming hotel in a former leather factory on the riverfront, convenient to the old port and downtown. It has the look and feel of a B&B – 19th-century architecture, post and beam ceilings, oak floors – with four-star service and modern amenities (multi-jet rainfall showers, Le Labo bath products). Be sure to ask for a room with water views. _aubergeduvieuxport.com_

Opposite: The Drake Hotel in Toronto

This page, clockwise from top: Montreal's Hôtel Gault, inside and out; a corner suite at Auberge du Vieux-Port

MEXICO

BAJA CALIFORNIA SUR
Drift San Jose, San José del Cabo
Located in the town center, Drift is the perfect accommodation for independent travelers seeking peace, quiet, and comfort in a tranquil and private setting. The contemporary, industrial-style rooms are comfortable and beautifully furnished with minimalist decor and surround a courtyard with a small pool in the center. Guests are encouraged to make themselves at home and get to know one another. The hotel's food cart and mezcal bar are open to the public on Thursday and Saturday evenings and live music is on the ticket regularly – a few more reasons to never leave this little urban oasis. *driftsanjose.com*

La Bohemia, Todos Santos
This eight-room boutique hideaway not far from Cabo has all the creature comforts of a great bed-and-breakfast – beds with beautiful headboards upholstered in bright Otomi fabrics; wool blankets imported from Peru; bathrooms with hand-painted tiles, beautiful Mexican sinks, and locally sourced bath products; and a lush tropical garden with hammocks, an honor bar, and a small but lovely swimming pool. *labohemiabaja.com*

GUANAJUATO
Hotel Amparo, San Miguel de Allende
A small, nicely designed boutique hotel with five guest suites run by passionate, travel-loving, textile-designing owners. Situated in the center of the historic colonial city inside a heritage building that was once a private residence for the mayor, this stylish hideaway is outfitted with mid-century furnishings, original tiling, and custom-made towels and bedding from the owners' company, Hibiscus Linens. *hotelamparo.com*

GUERRERO
Encanto Acapulco, Acapulco
Set high on a hilltop, with sweeping vistas of Acapulco Bay, this chic, geometric hotel is known for its all-white exterior and interconnected water features, which sweep past private suites and smaller pools and lead to a jaw-dropping infinity pool, reflecting silhouetted trees and the cove below. The property, which has won several architecture awards, was designed by Miguel Angel Aragonés, a self-taught Mexican architect responsible for more than a dozen buildings in Mexico City, who, when not designing residences and hospitality projects, aims to change the aesthetic of low-income housing. *encantoacapulco.mx*

JALISCO
Hotel Demetria, Guadalajara

A moody, minimalist design hotel attached to the landmark Art Deco Casa Quiñones, the Demetria incorporates contemporary steel-and-glass architecture with a restaurant, bookshop, and rooftop pool, plus contemporary art installations. The Demetria also operates apartments in a Luis Barragán–designed building around the corner. _hoteldemetria.com_

MEXICO CITY
Las Alcobas, Mexico City

An elegant, impeccably stylish, and discreet hotel on a quiet street in Polanco, the city's swankiest neighborhood. The hotel over-delivers on all counts: the thirty-five rooms have custom furniture and Italian linens on heavenly beds; spa-like bathrooms have rain showers, whirlpools, steam jets, and Naturopathica products. The thoughtful amenities include personal butlers, complimentary Mexican snacks in the mini bar, and the Aurora Spa on the second floor offers massages, scrubs, and wraps. The small hotel claims two restaurants, both excellent. Anatole is seasonal and casual; Patria, where chef Martha Ortiz does modern takes on contemporary Mexican cuisine, is one of the city's best. _lasalcobas.com_

Ryo Kan, Mexico City

The coolest, most Zen-inducing ryokan is located where you least expect it – about ten minutes from Chapultepec Forest in the heart of Mexico City. It's got everything you'd expect from a traditional Japanese inn: tatami mat floors, sliding walls, a garden with a koi fish pond, and even an onsen of sorts on the rooftop terrace. But with ten blond-wood-bedecked rooms starting at $150 a night and a great location in the city's up-and-coming Little Tokyo – don't miss whiskey-sake bar Le Tachinomi Desu (_edokobayashi.com_) nearby – this place is anything but stuck in the past. _ryokan.mx_

OAXACA DE JUÁREZ
Hotel de la Parra, Oaxaca

The location, mere steps from the Zócalo town square and the cathedral, couldn't be more convenient, and the hotel staff couldn't be lovelier and more thoughtful. The thirteen rooms and suites are simple in style, with traditional artisanal blankets at the foot of the bed. When you want to stay in, the courtyard pool is beautiful, the lounge is super relaxing, and the in-house restaurant serves local specialties made with ingredients from the nearby markets. _hoteldelaparra.com_

DESIGN ON A DIME

Who says a stay in the city has to be expensive? These US hotels deliver on style and service, not on price tag.

The Dean, Providence, Rhode Island
Designed to reflect the city's history and culture, this masculine boutique hotel is filled with locally made furniture and found objects from Europe. Pick up a mic and get down with your favorite tunes in a private room at The Boombox, Providence's first and only karaoke lounge. *thedeanhotel.com*

The Marlton Hotel, New York, New York
Channeling a Parisian hôtel particulier in Greenwich Village, this place is elegant without having an ounce of snobbishness. The cozy lobby living room has lots of seating, a cafe kiosk, free WiFi, and a roaring fire; bistro Margaux has a solarium perfect for quiet breakfasts and two-top banquettes for buzzy dinner dates. The rooms are bright and feminine, but tiny, so come in a cozy state of mind. *marltonhotel.com*

The Asbury, Asbury Park, New Jersey
The town's Victorian-era past will mix with its rock'n'roll present on the Jersey Shore. Bunk with friends in dorm-style rooms that sleep up to eight or stick with a king or queen room for privacy. The beach is two blocks away, but a pool is right at hand. The fun scene on the rooftop includes yoga classes, an outdoor drive-in-style movie theater, and a cocktail bar that hosts a rotating list of DJs. *theasburyhotel.com*

From top: a room at The Dean in Providence, Rhode Island; a world of volumes at The Asbury in New Jersey

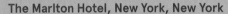

Clockwise from top: two relaxing setups at the beach-happy Dreamcatcher in Puerto Rico; two interiors at the city-chic Robey in Chicago

The Dreamcatcher, San Juan, Puerto Rico The capital's only vegetarian bed and breakfast delights with twelve boho-chic rooms, each equipped with a dreamcatcher, just steps from the beach in the residential Ocean Park area. Morning yoga, a luscious breakfast and brunch, tarot card readings, and adventure tours ensure you're blissed out from the moment you arrive. *dreamcatcherpr.com*

The Robey, Chicago, Illinois Mexican hoteliers Grupo Habita continue their tradition of repurposing old structures in clever, contemporary ways. Here, Art Deco designs are fused with mid-century modern furniture in a sleek, minimalist palette of lights and darks, resulting in a confident mix of Americana. Two onsite watering holes and a triangular rooftop pool round out the offerings on the border of Wicker Park and Bucktown. *therobey.com*

Hotel San José, Austin, Texas This cool, mid-century motor lodge in South Congress got a stylish minimalist makeover in forty bungalow-style rooms. Subdued spaces are punctuated with bold decor like colorful serape-patterned pillows and cowhide rugs. If the design doesn't leave you feeling rejuvenated, the onsite pool, courtyard, and gardens are guaranteed to do the trick. Custom-made kimono bathrobes and old-school tech on loan (think typewriters and Polaroid cameras) are just a few of the quirky, thoughtful amenities. _sanjosehotel.com_

Hotel Eleven, Austin, Texas This fourteen-room boutique in the up-and-coming East 11th Street neighborhood strikes a careful balance between the city's alternative spirit and contemporary design principles. Every space is unique, but you can count on cozy interiors, ample natural light, and sleek bathrooms throughout. Most guest rooms include private Juliet balconies, but for more fresh air head up to the rooftop and take in the 360-degree city views. Because the hotel is just down the street from Franklin Barbecue – the best BBQ joint in town – there's no excuse not to be first in line. _hotelelevenaustin.com_

Boon Hotel + Spa, Guerneville, California This Russian River Valley hotel is clean and cozy, fun and free-spirited, and well-positioned near the farm-to-table restaurants of Healdsburg and the vineyards of Sonoma County. Grab a bike and go exploring, hit the saltwater pool and spa for hangover relief and the outdoor hot tub for midnight smooching. _boonhotels.com_

Clockwise from top left: the ivy-covered entrance and the pool at Hotel San José in Austin; a perch in the sun and at the pool at Boon Hotel in Sonoma

Hotel Normandie, Los Angeles, California Bohemian minimalism prevails in this budget-friendly Koreatown hotel where tiny rooms make up for the lack of space with beautifully restored wood floors, plush bedding, and glimmering white tile. The charming lobby is a wonderful place to sip an espresso while taking in the wood beam ceilings, glowing chandeliers, and the public-use typewriter. *hotelnormandiela.com*

Farmer's Daughter, Los Angeles, California A trendy boutique with a flirty vibe and down-home country stylings (rooms have denim duvets, plaid curtains, and custom-made wooden chairs) on a happening strip in West Hollywood. Perks include an outdoor pool and sundeck, discounts at a nearby fitness center, and easy access to big-ticket museums, indie shopping, and the historic farmers' market at The Grove. *farmersdaughterhotel.com*

Hotel Valley Ho, Scottsdale, Arizona The desert hideaway that used to welcome Bing Crosby and Zsa Zsa Gabor is now a vibrant and stylish hotel where vintage charm and updated luxury meet around the corner from some of the best dining, shopping, and entertainment in town. Two buildings offer different experiences: The Tower has a pool, mountain views, and rooms with private balconies, while The Hotel is dressed in Arizona artwork and floor-to-ceiling glass walls that open onto a sizable patio. *hotelvalleyho.com*

Pacific Edge Hotel, Laguna Beach, California Playful and nautical, laidback and family friendly, it's essentially a beach pass with benefits on a perfect stretch of Southern California sand, with waterfront views, beach bungalows, open-air dining, and an ocean-to-table restaurant. *pacificedgehotel.com*

From top: Arizona's Hotel Valley Ho is welcoming both outside and in

BETTING ON MICROBRANDS

Small hotel groups are tapping into the modern traveler's needs by setting up in the right locations with nice design details, cool intel, and quality amenities at (mostly) affordable prices. Here's what else they've got going for them:

1 Hotels
Inspired by nature, driven by wellness, bringing the outdoors inside.
1hotels.com

Arrive Hotels
Low-key luxury neighborhood vibes, welcoming bars, and free high-tech amenities.
arrivehotels.com

Generator
Awesome social spaces, fun food and beverage scenes, cute communal atmosphere.
staygenerator.com

Germain Hotels
Bringing family-run chic and approachable luxury to Canada's top markets.
germainhotels.com/en

Graduate Hotels
A stylish option for friends and families visiting university towns.
graduatehotels.com

Grupo Habita
Contemporary and clever designs in fashionable neighborhoods across Mexico (and the US).
grupohabita.mx

Hotel June
A pared-down (yet whimsical) interior design overseen by Kelly Wearstler, who is the creative force behind June's parent microbrand, Proper Hotels.
thehoteljune.com

Life House Hotels

Connecting visitors to neighborhoods with fun and easy decor in vacation destinations like Miami and Nantucket.
lifehousehotels.com

Makeready Hotels

Craftsmanship and connection with local artisans, architects, and designers in redesigned and reinvigorated spaces.
makereadyexperience.com

Moxy

Affordable and central and notable for cool looks by top-name designers who clearly had fun with the "go for it" brief.
moxy-hotels.marriott.com

NoMad Hotels

Ornate design meets an obsessive attention to bespoke service, with award-winning namesake restaurants and bars.
thenomadhotel.com

Palisociety

LA-based, family-run, bringing the California spirit to neighborhood-centric boutiques that are plush and cheerful, with in-house dining and drinking spots to match. *palisociety.com*

Pendry

An approachable offshoot of luxury Montage resorts in smaller-market towns.
pendry.com

Salt Hotels

Stylish digs in north-east US beach towns not known for boutique options.
salthotels.com

Sister City

Urban bohemian efficiency, inspired by Japanese bento boxes (among other things) and a "less, but better" motto, brought to you by the folks behind Ace Hotel.
sistercitynyc.com

The Hoxton

The "open house" policy lures locals as well as travelers to cozy corners of their lobbies and rooftop bars.
thehoxton.com

The Line

Shaped by the neighborhood, followed by foodies, building a buzz.
thelinehotel.com

Urban Cowboy

Over-the-top and totally funky design elements, B&B vibes, and plenty of communal charms.
urbancowboy.com

Opposite, from left: a warm welcome at Hotel June in Los Angeles; Empire State Building views at Moxy Chelsea in NYC

This page, from top: The Asbury, a Salt Hotel, in New Jersey; good cheer at Graduate Nashville

WHERE MILLIONAIRES SHARE THE WEALTH

These cultural institutions include the former homes of the wealthy and the centers they endowed when their collections outgrew their wall space.

The Morgan Library, New York City, New York, USA
J.P. Morgan's former home includes his stunning original library and a modern Renzo Piano–designed museum dedicated to the literary arts. *themorgan.org*

The Broad, Los Angeles, California, USA
This LA newcomer has a stunning modern art collection, notably Yayoi Kusama's always-packed *Infinity Mirrored Room–The Souls of Millions of Light Years Away*. *thebroad.org*

Isabella Stewart Gardner Museum, Boston, Massachusetts, USA Modeled on a 15th-century Venetian palazzo, this serene home and garden is notable for its European paintings and tapestries. *gardnermuseum.org*

Museo Soumaya, Mexico City, Mexico A cutting-edge architectural stunner with more than 66,000 pieces, ranging from Pre-Hispanic Mesoamerican work to the biggest collection of Rodin sculptures outside France. *museosoumaya.org*

PAMM | Pérez Art Museum Miami, Miami, Florida, USA This massive waterfront Downtown Miami museum showcases international art from the 20th and 21st centuries in its many formats. *pamm.org*

The Breakers, Newport, Rhode Island, USA
Cornelius Vanderbilt II's 1893 oceanfront summer cottage is a stunning living museum, with attending stables and a carriage house. *newportmansions.org*

UNDERSTANDING OUR PAST TO BUILD A BETTER FUTURE

These institutions help us understand where we came from and how to make tomorrow more inclusive, understanding, and decent.

Canadian Museum for Human Rights, Winnipeg, Manitoba, Canada
The first museum in the world dedicated exclusively to human rights everywhere, with a special focus on Canada's collective history. *humanrights.ca*

National Center for Civil and Human Rights, Atlanta, Georgia, USA
A museum and cultural center exploring the American civil rights and global human rights movements and the legacy of Dr. Martin Luther King, Jr. *civilandhumanrights.org*

National Museum of African-American History and Culture, Washington, D.C., USA Years in the making, the stunning new Smithsonian museum relates the history of Black Americans from the earliest days of slavery to today. *nmaahc.si.edu*

The Legacy Museum, Montgomery, Alabama, USA Owned and operated by the Equal Justice Initiative, this museum tells the history of African-American oppression in the United States, from enslavement to segregation to mass incarceration in the modern day. *museumandmemorial.eji.org/museum*

Whitney Plantation, Wallace, Louisiana, USA This 2000-acre (809-hectare) complex includes a museum, main house, slave quarters, French Creole barn, and sculptures that tell the story of slavery in the Southern United States. *whitneyplantation.org*

Museum of Anthropology at the University of British Columbia, Vancouver, British Columbia, Canada
Built on the traditional land of the Musqueam people, this museum focuses on and collaborates with First Nations communities from around the world, displaying collections according to Indigenous criteria. *moa.ubc.ca*

Mémorial ACTe Museum, Pointe-à-Pitre, Guadeloupe This $92 million, state-of-the-art interactive museum and memorial paints a breathtaking picture of the history of slavery in the Caribbean. Various low-fi and high-fi installations are very powerful in surprising ways – from animated scenes to text projections to objects of the oppressor – and are interspersed with modern and contemporary artworks that break up the chronological telling of this horrendous history. *memorial-acte.fr*

The majestic and timeless
Morgan Library in NYC

GLORIOUS URBAN RUINS

We're not the only ones obsessed with old, decaying buildings. (Just look at Instagram.) Note that trespassing may not be allowed, which may or may not stop you.

Jazzland, New Orleans, Louisiana, USA
This former amusement park never recovered from Hurricane Katrina flooding.

Michigan Central Station, Detroit, Michigan, USA
This 1914 train depot has been closed since 1988, its future use or demolition long debated. The latest: Ford Motor Company is planning to convert it into offices.

La Guarida Restaurant, Havana, Cuba
The dramatic and decaying staircase that sweeps up to the third-floor restaurant is the site of countless photo shoots.

Staten Island Boat Graveyard, Staten Island, New York, USA
This 1930s scrapyard is where 100 tugboats, ferries, and cargo ships have gone to die their slow, sinking death. That it's hard to access and is technically off limits only adds to its creepy appeal.

Windsor Ruins, Claiborne County, Mississippi, USA
Built in 1859 and used as a Union hospital during the Civil War, the only thing remaining from the plantation are twenty-three supporting columns.

Mormon Row, Jackson Hole, Wyoming, USA
The remaining homes and barns originally settled by a community of Mormons in the 1890s are in the middle of Grand Teton National Park.

Opposite: the staircase to La Guarida in Havana, Cuba

THE KITCHEN HEROES

Whether they're pioneering new foodways or just serving their standbys, these chefs help put their cities on the map.

Minneapolis, Minnesota, USA

Chef **Sean Sherman** grew up on Pine Ridge Reservation in South Dakota and cooked around the world for thirty years before turning his attention to the cuisine of his Oglala Lakota ancestors. Through The Sioux Chef, his catering company, cookbook, and community, he collaborates with Native American chefs, ethnobotanists, foragers, and artists to celebrate and revitalize North American culinary traditions.

Guadalajara, Jalisco, Mexico

Mexico's second largest city is in the midst of a renaissance fueled by chefs with hometown credentials and outsiders coming into the city with an openness to experimentation. **Alfonso Cadena**'s family-style platters of internationally influenced dishes encourage a communal vibe at Hueso, the dramatic restaurant where the white-washed walls are lined with bones. Noma alum **Francisco Ruano** is combining respect for tradition with full-blown culinary creativity at Alcalde in the business district. Australian **Paul Bentley** brings an exacting technique for house-made charcuterie and pastas at the impressively designed Magno Brasserie.

Washington, D.C., USA

It's a veritable United Nations of cuisines in the US capital, represented by the inventive Spanish cuisine of humanitarian **José Andrés**, the compulsively delicious Laotian meals by **Seng Luangrath**, the fine dining and easy spaghetti of Italian **Fabio Trabocchi**, and the Venezuelan specialties of **Enrique Limardo** – all have multiple outposts around town. **Kwame Onwuachi** established himself as a national talent and advocate for Black workers in the restaurant industry through the African and Caribbean foods he originally showcased at Kith/Kin. **Peter Prime** does inventive takes on street food from his native Trinidad and Tobago at Cane, the restaurant he owns with his sister, **Jeanine Prime**.

Philadelphia, Pennsylvania, USA

Another north-east US city that's home to a world of great cuisines. **Jezabel Careaga** puts her spin on Northwest Argentine empanadas and tartas at Jezabel's. **Kate Jacoby** and husband **Rich Landau** cook elevated vegan fare at Vedge. **Michael Solomonov** sealed his reputation as one of the country's best chefs at Zahav and has since gone on to open a handful of other Israeli-ish restaurants around town. Highly lauded chef and immigration activist **Cristina Martínez** serves Mexican cuisine at her casual eateries South Philly Barbacoa and Casa Mexico. Restaurateur **Ellen Yin** is the force behind the New American cuisine at fine dining Fork, casual High Street Philly, and wine-driven bistro a.Kitchen and a.Bar. Local boy **Greg Vernick** wows with a new American menu at Vernick Food & Drink. The best refined Italian may be at the hands of another native son, chef **Marc Vetri**, at his namesake Vetri Cucina, among other outposts.

Opposite: Greg Vernick (center) in his kitchen in Philadelphia

This page: Enrique Limardo's work in Washington, D.C., is (almost) too pretty to eat

A SPECIAL NOTE ABOUT EXTRA SPECIAL MEALS

Philadelphia is a sandwich town, and no trip would be complete without tasting a few of the many (many) options, all of which claim to be the best in town. In the winner's circle, **Pat's** and **Geno's** vie for the title of best cheesesteak, **DiNic's** wins for its beef sandwich, and **Duke's of Marlborough** and **John's Roast Pork** take the prize for the other local classic: roast pork with provolone and broccoli rabe.

Farther south, we couldn't imagine being anywhere near **Miami** without stopping for a meal at **Mandolin Aegean Bistro**, and especially their Greek and Turkish Samplers meze appetizers. They're listed separately on the menu, but there's no contest. Get both.

Clockwise from top: unforgettable wood-fired oysters at Cochon in New Orleans; mezze at Mandolin Aegean Bistro in Miami; a beautiful plate at Vernick in Philadelphia

New Orleans is the place for Gulf oysters – freshwater mollusks that are tender and meaty but mild in flavor. They're also entirely democratic – cheap and plentiful and available at dive bars (oyster shooters!) and fine dining establishments (oysters Rockefeller) alike. At French Quarter institutions like **Felix's**, you'll find them shucked and fixed with horseradish, cocktail sauce, and crumbled saltines. At chef-centric **St. Roch Market** in the Marigny, the best of the bunch are bright and delicate and spritzed with lemon and mignonette. You'll find them dusted with cornmeal, fried, and stuffed into po' boy sandwiches at no-nonsense corner stores, grocers, and seafood markets from the Metarie to the Garden District. Our vote is for **Liuzza's by the Track**, which serves a sammie overflowing and doused in garlic butter. For straight-up old-school charm, charbroiled oysters, and oyster stew with toast, seasonally open **Casamento's** (since 1919) cannot be beat. But the oysters at **Cochon**, tossed in a butter-anchovy-garlic-chili paste, then wood-fired until bubbling, are simply sublime.

Many of us take for granted the idea of eating simple, incredibly flavorful ingredients grown with care, harvested at the right time, and brought to the dinner plate quickly, with little fanfare. But that's mostly thanks to Alice Waters, whose 1970s food revolution continues every day at her lauded **Berkeley** restaurant and sweet cafe. Every meal at **Chez Panisse** feels like starting your food education from scratch.

Los Angeles sure knows how to make a meal out of a salad, and the greatest salads really do make you feel like you've got life down pat. On one end of the spectrum, the classic chopped salad from institutions like **The Ivy** or **La Scala** in Beverly Hills. On the other end, the extremely plentiful, plant-based plates from **Cafe Gratitude**. And there's no shortage of fresh, bold salad combinations from new-school favorites **Botanica**, **Gjusta**, **Huckleberry**, **Kismet**, **Honey Hi**, and **Bondi Harvest**.

From top: salad heaven at Botanica in Los Angeles; more sublime oysters at Casamento's in New Orleans; a seat in the sun at Botanica

FIND NATURE NEAR AMERICAN CITIES

Lesser-known escapes are closer than you think.

Channel Islands State Park, California
Close to: Los Angeles
Even by California standards, these five pristine islands off the coast of Los Angeles shine for their natural beauty and rich populations of birds, seals, and whales, making a water sport weekend an enticing prospect for urbanites.

Lassen Volcanic National Park, California
Close to: San Francisco
This smaller version of Yellowstone has ample snow for winter sports through July, hiking routes within hydrothermal areas, and one of the world's largest plug dome volcanoes, which form when lava extrudes from the earth but doesn't flow. And it's all just four hours from the Bay Area.

Great Sand Dunes National Park and Preserve, Colorado
Close to: Denver
What looks like a scene from Arabian Nights are actually the tallest sand dunes in North America. Sandboarding options and a creek flowing at their base make this the closest Colorado will ever get to having a beach.

Biscayne National Park, Florida
Close to: Miami
Across the bay from South Beach, there are more adventurous ways of staying cool – kayaking past mangrove forests, scuba diving for shipwrecks, and snorkeling over one of the largest tracts of coral in the world.

Valley of Fire State Park, Nevada
Close to: Las Vegas
Clark County is known for its petrified trees and bright red Aztec sandstone outcrops made from 150-million-year-old shifting sand dunes. Rainbow Vista is one of the most spectacular hiking areas come spring, when the desert mallow and indigo bush bloom. State park rangers offer a variety of guided wildflower walks. The trail is an easy, short hike for Vegas day trippers, with big views from the start.

Bryce Canyon National Park, Utah
Close to: Salt Lake City
The state's smallest and least-trafficked national park is worth the weekend camping trip, if only for the opportunity to marvel at hoodoos, skinny rock spires that prove erosion has a sense of humor.

Cuyahoga Valley National Park, Ohio
Close to: Cleveland (and not far from Detroit, Michigan)
You can boat, bird watch, and bike on Towpath Trail, an old portion of the Ohio and Erie Canal. But the best pastime here may be appreciating the natural and geological diversity of the park, which is sandwiched between the urban sprawl of Cleveland and Akron.

Congaree National Park, South Carolina
Close to: Charleston
It's a pleasant surprise to find a national park near one of the most charming cities in the American South, especially one with swamp trails, top-notch bird watching, and some of the tallest trees on the East Coast.

Big Thicket National Preserve, Texas
Close to: Houston
Though not as visually arresting as Big Bend, Big Thicket has plenty going on under its brush – the densely forested preserve is one of the world's most biodiverse areas outside the tropics.

North Cascades National Park, Washington
Close to: Seattle
Though most popular with off-roaders, casual naturalists can drive through to Ross Lake National Recreation Area for camping and picnicking. Those who wander deeper into the wilderness will find the highest number of glaciers in the US outside Alaska.

Anacostia Park, Washington, D.C.
Close to: Washington, D.C.
Everyone always focuses on Rock Creek Park, but this tract of land, wrapping around the Anacostia River, is the best urban park in the city. You can run, skate, bike, and picnic all along the urban national park land.

Hot Springs National Park, Tennessee
Close to: Memphis
The oldest preserved park in the country is a therapeutic water source that flows from Hot Springs Mountain outside the Arkansas city of Hot Springs. Visitors can test the water's medicinal effects in town on Bathhouse Row, a boulevard of grand bathhouses, including some from the Gilded Age.

Mother Nature shows her sense of humor at Bryce Canyon in Utah

CHAPTER 7

THE COMPANY YOU KEEP

So often when you travel, *what* you take matters less than *who* you take. Because the company you keep can make or break a vacation, it's important to consider your travel companions carefully.

The options are not limitless. You can travel alone or with a partner, friends, family, colleagues, and strangers, or in small or large numbers. That's it. Every trip you ever take will be some variation of one of these arrangements.

When the impetus for the trip is a special occasion – a landmark birthday, a destination wedding, a reunion, a bachelor/bachelorette weekend or babymoon or naughty weekend – you'll be in company. When your motivation is more internal – recovering from heartbreak, surviving a death or loss, seeking transformation, celebrating a milestone – you may prefer your own company or that of strangers. If you travel regularly for business, you're used to the solo path and probably have your routine well-oiled and your time-saving hacks down pat. Go, road warrior, go.

We'll get to where you should go in a minute, but first, a quick public service announcement: remember to be considerate of other people when you travel. This simple rule will make any trip so much easier, better, and more meaningful, to just scratch the surface of the benefits of following this simple guideline. "Other people" in this case refers not only to the people you're traveling with – although they may be the most important ones to consider, since they are with you the whole journey – but also the people you encounter along the way: the ticket-takers, the bus drivers, the flight attendants, the hoteliers, the tour guides, the locals at the bar, the other travelers you meet. You're not going to get very far by being selfish or self-absorbed. But you'll go the distance by being kind and thoughtful. This can be as simple as acknowledging a nice gesture from a stranger – a door held open, a smile on a train – or being the one to initiate the interaction. Your vacation may be your time, but you can find a way to take care of others along the way.

Now that you have the right attitude, here are excellent destinations for trips with friends, with special someones, and by yourself – with a focus on special occasions.

Previous page: coming in for a landing at Clayoquot Wilderness Lodge in British Columbia

Opposite: fishing for fun at GoldenEye in Jamaica

BRING YOUR CREW

Meadowood Napa Valley, St. Helena, California, USA
Meadowood is arguably the nicest resort in Napa Valley, where everything is as well-executed as can be, and the extreme luxury is low-key and unfussy. Let's start with the setting: 250 private, woodsy acres (100 hectares) that feel removed from Napa tourism, though the town is only a few miles away. The well-marked trails through the surrounding hills on the property can lead you on a leisurely stroll or a heart-pumping workout. Treehouse-style cabin accommodations, with separate living rooms with fireplaces and patios with deck chairs, afford maximum privacy. The world-class restaurant is one of the country's best, with a wine cellar to match. The award-winning spa, new fitness center, and three swimming pools will restore your body. The nine-hole golf course is sporty and zippy, as is the professional-grade croquet pitch (don't forget to pack your whites). With so much to do, all overseen by a staff that's attentive but not obtrusive, this is one for a special (older) birthday celebration, a business retreat (when you've had a really good year), or a multi-generational family trip. *meadowood.com*

La Bohemia Baja Hotel Pequeño, Todos Santos, Mexico
This six-room boutique hideaway has all the creature comforts of a great B&B – beds with beautiful headboards upholstered in bright Otomi fabrics; wool blankets imported from Peru; bathrooms with hand-painted tiles, beautiful Mexican sinks, and locally sourced bath products; and a lush tropical garden with hammocks, an honor bar, and a small but lovely swimming pool. But you'll want to spend your time together outside, swimming with whale sharks and sea lions, hiking and exploring Baja trails, releasing endangered sea turtles to safety. The lovely owners will hook you up with everything Todos Santos has to offer. *labohemiabaja.com*

Taylor River Lodge, Almont, Colorado, USA
Open from late May through mid-October, this off-grid locale on the Western Slope of Colorado is a woodsy wonderland ideal for families. There are private cabins with various set-ups – lofts, bunk beds, kitchens, and a teepee lounge. The all-inclusive rate (which really makes life easier when splitting costs with friends) includes not only food and drink (and an awesome mini bar), but activities like river rafting, axe throwing, fly fishing, mountaineering, shooting BB guns (don't shoot yer eye out, kid), and access to the beautiful pool cabin. *elevenexperience.com/taylor-river-lodge-colorado*

GoldenEye, Oracabessa, Jamaica
Ian Fleming created James Bond and wrote all his adventures at GoldenEye, and creative spirits have been finding their inspiration here ever since. The resort, now overseen by music producer-turned–Island Outpost hotelier Chris Blackwell, has freestanding villas overlooking the beach or the lagoon. Everything here exudes boho cool, including the outdoor showers and bathtubs surrounded by palm fronds and discreet shrubbery. Have a rum cocktail at Bizot Bar or a Red Stripe at Shabeen. Pull a banana off a bunch; they're hanging right in front of you. Meet your friends for a paddle around the lagoon, a swim in one of the pools, or massage treatments at the spa. Music is everywhere and always at the perfect volume; every minute here feels like a celebration. (Don't be surprised if you stumble across an indie movie star reading a book to his toddler.) If GoldenEye is beyond the budget, try Island Outpost's other Jamaica options: Strawberry Hill in the mountains and The Caves along the cliffs in Negril. *goldeneye.com*

Opposite, from left: on the water at Clayoquot Wilderness Lodge, British Columbia; the table is set at Tordrillo Mountain Lodge in Alaska

Stay fireside and slopeside at
Caldera House in Jackson Hole

Opposite, from left: an elegant
table and an elegant bird at
Cuixmala in Mexico

Caldera House, Teton Village, Wyoming, USA

Located at the base of Jackson Hole Mountain Resort,
this hotel and members club was built by a financier who
worked the chairlift when he was younger. As an adult he
decided to make his ski slope wishes come true, which
explains why the whole building feels like a fancy, dreamy
winter sports HQ. The highly designed two- and four-
bedroom suites have chef's kitchens, gas fireplaces, and
private balconies, and can be combined for a buyout for
up to sixty guests. Just the thing when you want a holiday
bonanza of sports, nature, and chilling. You won't need
to leave the building too often, as the spa, restaurant,
lounge, ski valet, and ski shop are all on site. When you
do walk outside, the dedicated staff can arrange wildlife
safaris through Yellowstone National Park in the summer
and heli-skiing excursions in the winter. *calderahouse.com*

Blackberry Mountain, Walland, Tennessee, USA

If a choose-your-own-adventure experience set among
5200 acres (2104 hectares) of protected land in Eastern
Tennessee's Great Smoky Mountains sounds appealing for
a family, friend, or foodie vacation, this relative newcomer
is the mountainside resort for you. The rustic-chic retreat
(sister property to beloved and highly awarded restaurant
Blackberry Farm) offers a lengthy roster of immersive
outdoor and wellness activities (aerial yoga, sound
bathing, mountain biking, trail running, fly fishing), two
restaurants, and several types of lodging (cabins, cottages,
private homes). *blackberrymountain.com*

Cuixmala, Jalisco, Mexico

This estate, nestled amid the 30,000-acre (12,141-hectare) Chamela-Cuixmala Biosphere Reserve, was once the home of an eccentric, nature-loving English billionaire. Today, the heavenly hideaway deep in the Jalisco state of Mexico on the wild Pacific Coast is more guest house than hotel, with options for small or large parties in Morocco-meets-Mexico-inspired casitas, villas, suites, and bungalows set amid forests, lagoons, and beaches. Did you walk onto a magical movie set? It sure will feel like it. The beauty of Cuixmala lies in the fact that it can be whatever you want it to be: a relaxing place to switch off, a romantic getaway, an adventure holiday, or the perfect spot for a celebration. _cuixmala.com_

Tourists, North Adams, Massachusetts, USA

An all-star team – including key players from the band Wilco, Brooklyn Magazine, and MASS MoCA – is behind this reimagined motor lodge–cum–riverside retreat just moments from a trio of significant art institutions in the northern Berkshires. A big hit with the young and the Instagramming, the forty-eight motel rooms here have high-vaulted ceilings, king-size beds, and picture windows with built-in lounge seats. Handsome woodlands, rivers, and mountains abound. A 220-foot (67-meter) suspension footbridge connects the hotel with a 30-acre (12-hectare) network of trails, glens, and forest clearings used for open-air concerts and private events. Bring your college friends for a reunion or your family for an outdoorsy and artsy weekend. _touristswelcome.com_

Paradise Beach Nevis, Nevis

With seven two- to four-bedroom villas, this beachfront resort is ideal for large groups looking for individual accommodations or a close-knit crew who wants to pile in together. Each villa comes with a full kitchen, a personal butler, a private pool, and wild monkeys as neighbors. Spend your days lounging by the beach or head into town for a glimpse of perfectly preserved 18th-century buildings, including Founding Father (and Broadway inspiration) Alexander Hamilton's birthplace. _paradisebeachnevis.com_

Nestled into Suttle Lodge
in Oregon

Opposite: family fun at Mohonk
Mountain House in New York

Suttle Lodge, Sisters, Oregon, USA

Nostalgists looking to impart a classic American vacation experience to their kids will find a rose-tinted version of camp life at this 15-acre (6-hectare) rustic resort on the shores of Suttle Lake in the Deschutes National Forest. The large timber lodge, which has been running in some capacity since the 1930s, has been revived by The Mighty Union, the hospitality group behind The Ace Hotel Portland. It has wildly comfortable leather couches, a cocktail bar, a lending library with books and games, and a highly curated vinyl selection (guests act as record selectors). Groups can book fully equipped lakeside cabins or very rustic camping cabins among slender pines. On brisk summer mornings, you'll pad down to the Boathouse restaurant for house-made hash browns, egg sandwiches, and many refills of hot coffee in tin mugs while watching quiet canoes paddle by. There are shady, toddler-friendly trails around the lake, lawn games, and live outdoor music. Off-property, you'll find state parks with refreshing waterfalls, rock-climbing scrambles, a night sky observatory, and the funky little town of Sisters – which has all the necessities a sentimentalist needs (homemade ice cream shop, pottery studio, stitchin' post) for a vacation to remember. _thesuttlelodge.com_

Rosewood Mayakoba, Riviera Maya, Mexico

The Mayakoba development – a 1600-acre (647-hectare) gated community amid jungle, lagoon, and beach – is home to a handful of luxury resort hotels. Casual Caribbean beaching, in other words, this is not. But Rosewood Mayakoba strikes a lovely balance, delivering over-the-top luxury with warmth and ease. And a sense of heightened drama that begins when staff welcome you at the lobby and escort you to the skiff that glides you through mangroves and waterways to the lagoon entrance of your villa, where a warm, outdoor plunge pool awaits. You'll hop on bikes and weave your way through palms and over bridges to get to morning yoga under a palapa surrounded by the lagoon. Maybe you'll follow that with a shaman-led ritual in the temazcal sweat lodge at Sense Spa. For sure lunch will be tacos from the shack in the sand at the dedicated family club or the adults-only beach club, depending who you're with. You'll end the day with cocktails and a fire-roasted meal sitting under twinkly lights at long picnic tables between the open grill and the herb-and-vegetable garden. _rosewoodhotels.com/en/ mayakoba-riviera-maya_

10th Mountain Division Hut Association, Aspen, Colorado, USA

Does your sporty crew need a holiday challenge? This one is as unbeatable as it is unusual. Colorado is home to several systems of backcountry huts reachable in the summer by hiking and biking and in the winter by skiing or snowshoeing. The cozy huts in the 10th Mountain Division Hut Association, named in honor of the Army division that trained in the area, are among the best in the Rocky Mountains. They may be very basic (think bunk rooms for communal sleeping, a wood-burning stove, an outhouse, and sketchy, if any, WiFi), but they achieve Taj Mahal–like status when the journey to reach them is, on average, 6 or 7 miles (10 or 11 kilometers) and climbs roughly 2000 feet (610 meters) in elevation. The huts can be strung together for an epic journey – a "hut-to-hut trip" in local parlance – or single huts can be accessed for a one- or two-night adventure. Make all the noise you want: You're probably the only people around for miles and miles, and on a clear night, the Milky Way will feel like it's all yours. _huts.org_

Mohonk Mountain House, New Paltz, New York, USA

What began in 1869 as a ten-room tavern has become, five generations later, a 265-room compound surrounded by the largest private nature preserve in New York State. Set along Lake Mohonk, with views of the forest, Catskill Mountains, and Shawangunk Ridge, the destination's list of things to do year-round is endless. This is an innocent, go-back-in-time, Americana-at-its-best getaway, where the action ranges from lazy (a nap on a rocking chair, a massage at the award-winning spa, outdoor movies at the barn) to heart-thumping (cross-country skiing, rock-climbing, kayaking in front of your napping friends). You'll have fun when you're on your own and when you're all together. Everyone feels at home at Mohonk. _mohonk.com_

MIND YOUR ELDERS

You love your parents and grandparents and want them to be part of your vacation. Just don't forget to be sensitive to their needs and any restrictions and try to work around them – especially if they don't want to cop to their limits or feel like they are cramping your style. A few simple guidelines will go a long way:

Reconsider the Journey For you, it's a five-minute walk on cute cobblestone streets to the terrific taco restaurant. For Grandma and her cane, the slight uphill ascent may as well be Everest. Make sure she can be driven to the door, even if it means renting a car you wouldn't have otherwise rented. Similarly, staircases can become unexpected land mines when elevators aren't available or aren't working. A teenager's quick flight down a subway platform is an impossible stretch when your knees aren't what they used to be. Plan ahead for alternative transportation methods just in case.

Get a Wheelchair at the Airport Let's talk about the bright side: request a wheelchair to help them get through the airport. Their travel companions are typically waved in with them. You'll never breeze through security checkpoints faster.

Clockwise from top: the boathouse at Suttle Lodge, Oregon; chilling at Tourists in the Berkshires; pondering the Caribbean at Hotel Esencia, Mexico

Add Time to the Trip What takes you no time takes them longer. If you're traveling by train, it might take you five minutes to zip from track 1 to track 18, but if you use a walker, it will take a half hour. When planning the itinerary and the logistics, prioritize their comfort over saving time.

Get Ready to Change Your Best-Laid Plans Your friend had planned a glorious afternoon at a nearby vineyard: luncheon feast, cellar tour, wine tastings. When your father wakes up, he isn't feeling well. His legs ache and his stomach is upset. "Go without me," he insists. "I'll be fine here alone." This is generous of him, and you'll consider it for a second because you *really* want to see the vineyard. But no. Spend the day with him instead. Whip up a meal, watch a movie, play poker, and tell stories under the stars until the wee small hours.

Recognize Their Limits, Because They Won't Or maybe they can't. It's no fun to feel weaker or slower or less capable than you want to feel. So don't point it out to them directly in case it's too painful for them to hear and admit. Let this be the wordless thing no one talks about that you work around and never let get in the way of a wonderful time together.

What About the Little People? Generally speaking, the same rules apply when traveling with small children. Only there's a different, bittersweet emotional tenor: You slow down with little kids because their capacities haven't developed. You slow down with the elderly because their capacities are diminishing. The biggest difference when your companions are little children? You need a lot – a lot! – more snacks. At all times.

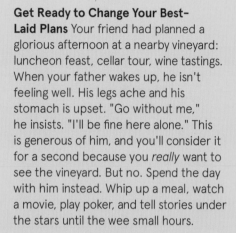

ROMANTIC INTERLUDES

Wheatleigh, Lenox, Massachusetts, USA

This gorgeous Berkshires estate, a few hours from both New York City and Boston, was built in 1893 by a railroad tycoon as a wedding present for his daughter. Modeled on a 16th-century Florentine palazzo, the house has a timeless grandeur, with high ceilings, elegant decor, a column-lined patio, and arched windows with mountain views. The cuisine is among the best in the state, and access to nearby Tanglewood makes it extra special for couples who love music. (Perfect harmony, awww.) _wheatleigh.com_

Hasbrouck House, Hudson Valley, New York, USA

A super attentive staff oversees a no-expenses-spared (but non-bank-breaking) vacation home for New Yorkers in need of an escape. The 18th-century Dutch Colonial mansion is luxe but not louche, high-end but not stuffy, foodie-focused but not myopic when it comes to guest desires. And there are many activities and paths for rest and relaxation. Start the day with yoga, end at a campfire by the lake, pick apples in the orchard next door, dine at an incredible farm-to-fork restaurant, and take a dip in the 55-foot (17-meter) 1920s swimming pool – to list just a few highlights. _hasbrouckhouseny.com_

Tordrillo Mountain Lodge, Judd Lake, Alaska, USA
A five-star, multi-sport wilderness lodge for couples who love adrenaline. A forty-five-minute floatplane flight from Anchorage lands guests in the remote Tordrillo Mountains, where stylish digs, fancy chefs, a lakeside sauna, and in-room massages are rounded out by helicopter-based adventure experiences. In the winter, an accomplished guide team leads guests in skiing and snowboarding through steep gullies and powder fields – and if you're lucky you'll catch the Northern Lights at night. Summer calls for glacier hiking, wake surfing, waterskiing, and primo wildlife viewing. *tordrillomountainlodge.com*

The Other Side, Eleuthera, Bahamas
A romantic compound of exquisite tented structures (think *Out of Africa* meets Mustique), this is the place to truly disconnect from the outside world. Accessed by private launch, the property has a chic house-party vibe; guests wander in and out of the great house for simple meals of grilled fish before retiring into the stunning pool that juts out over the turquoise bay, with views of Harbour Island beyond. Proprietors Ben Simmons and Charlie Phelan have thought of every understated detail so the food is delicious, the honor bar is well-stocked, and morning yoga is available for those who don't sleep in. Low-key luxury at its very finest. *ontheos.com*

Opposite: a deep soak in the Carriage House and the entrance to the Stable House at Hasbrouck House, New York

This page: palazzo style at Wheatleigh, Massachusetts

Opposite: a hammock equals bliss at Hotel Esencia on Mexico's Riviera Maya

Casa Vitrales, Old Havana, Cuba

Havana's slow pace, unreliable WiFi, narrow streets, and vibrant spirit make it a romantic getaway for exploring (both the city and each other). Because the traditional hotel options here are nothing to brag about (either too expensive or too lacking, and usually state-run), a local guesthouse is the way to go, especially one run by a charming and helpful team who will give you invaluable advice about what to do. This nine-suite bed and breakfast is centrally located in an old colonial building in Old Havana, making it conveniently close to everything you'll want to do. *cvitrales.com/EN*

Hotel Esencia, Riviera Maya, Mexico

You land in Cancun and drive an hour south. You turn left into the edge of the jungle and are escorted via golf cart through a thicket of vines – cue the peacocks calling out their welcome – emerging onto the quietly grand former estate of an Italian duchess, who built this place so she could be near her lover. You pass turtles swimming in a small cenote, pause for afternoon tea in the sitting room, and check into your room – a sea of white punctuated by a colorful pillow, a dramatic palm frond. Two pools await, as does a secluded beach along a gentle bay. The wild Tulum scene is close by, as are excellent archaeological and ecological sites, but if all you want to think about is morning yoga, another bottle of Casa Madero rosé, the guacamole and tacos at Mistura restaurant, and getting back to your day bed on the beach, you're making the right decision. *hotelesencia.com*

Cambria Beach Lodge, Cambria, California, USA

If you think there's nothing quiet, private, and secluded on the California coast, then you don't know Cambria, one of the state's last under-the-radar coastal destinations – and they'd be happy to keep it this way. But when you want your trip for two to be less about rose petals in the bathtub and more about beach walks during a stunning sunset, this cute seaside lodge will more than fit the bill with its ocean views, in-room fireplaces, and local wines in the minibar. That doesn't mean the vibe here falls flat. Complimentary adventure kits, stylish Linus bikes, and access to Moonstone Beach and the wineries of Paso Robles mean there's plenty to do when you're not lounging in your sun-drenched room or taking in Pacific views from the sky deck. *cambriabeachlodge.com*

From left: a porch and a beach suite at Cheval Blanc St-Barth Isle de France

Quinta Real Zacatecas, Zacatecas, Mexico

The San Pedro bullfighting ring hosted some of the best toreros Mexico has ever known from 1866 to 1975. The formerly violent arena has been cleverly (and beautifully) restored and converted into a hotel. So why are you coming for romance? Because the past comes alive here in dramatic form, and the spirit of danger that lingers from the bullfights is, frankly, exciting. (You're sipping your late-night cocktails in the space that used to house the bulls before they fought!) On the more genteel side, your passions will be more soothingly stoked by the spacious luxury suites furnished with period pieces and bubbling baths. *historichotels.org/hotels-resorts/quinta-real-zacatecas/history.php*

Clayoquot Wilderness Lodge, Tofino, British Columbia, Canada

This is a stunning Vancouver Island eco-safari where they craft bespoke expeditions in the remote wilderness of British Columbia, like mountain river kayaking, hot spring hiking, and bear and whale watching, to name a few. When you're not out in the temperate rainforests of Pacific Rim National Park, you and your favorite travel companion are snug between the covers in one of twenty-five luxury canvas tents furnished with old-world rugs, antiques, and heirloom china. *wildretreat.com*

The Lowell, New York, New York, USA

Evoking everything that's wonderful about old-school, discreet uptown Manhattan, this intimate boutique hotel feels so timeless that it would be so easy to ignore Central Park and Museum Mile, mere steps away, and lose yourself inside. Start with cocktails at Jacques Bar, followed by a Mediterranean-infused French meal at Majorelle. Settle in for a nightcap in the deep sofas in the Club Room, then wander upstairs, where the fireplace is roaring at the foot of your bed. Wake up, have room service on the terrace, and do the whole thing all over again. _lowellhotel.com_

Cheval Blanc St-Barth Isle de France, Baie des Flamands, St. Barts

St. Barts is where French people go when they want to feel sexy and act naughty. Tucked away amid lush gardens on a private stretch of white sand on Flamands Beach, this newcomer is the ultimate combination of luxury and simplicity. Serene rooms designed by Jacques Grange in a palette of whites, turquoise, and blues overlook the Caribbean. While away the days on the discreet beach or in the shimmering saltwater infinity pool. Open-air massages for two and beachside picnics at dawn can be easily arranged, or you can make your own magic. _chevalblanc.com_

Exploring icebergs at Tordrillo Mountain Lodge, Alaska

GO IT ALONE

Troutbeck, Amenia, New York, USA

This 250-year-old inn-cum-gathering spot in Amenia has played host to Ralph Waldo Emerson, Henry David Thoreau, Mark Twain, Ernest Hemingway, Teddy Roosevelt, and such giants of the civil liberties movement as Sinclair Lewis, W.E.B. Du Bois, Thurgood Marshall, Dr. Martin Luther King Jr., and Langston Hughes. You're swept up in the history from your first approach across a glorious lawn leading to a massive slate-covered manor house. The building has seventeen highly individualized rooms, some sprawling, some intimate, put together by storied designer Alexandra Champalimaud, whose son Anthony Champalimaud is the welcoming hotelier running this luxurious compound. Walk the grounds, polish your TED Talk, read a book by the fire, treat yourself to a delicious meal. *troutbeck.com*

BodyHoliday, Cariblue Beach, Saint Lucia

Don't be turned off by the name or the fact that it's a Caribbean all-inclusive. Your prejudices will be dashed at this resort that wins awards not only for its spa but also for its wine list. The vibe is relaxed throughout the retreat, a picturesque beachfront cove encircled by forested hills. Stimulation here comes from yoga classes, archery lessons, private training sessions, Ayurvedic treatments, and infrared massage chairs – not to mention cooking classes at the organic hilltop farm and open-sea swims with Olympic athletes. Their spot-on motto? "Give us your body for a week and we'll give you back your mind." *thebodyholiday.com*

Opposite, from top: serenity at Chablé Yucatán; the Ayurvedic Temple at BodyHoliday in Saint Lucia in the Caribbean

This page: taking the plunge at The Caves in Jamaica

Basecamp Hotel, Boulder, Colorado, USA

This handsomely furnished and affordable boutique hotel is the perfect jumping-off point for adventurous solo travelers looking for a well-rounded winter vacation. The property's communal vibe is great for making friends, whether at the indoor pool, sauna, rock climbing wall, or around the tables at the coffee-slash-juice bar. Another option: connect with like-minded spirits at one of the city's many pot dispensaries (hang loose!). Once you're ready to venture out, ski resorts, hiking trails, restaurants, coffee shops, grocery stores, craft breweries, museums, and shops are just a short drive away. *basecampboulder.com*

Esalen Institute, Big Sur, California, USA

A community-minded farm center for personal retreats located on a breathtaking stretch of the Pacific coastline. Book a cabin, sign up for workshops, work the land, eat healthy meals, and embrace the bathing rituals of the cliff-side springs (which you can relax in until 3 in the morning). Esalen is where *Mad Men's* Don Draper dreamed up his Coke ad. What will you be inspired to create or become? *esalen.org*

Cave Hill Farm, McGaheysville, Virginia, USA

Hiking the Appalachian Trail is one of those life-changing solo adventures that myths are made of, but it's not one for the faint of heart or the weak of will when it comes to outdoor camping. To dip into the experience in a safer and less intimidating way – but still reap the rewards of Being in Nature and Thinking Big Thoughts – spend a few days "riding the sky" along the 105-mile (169-kilometer) Skyline Drive atop the Blue Ridge Mountains. There are seventy-five scenic overlooks along the journey, and you don't need to hit them all, though you should park and hike along the paths down to the many picturesque and relaxing waterfalls and streams. Your welcoming home base at the end of the thought-filled days is this 1830s bed and breakfast in the heart of the Shenandoah Valley. Check into one of five antique-filled rooms named for characters like Uncle Charlie, Aunt Emma, and Grandmother and sink into a deeply cozy sleep in an Amish-made bed by the fireplace. If you time your visit right in the summer or winter, you might see a fog ocean roll in below you – a purple mountain majesties experience if ever there was one. *cavehillfarmbandb.com*

The Ranch, Malibu, California, USA

This sprawling 1920s hacienda-style estate, a former summer camp, sits on 100-plus acres (40-plus hectares) that have been transformed with well-appointed private cabins, indoor and outdoor dining areas, two workout facilities, and a year-round organic farm with goats and chickens. You're coming here for a jumpstart at a luxury boot camp, through four-, seven-, or ten-day programs of daily hikes, fresh and healthy meals, and wellness classes. You'll go home a little refreshed and a lot healthier. *theranchmalibu.com*

Chablé Yucatán, Chocholá, Mexico

If your idea of a heavenly solo experience involves a combination of seeing new places, stepping back in time, and being pampered enough to feel restored deep in your bones – all while being ensconced in a beautiful hotel with outstanding service – Chablé Yucatán is your Mexico fantasy come to life. Start with the stunning setting, where the winning elements include a jungle spa built around a cenote (sinkhole) and a restored hacienda with old-meets-modern design. You'll live total relaxation in discreet casitas, feast on incredible cuisine, and delight in authentic Maya influences throughout. The hotel alone could keep you for days, but you'll want to make time for the area's excellent attractions, especially the rich cultural scene in Mérida (a town rising in popularity among insiders), the charming colonial town of Campeche, the ancient Maya ruins at Chichén Itzá, and the flamingos at Ría Celestún Biosphere. *chablehotels.com/yucatan*

Opposite: look within at Esalen Institute in Big Sur

This page, from left: Troutbeck in New York, seen outside and in a cozy nook

Mobile Homes The new trend in house rentals? Mobile homes. For the classic option, search online for "Airstream rentals" or work with a company that can handle the details, like LivMobil (*livmobil.com*), which rents decked-out trailers attached to tow vehicles from Los Angeles, Denver, Washington, D.C., and San Francisco. Goss RV (*gossrv.com*) tricks out motor coaches that would satisfy the most demanding rock stars, providing white-glove service to make them five-star hotels on wheels.

Lighthouses Make nautical magic in an old lighthouse. The United States Lighthouse Society (*uslhs.org*) rents lighthouses throughout the United States and Canada, with options like Lake Superior Lighthouse (room for fourteen on Michigan's Upper Peninsula), Two Harbors Light (the oldest working lighthouse in Minnesota), and Little River Lighthouse in Maine (the easternmost option in the United States, built in 1888).

UNCONVENTIONAL ACCOMMODATIONS

Who says you have to stay in a hotel or a house?

Houseboats Live on the prettiest lakes on the continent – Lake Koocanusa in Montana and British Columbia, Lake Cumberland in Kentucky, Crater Lake in Oregon, Lake Winnipesaukee in New Hampshire, Lake of the Woods in Ontario – by renting a houseboat kitted out with comfy beds, big TVs, kayaks, and full bars. Sailing experience isn't a requirement, as many come with pilots.

Tents Glamping is going even more mainstream with the emergence of boutique companies that have operations throughout the United States. We especially love the eco-minded ethos of Collective Retreats (_collectiveretreats.com_) – which has camps in destinations like New York City's Governors Island, Texas Hill Country, and Big Sky, Montana – and Under Canvas (_undercanvas.com_), with outposts in national parks like Mount Rushmore, Acadia, Glacier, and Yosemite.

Trains A scenic train is an excellent option for travel with family members who are elderly or have limited mobility, as the beautiful scenery comes to you at a slow and easy pace. Options include multi-day trips through north-west Canada on the glass-covered upper deck of a Rocky Mountaineer train (_rockymountaineer.com_), or a few picturesque hours through Alaska on a White Pass & Yukon Route Railway tour (_wpyr.com_).

Clockwise from top: an Under Canvas camp in the Smoky Mountains; riding the rails on Rocky Mountaineer; an Under Canvas bedroom tent; Collective Retreats on Governor's Island in NYC

HOW TO TRAVEL IN A GROUP – WITHOUT BEING A JERK

Raise your hand if this sounds familiar. You're at dinner with an intimate group of friends and, somewhere between the second and third bottles of wine, someone suggests you all go on vacation together. That you rent a cottage on a lake in Ontario. A houseboat on Lake Mead. A ski condo in Vail. Or that reliable standby, a farmhouse villa in Italy or France. It's such a great idea! Before dessert, it's settled: this *will* happen.

Within a few days, someone sends a follow-up email to the gang with links to rental options around the world. Let's call her Jasmine, because 90 percent of the time, it's going to be a woman. (Sorry, chaps, the truth hurts.) A flurry of emails later, it's settled: next summer, you're renting that gorgeous house everyone loves in San Miguel de Allende.

In the ensuing ten months, Jasmine is the one who forwards the email alert about the Delta sale on airfare to Mexico City. Who reminds everyone how much they still have to Venmo her for the deposit she placed on the villa – five months ago. Who coordinates the information that Oliver has gone paleo, that Carmen is gluten free, and that Pablo is now vegan, and sends it to the rental company so the chef she arranged can prepare a menu that's not only totally locavore but good for everyone's dietary peccadillos. In the weeks leading up to the trip, Jasmine gets texts at 3am from Keysha, asking her to resend the link to the car service she found because she's joining the gang from Mérida.

Don't stand out in the wrong way. (Not that anyone does on Mount Rushmore.)

THE STUFF TO BRING

You'll be glad you packed:

A corkscrew for an impromptu bottle of wine

A box of granola bars to fend off the munchies when food isn't at hand

A headphone splitter so two people can watch a movie together

Two decks of cards for canasta, blackjack, hearts

Bananagrams because not everyone likes Scrabble

Matches for candles and campfires and also ...

Incense or travel candle as a buffer for shared bathrooms

A playlist to share with everyone afterward to stoke good memories

A compass so you'll never get lost on a meander

A small outlet strip so no one has to fight over who gets to charge their phone

Don't forget the souvenir. Everyone should buy the same small, locally made token – huarache sandals, a woven bracelet, a coffee mug, a scarf – as a memento of the trip you took together.

Once settled into the villa, Jasmine gets a daily onslaught of questions. "What's the plan for dinner?" "When are we going to the ruins?" "What time is the concert in the cathedral square tonight?" "Did you put my matcha on the list for the supermarket run?" "Where are the clean towels for the pool?"

In the end, everyone has an amazing vacation.

Except one person.

This is, of course, an exaggerated version of what we're talking about. But if you've ever gone on a bachelorette weekend or a boys' ski trip or a family reunion or even a getaway for two, you're familiar with the situation: one person usually ends up doing a disproportionate amount of the heavy lifting in planning and coordinating the vacation the whole group is going to enjoy.

This is totally unfair.

The next time you're involved in planning a vacation – whether it's with a big or small group of friends or family – be the one who reminds everyone that you should all chip in on the planning. Break it down depending on the kind of trip, and suggest that you all divide the tasks: researching the destination, accommodation options, transportation logistics (how to get there and how to get around), activities, places to eat and drink, and travel essentials like where to buy the supplies you'll need once you're there – groceries and wine, sunscreen and insect repellent, lift tickets and spare flip-flops. Give yourself bonus points for circulating in-case-of-emergency info like the nearest hospital, rescue resources if you're deep in nature, and the closest embassies if you're in a foreign country. (Isn't there a travel superstition that says disaster only strikes if you didn't plan for it? If not, there should be.)

Bring everyone in on the action, no matter how young they are or how "totally hopeless at planning" they claim to be. Children will be glad they were asked to contribute and will take particular pride in knowing they planned certain days – and it might make them more willing to spend an afternoon exploring that boring old museum. All-ages planning taps into a (terrific) growing trend we've seen in recent years: young children are playing a bigger and bigger role in organizing family vacations.

As for those so-called "incompetent planner" types, they might be surprised and delighted to learn that they *can* coordinate an unforgettable dinner or arrange an afternoon excursion to the underwater caves. Those

Opposite: the pool at Cheval Blanc St-Barth Isle de France

Clockwise from top: chasing waterfalls in the Berkshires at Tourists in Massachusetts; traipsing among lily pads at BodyHoliday in Saint Lucia; chilling at Bar Bizot at GoldenEye in Jamaica

hopeless planners, by the way, tend to use their alleged hopelessness as an excuse to avoid doing any work. Don't let them get away with it.

Even with all this democratic division of labor, the Jasmine in the group will still end up doing a little more because, well, groups tend to need a leader (and Jasmine might, let's be honest, be a control freak). But encourage her to assign tasks rather than shoulder them all herself, and keep track of the master task list or Google doc where everything is being recorded. She can assign Becky and Daniel the job of arranging a kayaking afternoon and beach barbecue, and ask Callum to circulate a list of Mexican movies everyone can watch before the trip to get psyched about where they're going. The more hands at work, the lighter the labor. By the way, this counts when it's just a couple traveling. Don't let your special person do all the work.

Because here's the bottom line when it comes to group travel: if everyone helps plan, everyone is that much more invested in the trip being a success.

If, for all these good intentions, you do end up on a trip that has been largely planned by one person, then be grateful. REALLY grateful. Get everyone to chip in to give Jasmine an afternoon at a spa, or buy her the beautiful blanket she admired at the artisan's market in town. She's your friend (or your cousin or your mom): you should know what would make her happy. And don't forget to raise a glass to her – at least once! – to acknowledge and thank her for the work she put into the vacation.

TOOLS OF THE TRADE

Organize your trip with these digital assistants.

Dropbox
Create a folder for everyone to upload their pics. (A shared iPhone, Google, or Flickr album works as well and can be uploaded right from your phone.) This will help everyone relive the trip while you're on it, and avoid turning the photo project into a chore when the vacation is over. The long flight or drive home is another great time to organize photos.

Venmo
Create accounts and pay each other as you go.

Google Docs
Make one document with the itinerary, the address, and contact information for the places you'll be staying, along with other essential information like flights and car services.

A shared spreadsheet is where you can keep track of the things you want to see and do, and will be most useful if organized by category: restaurants, bars, sites, shops, cafes, neighborhoods to explore.

A doomsday document of emergency info has everyone's in-case-of-emergency contact back home, passport numbers, insurance info, etc.

Whatsapp
Create a group so everyone on the trip can communicate by phone or text.

Social Media Hashtags
If you're active on social media and are planning to share your trip, settle on a shared hashtag for your posts. And don't forget to establish ground rules on what is and isn't okay to post.

CHAPTER 8

ON THE ROAD

Is there any better way to experience the multilayered culture of the USA, the sweeping landscapes of Canada, or Mexico's endless variations on a roadside taco than on a good old-fashioned road trip?

There's so much romance and adventure inherent in driving long distances. The freedom of exploring on the road gives travelers the chance to see not only the wide-open ranges and the ancient sites, but also the community thoroughfares, the miracle miles, the desolate edges, the tourist traps, and all the regular stuff that surrounds the amazing stuff and makes it even more special.

Whether you're zipping around in a convertible, packing up a motorcycle, piling everyone into a minivan, or lugging an Airstream behind you, road trips can make you feel alone in your bubble and alive in the world all at once. Tracing routes as you go and making stops on the fly afford the out-of-the-comfort-zone journeying that changes lives.

You might think you need to be of a certain age or in a certain place or have a certain amount of time, but there are many ways to build a vacation on the road – if you are up for the journey.

Previous page: looking forward to the long and winding road ahead

Opposite: home on the range in White Sands, New Mexico

This page: nature meets farmy Americana

MINI ROAD TRIP ITINERARIES

Zooming in on little areas with a lot of personality.

Opposite, clockwise from top: maritime charm in spades at Peggy's Cove; nautical feasting at Grand Banker; seeing lunch eye to eye at Captain Kat's; a picturesque beacon on Peggy's Point Shoreline; Lunenberg Anglican Church, one of the oldest in Canada

Nova Scotia for Lobster Lovers
Food-obsessives, bundle up: Winter is lobster season on Nova Scotia's southern coast.

Arrive in Halifax and whet the whistle at Obladee (*obladee.ca*), a dimly lit bar serving Nova Scotia oysters (so fresh and so clean) and impressive natural wines. The official driving tour begins in Peggy's Cove – Wes Anderson himself couldn't design a quainter spot, with its colorful fishing shacks and charming red-and-white lighthouse. Drive to Lunenburg, a fishing town and UNESCO World Heritage Site, and learn the lay of the land from the locals at Lunenburg Walking Tours (*lunenburgwalkingtours. com*), breaking for a seafood feast at Grand Banker (*grandbanker.com*) and warming beverages at Ironworks Distillery (*ironworksdistillery.com*). Spend the night in Summerville at the oceanfront Quarterdeck Resort (*quarterdeck.ca*). The next day, day-trip it in fishing town Barrington for Captain Kat's bang-up versions of every imaginable lobster dish (*captkatslobstershack.weebly. com*). Make your way back to Halifax for a glass of Acadie pét nat and mussels at Gio (*giohalifax.com*) in the Prince George Hotel (*princegeorgehotel.com*) – or maybe just a warm bath and a bag of lobster-flavored chips from New Brunswick-based snack company Covered Bridge.

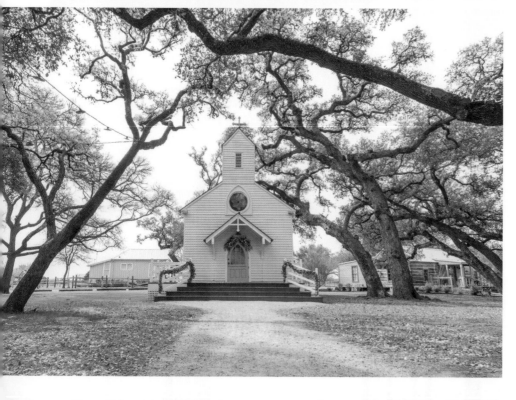

Texas Hill Country for Retrophiles

Your own antiques roadshow, with cowboy duds and artisanal baked goods.

The Original Round Top Antiques Fair (*roundtoptexasantiques.com*) is a half-century-old extravaganza for sentimentalists and treasure hunters whose idea of a good time involves digging through thousands of vendor booths set up in tents, barns, and dance halls along a 25-mile (40-kilometer) stretch of Highway 237 between Burton and La Grange. Located about an hour and a half from Austin or Houston, the show lasts for roughly a week or two every fall and spring. Make your home base Rancho Pillow (*ranchopillow. com*), a kooky 20-acre (8-hectare) compound in the tiny town of Round Top, flush with cows and bluebonnets. And don't attempt to navigate the fair without a plan of attack: Warrenton for funky, eclectic, inexpensive finds; Marburger Farm for a more curated (expensive) edit. The nearby town of Carmine has dusty little shops brimming with bric-a-brac and fun kitsch. At the other end of the shabby-chic spectrum is the Magnolia empire in Waco. The incredibly manicured and always TV-ready Magnolia Market at the Silos (*magnolia.com/silos*) has a food truck garden, restaurant, shopping area, and, should you want to stay a while, nearby rental cottages decked out in their signature modern farmhouse aesthetic. Stock up on baked goods and more vintage wares before the drive back to the airport.

Opposite, clockwise from top: Rancho Pillow's front porch and their photogenic Studebaker; a picture-perfect Texas church, one of many treasures along the way; cocktail hour at Rancho Pillow after a day of thrifting

Opposite, clockwise from top: a local farmscape; mum's the word; the promise of new-fallen snow; Norman Rockwell–approved holiday vibes at Woodstock Inn & Resort; the best loaves in town, fresh from the oven at August First Bakery; a well-appointed sitting room at Woodstock Inn & Resort

Vermont for Yankee Enthusiasts
Beat cabin fever with big snow and big leg workouts.

If you start in NYC, take the Taconic Parkway and stop at the old-school Millbrook Diner (*millbrookdiner.com*) for sustenance before making your way to New England's most postcard-perfect town, Woodstock, Vermont, to stay at the grand Woodstock Inn & Resort (*woodstockinn. com*). Head across the quaint village green outside the front door for stops at the old-school F.H. Gillingham and Sons general store (*gillinghams.com*) and Yankee Bookshop (*yankeebookshop.com*), and have a bite at the beloved local, The Prince & The Pauper (*princeandpauper.com*). Then it's on to Burlington, with a pit stop along the way at Shelburne Farms (*shelburnefarms.org*), a nonprofit focused on sustainability education, for tours of their historic barns, tons of scenic walking trails, and classic Vermont foodstuffs from the farm store. Once you get to town, have a meal at chef Eric Warnstedt's revered restaurant Hen of the Wood (*henofthewood.com*). Do your boutique shopping on Church Street or head down the hill to walk along Lake Champlain. Break for maple biscuits at August First Bakery (*augustfirstvt.com*) – they also have the best bread. Take a little drive to Vergennes, which proudly calls itself the Smallest Town in the US, or move your base to Stowe (*stowe.com*) to hit the slopes. Snowshoe or cross-country ski to the rustic Slayton Pasture Cabin (*trappfamily.com/slayton-pasture-cabin.htm*) deep in the woods for hot soup and cider. (*Sound of Music* fans, this is where the real Von Trapp family ended up.) Hit the trails in Sterling Forest for back-country skiing, or mix up cruiser runs, expert trails, and off-piste fun on Stowe Mountain. Spend après getting a Swedish massage, craft beer, or hearty farm-fresh meal in downtown Stowe.

CANADIAN ROCKIES FOR CHIONOPHILES

Glittering blankets of snow, pristine air, lots of layers, and the swish of skis on untouched powder.

The Canadian Rockies, which splinter the western part of the country, are home to a host of national parks, including Kootenay and Yoho. But the most magnificent views – and the best breweries – are tucked away within **Banff** and **Jasper**, two parks that can be wrapped into a picturesque weeklong road trip. If there's one place in the world that truly resembles a shook-up snow globe, it's Lake Louise – a hamlet in Banff National Park known for its turquoise, glacier-fed lake ringed by high peaks and overlooked by the stately Fairmont Chateau Lake Louise. In winter, the property creates its own winter village on the snow-covered frozen lake, with a hockey and ice-skating rink, snowshoeing and cross-country skiing trails, and an ice bar serving hot toddies in a space kitted out with blankets and fire pits. Maligne Canyon, the deepest canyon in Jasper National Park, descends 164 feet (50 meters), shaped by rushing water for millions of years and framed by gigantic waterfalls and ice pillars with great names like Queen of Maligne and Angel. Make your way through the self-guided interpretive trails on the short loop reaching the upper levels of the canyon or the longer trail at the base of the gorge. Ice cleats for traction are available at mountaineering shops in town or are provided during guided tours with a company like Sundog Tours (*sundogtours.com*). After a morning wildlife excursion, warm up at Jasper Brewing Company (*jasperbrewingco.ca*), Canada's first national park brewery, with a six-pack sampler of the latest on tap and Jasper's take on classic poutine.

Opposite, clockwise from left: cozy cabin living on Lake Louise; skis in the snow; Fathom editor California, all bundled up

This page, from left: Jasper Brewing's retro van; go big, or go home cold

The crown jewel of Banff is Moraine Lake, a vivid stretch of turquoise water nestled in the Valley of the Ten Peaks. Snow-capped mountains, waterfalls, and jagged rocks surround the lake, creating an unreal scene sure to break Instagram. Canoe rental stands pepper its shores, and a one-hour paddle is well worth the exorbitant price tag. In winter the town of Banff is a ski lover's dream, with access to three world-class ski resorts and a lively après scene. It's also the town with the most action, including a variety of cozy restaurants, breweries, distilleries, cannabis dispensaries, and hot springs. Perched on the summit of Sulphur Mountain at 7510 feet (2289 meters), Sky Bistro (*banffjaspercollection.com*) is a dining sanctuary in the sky. Accessed via the Banff Gondola, the scenic alpine restaurant is ideal after an afternoon strolling the mountain boardwalk, hanging in the heated igloo lounges, or hiking up the zigzagged trail to work up your appetite.

The ultimate way to reach solitude and unplug in the majestic Rocky Mountains is on the scenic route aboard VIA Rail's (*viarail.ca*) The Canadian: a glass-domed train that winds through the mountains and ice valleys with luxury sleeper cars, dinner on board, and cozy nooks for staring at the scenery. With frequent departures from Vancouver or Toronto, adding a night or two on the train to your itinerary is easy, with rail tour operators like Vacations by Rail (*vacationsbyrail.com*) offering packages that include transportation to and from the parks, hotel accommodations, and guided wildlife tours and expeditions.

If you're looking for a remote stay, the 1930s-era Skoki Lodge (*skoki.com*) is 7 miles (11 kilometers) from the nearest road and only accessible via back-country skis or snowshoes (while carrying your overnight pack) – a trip that takes about three to five hours. There's no electricity or running water, but the log cabins are cozy and the family-style gourmet dinners are served by candlelight.

Prefer a more refined option? Fairmont Jasper Park Lodge (*fairmont.com/jasper*) stretches across the shores of emerald-green Beauvert Lake with a number of well-appointed cedar chalets and signature log cabins connected by picturesque walking paths. The Jasper Planetarium (*jasperplanetarium.com*) dome theater offers nightly telescope expeditions and live Dark Sky tours.

Towering above Banff at super high altitudes is Fairmont Banff Springs (*fairmont.com/banff-springs*), a.k.a. The Castle of the Rockies, built in 1888 by the Canadian Pacific Railway. Luxury amenities here include mineral soaking baths and spa treatments to ease aching joints after a day on the slopes.

Steps from the quaint streets of Banff and a ten-minute ride to the gondola, Elk + Avenue Hotel (*banffjaspercollection.com*) is a minimalist modern lodge great for groups of friends, couples, or solo travelers who are looking for the après ski scene and want to be close to the happenings in town.

Opposite, from left: an elk mugs for the camera; a snow-dusted Fairmont Banff Springs

This page, from top: alpine backcountry Skoki Lodge in Banff National Park; a log cabin at Fairmont Jasper Park Lodge

Pit stop for: moose – whiskey – big bowl o' poutine – bighorn sheep – bison burgers – axe throwing – pint of local Albeerta

Tasty fact: A must-have cocktail while in Alberta is the Caesar, the Canadian version of a Bloody Mary, made with a blend of tomato and clam juice, Worcestershire, hot sauce, and a spiced celery-salted rim.

Snow and ice enthusiasts can maximize their time outside in a few ways:

The Icefields Parkway, a 144-mile (232-kilometer) stretch of road linking Jasper and Banff, is known as one of the most scenic drives in the world, winding through two national parks, jagged mountains, pine forests, glaciers, and frozen lakes. It takes approximately three hours to drive from Banff to Jasper (the most common direction if flying in from Calgary), but you'll want to plan for one full day with various scenic lookouts, hiking trails, and wildlife sightings along the way. Here are the top stops.

Herbert Lake may only be a five-minute drive north from Lake Louise, but it's quiet and tranquil, especially in the early morning when the lake is still and glassy, making for great reflection photos. It's the perfect place to start the day's drive.

When you're ready to stretch your legs, pull off at Bow Lake, known for its bright blues and glacial reflections with an easy hiking trail up to Bow Glacier Falls. Snap a pic as you climb across the fallen boulder, known as Chock Stone, wedged in place over the top of the canyon, forming a boulder bridge.

An hour from Jasper, explore the largest expanse of glacial ice in the North American Rockies: the ancient Columbia Icefield, where time is measured in millennia. From the highway, the plateau of Athabasca Glacier is visible as well as the ice cliffs on Snow Dome, Mount Kitchener, and Stutfield Peak.

Just a short walk from the parking lot off the highway is the turquoise jewel that is Peyto Lake. Canada boasts a lot of blue glacial lakes thanks to the abundance of rock flour in glacial meltwater, however this takes the crown: there is no bluer lake anywhere in the Rockies.

The upper end of the two waterfalls at Sunwapta Falls is easily accessible from the viewpoint parking lot and has an impressive drop-off of nearly 60 feet (18 meters). A short loop takes you down to the lower falls through a lodgepole pine forest. Stop just north of the falls to see the kooky Kerkeslin goat lick, where mountain goats congregate for salty mineral deposits right by the road.

Ski the Big 3 – Banff National Park's three ski resorts, Lake Louise, Sunshine, and Mount Norquay – conveniently located less than an hour from each other, making it possible for the avid skier to hit each slope, especially in the spring, when the sun doesn't set until 8pm or later.

Most hotels in town provide shuttle service to Marmot Basin Ski Resort, a smaller mountain with more affordable prices and way fewer crowds, making it ideal for families with small children.

The best destination for a spa day or late-night soak is the large outdoor geothermal baths at Banff Upper Hot Springs (*hotsprings.ca/banff*).

Opposite, from top: VIA Rail rolls through Canada; Bow Lake at night

This page, clockwise from top: iconic Spirit Island in Maligne Lake; a view of Lake Louise; come on in, the water's fine at Banff Upper Hot Springs; inside the ice lodge on Sulfur Mountain

Clockwise from top left: waving
palms in surf town Puerto
Escondido; geometric details at
Casa Antonieta; Oaxaca's signature
earth tones

Mexico for Hungry, Crafty Creatives
*For arts and culture both old and new, as well as artisanal
specialties and flavors.*

For such a small city, Oaxaca really packs a punch.
This UNESCO World Heritage Center is one of the most
beautifully preserved colonial towns in Mexico, known
for its cuisine and crafts. Fly straight to Oaxaca on a
connection through Mexico City or, for a true road trip,
start in the capital and drive two hours south-west
on highway 150D to Puebla, a colorful city filled with
churches (365 of them, one for every day of the year) and
stunning examples of Baroque architecture. Go from old
to new with visits at Biblioteca Palafoxiana (*en.palafoxiana.
com*), the oldest library in the Americas, and the Museo
Internacional del Barroco (*mib.puebla.gob.mx/en*), which
looks like a mini Bilbao. Check into La Purificadora
(*lapurificadora.com*), a high-design hotel with a rooftop
lap pool in a former water purification plant.

Then it's on to Oaxaca. Spend a day walking around the historical center with stops at Museo Textil de Oaxaca (_museotextildeoaxaca.org_), which promotes textile traditions (and has a terrific gift shop with local textiles and clothing); MACO, the art museum where the old meets the new in a beautiful, 17th-century colonial mansion; the renovated 1529 former convent San Pablo; and the Santo Domingo Cultural Center, which includes the Baroque Santo Domingo church, Museo de las Culturas de Oaxaca (in an old monastery), and an ethnobotanical garden.

Are you hungry and ready to shop? Mercado 20 de Noviembre (_mercado-20-de-noviembre.webnode. mx_) is open daily and specializes in traditional crafts and foods – come early in the morning and make a feast of hot chocolates and tamales. You'll notice that the moles here come in many varieties – red and yellow, made from seeds, and not just chocolate. For chocolate souvenirs, stock up at Mayordomo (_chocolatemayordomo.com.mx_) across the street.

Other markets are located outside the city on certain days – Monday mornings in Teotitlán del Valle (it's all over by 11am), Thursdays in Villa de Zaachila (one of Oaxaca's oldest markets), Fridays in Ocotlán de Morelos, and Sunday in Tlacolula de Matamoros. Spend a day touring the surrounding villages, which each have their own craft specialty – San Martín Tilcajete for alebrijes (small, colorful wooden animal figures); San Bartolo Coyotepec for barro negro black pottery; San Antonino Castillo Velasco for embroidered women's clothing; and Teotitlán del Valle for hand-woven rugs.

From left: cacti as singular landscaping feature and the beach, pool, and hammock – all at Hotel Puerto Escondido

**Clockwise from top left:
thatched-roof simplicity at Un
Sueño Cabañas del Pacífico;
colorful textiles are easy-to-pack
souvenirs; lush lagoon life; stairway
to heaven in Puerto Escondido**

A half hour outside the city are the pyramids,
palaces, and temple ruins at Monte Albán, the pre-
Columbian archaeological site that was once the capital of
the Zapotec civilization. If you're traveling with kids, they
will be thrilled to see the giant Montezuma cypress tree El
Árbol del Tule ("the tree of life") in Santa María del Tule –
deemed the largest tree in the world. The most charming
hotels in Oaxaca are the six-room Casa Antonieta
(_casaantonieta.com_) and Los Amantes (_hotellosamantes.
com_), which has incredible views of Santo Domingo from
the rooftop.

The can't-miss restaurants are Casa Oaxaca (*casaoaxacaelrestaurante.com*) for exceptional mole, Los Danzantes (*losdanzantes.com*) for Mexican fusion on a picturesque patio, and Criollo (*criollo.mx*) for innovative cuisine by star chef Enrique Olvera. Oaxaca is the capital of mezcal, and the best mezcalerías to learn the wonders of the agave plant are La Mezcaloteca (*mezcaloteca.com*), where they pour into traditional gourd cups, and In Situ Mezcaleria (*insitumezcaleria.com*), which claims to have the world's biggest collection of mezcals.

Top off the road trip with a cold cerveza on the beach down the coast. Give yourself plenty of daylight hours to drive the very windy Route 131 through minuscule towns to reach the beach at Puerto Escondido. The waves are the stuff of surf dreams (though too rough for swimming) at Playa Zicatela, whose epic break is considered the Pipeline of Mexico. It's a quieter scene at the bottom of a long stairway at Playa Carrizalillo, where shallow waters are great for swimmers or surf beginners. Take a short drive west to Laguna de Manialtepec to see the diverse wildlife in the lagoon and mangroves by day and the stunning bioluminescence at night. A forty-five-minute boat ride from here will get you to Lagunas de Chacahua National Park and a remote beach that's the perfect place to finish the last fifty pages of your novel. There's nothing to do here but swim, surf, and eat. When you are ready to go, tap your boat driver on the shoulder. He probably fell asleep in a hammock. Hotel Escondido (*hotelescondido.com*) has sixteen very chill, high-design, adults-only cabanas on a vast and unspoiled beach. Punta Pájaros (*puntapajaros.mx/en/*) is a collection of cute eco-villas on the water designed by architect Alberto Kalach and available on Airbnb. If you're here between October and March, you can see the magical turtle migration.

Continue down the coast along Route 200 for an hour to get to Mazunte and San Agustinillo, small beach towns favored by very cool surfers, hippies, and Europeans who came for a visit and decided to stay. (Which means a real Italian runs the pizzeria and an Argentine surfer made the empanadas.) Recognize the road you're on? You saw it in the excellent Mexican road trip movie *Y Tu Mamá También*. If this has you feeling frisky, lose your inhibitions at Playa Zipolite, Mexico's only legal nude beach. The rustic-chic beach hotels to book are Casa Aamori (*aamoriboutiquehotel.com*) and Un Sueño Cabañas del Pacífico (*unsueno.com*). Also, bring cash. Rather wonderfully, there are no ATMs around here.

Old meets new at La Purificadora in Puebla

From left: Jeralyn inside the Animal Flower swimming cave's ocean window; a breezy Barbadian beach shack

Barbados for Beach Babes

It's easy livin' on the rural, rustic, rogue side of the island.

Barbados is far east and south in the Caribbean. The first landfall from Africa and Europe (it was in possession of the British until 1966), it has deep roots in English and African cultures (and the Arawak and Carib peoples likely lived on the island before that). The west side is the one that's famous – for its gentle Caribbean waters, fancy-pants resorts, celebrities, golf courses, that kind of thing. The east side, on the Atlantic Ocean, feels totally different, with low-density population and high-density foliage, wild and rugged coast, wind-carved cliffs, radical surfer beaches, and small guesthouses and inns. The island is small enough to navigate in a day, but with a few days and a car you can get a really good feel for the land, the food, and Bajan pastimes.

After landing at the airport, start driving north to Bathsheba, the hilltop town with an impressive surf break. Huge limestone boulders look like meteors that hit the sand, making for a dramatic setting. Hardcore surfers are drawn to the clean, enormous wave known as the Soup Bowl, and spectators can unpack their picnic on the palm-fringed beach lawn (the currents are so strong that swimming is not advised for non-surfers). Check into a rustic rental or The Atlantis Historic Inn (*atlantishotelbarbados.com*) then head south to Crane Beach for a swim, or do some sopsing ("chilling," in local parlance) in one of the many nearby tide pools.

Another beautiful day would include cruising to St. Lucy on the northern tip of the island for a laidback West Indian cliffside lunch and an incredibly refreshing swim in the tranquil sea cave under the North Point cliff at Animal Flower Cave (*animalflowercave.com*). The natural window overlooking the ocean makes the experience very special.

Other great stops to hit are Andromeda Botanic Gardens (*andromedabarbados.com*) in Bathsheba and St. Nicholas Abbey (*stnicholasabbey.com*) in St. Peter for the rambling gardens and history of intrigue. Farther around the north-west coast, Fish Pot (*fishpotbarbados.com*) and Little Good Harbour inn (*littlegoodharbourbarbados.com*) serve cozy dinners smack dab on the water, Cobbler's Cove hotel (*cobblerscove.com*) has a great swimming pool scene, and Lone Star (*thelonestar.com*) offers a cool boutique stay and chic cocktail bar. At the southern tip, make your way to deAction Surf Shop (*briantalma. pro*) and Silver Sands beach for windsurfing lessons and Little Arches Boutique Hotel (*littlearches.com*) for a meal at Cafe Luna. Even if a flying fish cutter (sandwich) for breakfast does not sound like your thing, make it your thing and stop at Cuz's Fish Shack (*cuzsfishshack. restaurantsnapshot.com*) before you leave the island.

Clockwise from left: the family that surfs together; a serene pit stop on the southern coast; the colorful digs of deAction Surf Shop

Minnesota's North Shore for Naturalist Beer Drinkers

Sips and sights along Lake Superior's stunning, rocky shoreline, from Duluth to Grand Portage.

Start in north-east Minnesota in Duluth, the port city famous for its breweries, scenic views, hefty beards grown for warmth, and its most famous son, Bob Dylan. Get a glimpse of the rock'n'roll legend's Midwestern roots on a walk along the Bob Dylan Way (*bobdylanway.com*) through downtown and the vibrant arts district. Watch the saltie ships cruise into port under the famed Aerial Lift Bridge (a "saltie" is a ship visiting from the ocean). Pay homage to the region's Scandinavian immigrants at Vikre Distillery (*vikredistillery.com*), tippling aquavit, known as the Norwegian moonshine. Sample local brews at Fitger's Brewhouse (*brewhouse.net*), Bent Paddle Brewing (*bentpaddlebrewing.com*), Lake Superior Brewing, Canal Park Brewing Company (*canalparkbrewery.com*), and Endion Station Inn (*endioninn.com*), a "brewtique hotel" in a historic train station. The quality of Duluth's fresh drinking water is the reason the beer's so good.

Grab lunch from Northern Waters Smokehaus (*northernwaterssmokehaus.com*) and go agate-hunting along the North Shore's rocky beaches and find a perch at Brighton Beach. For an overnight stay, pick a great Airbnb in Two Harbors, an excellent base for exploring Gooseberry Falls, Minnesota's most visited state park, and Split Rock Lighthouse, one of the most popular spots for photographs. Further north in Grand Marais, the harbor has natural rock outcroppings that made it an inlet for the fur traders of Lake Superior. The land is sacred to the Ojibwe tribe, who were one of the earliest fur traders in North America. This is also the gateway to the Boundary Waters Canoe Area Wilderness. From there, you can hike up to Eagle Mountain (the highest peak in Minnesota) and sign the travelers' book at the summit. At the tippity-top of the state, you'll feel like you're at the end of the world, where the naturally jagged Hollow Rock arch appears as a deserted island off the shores of Grand Portage. If you appreciate the remoteness of the uncharted northern Midwest, consider a ferry transport to Michigan's remote Isle Royale National Park, the scenic end point of this North Shore excursion.

Opposite, clockwise from top: tumbling waters at Gooseberry Falls; an icy Lake Superior; Northern Lights in all their radiance; the beacon of Split Rock Lighthouse

AMERICAN SOUTHWEST FOR ART PILGRIMS

An eccentric and illuminating desert mission.

Donald Judd's iconic concrete cubes en plein air

Opposite: the multipurpose performing arts center ASU Gammage

The wide, wide open spaces, stark desert, and blue sky of the American Southwest made the perfect blank canvas for the land art movement of the 1970s. Far-out artists with madcap ambitions began producing site-specific earthworks on a monumental scale – using earth (and light, air, and water) as their medium.

The remoteness equaled freedom for the artists, permanence for their work, and pilgrimages for art lovers everywhere.

A Southwestern art tour starts or ends in the Far West Texas town of **Marfa**, a unique community with a ghostly appeal and a thriving contemporary arts community. At dawn, head to the massive Chinati Foundation (_chinati.org_), the ambitious contemporary art center founded by the late artist Donald Judd, whose concrete cubes are set against a painted sky. Reserve a tour indoors or take a self-guided one outdoors.

Drop into 1920s Mexican dance hall Ballroom Marfa (_ballroommarfa.org_), now a nonprofit space for contemporary art and culture and cultural events. Take a drive over to the large-scale outdoor _Stone Circle_ by Haroon Mirza. Inspired by ancient megaliths, the solar-powered sculpture is set in the high desert grasslands east of Marfa.

Marfa may be tiny, but the cool quotient is high. Visit Marfa (_visitmarfa.com_) is an excellent resource with a nicely made directory of mobile kitchens, cafes, coffee shops, food trucks, saloons, galleries, and boutiques.

Funky lodging befitting of a funky town include El Cosmico (*elcosmico.com*), which consists of teepees, safari tents, seasonal yurts, and beautifully restored 1950s-era trailers. You may want to stay put with a beer and a hot tub soak under the stars, but if you're up for a spook, head over to the Marfa Lights Viewing Station (9 miles/14 kilometers east of Marfa on Highway 90; look out for the sign directing you to the official observation area) to catch the mysterious light show that has fascinated people for over a hundred years. Paranormal phenomenon or atmospheric reflections? You decide.

For cushier accommodations, head to Cibolo Creek Ranch (*cibolocreekranch.com*), one of the oldest ranches in Texas, with secluded forts and haciendas and fresh-squeezed lime-juice margaritas. The next morning, pile into the hotel's Humvee and head to the Chinati Mountains to find abandoned Texas Ranger houses at Fort Davis, Native American rock art, and panoramic vistas perched high above the ranch.

It's back on the road. Drive north-west of Marfa, through Van Horn, to Guadalupe Mountains National Park. Make a pit stop at the iconic *Prada Marfa* in the tiny settlement of Valentine. Head to **Van Horn** for the historic Hotel El Capitan (*thehotelelcapitan.com*), designed by acclaimed architect Henry Trost in 1930. Hike to Guadalupe Peak, the tallest point in Texas, at the Guadalupe Mountains National Park. Come autumn, McKittrick Canyon has the best fall foliage. If the stars align, attend a Star Party at McDonald Observatory (*mcdonaldobservatory.org*).

Pit stop for: hatch chilies – turquoise – fry bread – nopales tacos – asado – kachina dolls – wild lavender

Tasty fact: Ever since the Spanish introduced pigs to the Río Grande Valle, the matanza has been part of New Mexico's culinary culture. It's a community event at harvest time that involves digging a hole in the yard, getting a hot fire going, and burying a pig in coals. Find your way to the tradition if you are driving through New Mexico in the fall.

Horseback riding in White Sands
National Park

Opposite: iconic
Southwestern teepees

Wake up and drive through El Paso into New
Mexico and stop at **Old Mesilla**, a cool little village of
Southwestern hopes and dreams, five minutes from
the city of **Las Cruces**. Rent an adobe. Find inspiration
at a little bookstore called Mesilla Book Center, which
specializes in the Southwest. Then spend some time
exploring Double Eagle (_double-eagle-mesilla.com_),
a former mansion-turned-bar-and-restaurant with
checkerboard floors, oil paintings, and chandeliers.
Fun fact: Billy the Kid was jailed here in 1881.

Spend a day and camp overnight in the awe-
inspiring gypsum dune fields of White Sands National
Monument. Create some artwork of your own – it's a
photographer's paradise.

Vintage shop your way through Tularosa (_tularosa.
com_) before heading to Japanese-inspired onsen Ten
Thousand Waves (_tenthousandwaves.com_) for a relaxing
soak, or The Inn of the Five Graces (_fivegraces.com_)
in **Santa Fe** for a colorful spa treatment and stay in a
luxurious jewel-box-like guest room. The cool El Rey
Court (_elreycourt.com_) is an updated Pueblo Revival motel
along the original Route 66, with a mezcal bar and great
recommendations for the area. It's close to the galleries
and antique shops in the Santa Fe Railyard Baca District
(_railyardsantafe.com_) and the interactive art collective
Meow Wolf (_meowwolf.com_). Santa Fe Vintage Outpost,
Shiprock Gallery, and Double Take are the best spots for
vintage wares.

Spend a summer evening at the Santa Fe Opera (*santafeopera.org*), a state-of-the-art outdoor amphitheater with views of the Tesuque Valley.

When you've had your fill of Santa Fe, take the mountainous, winding High Road to Taos. En route, make your way to the tiny, powerful shrine El Santuario de Chimayo, which was a sacred healing site of the Native Pueblo Indians long before the initial Spanish conquest of New Mexico. Stop by Rancho De Chimayo (*ranchodechimayo.com*) for comforting posole with shredded, slow-cooked pork. Feel like you're driving through a painting as you stop at small villages like **Cordova** (noted for its woodcarving), **Truchas** (the summit town), **Las Trampas**, and **Peñasco**.

In **Taos**, pick up a hand-loomed rug at Starr Interiors (*starr-interiors.com*); trinkets and decorative items at Taos General Store; and pottery, jewelry, and talismans from Taos Pueblo (*taospueblo.com*), a multi-storied adobe compound continually in use by the Red Willow Native American community for 1000 years.

Book tickets in advance for a private tour of Abiquiú (*okeeffemuseum.org*), the 18th-century, cliff-top adobe house that Georgia O'Keeffe lived in from 1949 until her death in 1986. Walk in her footsteps at Ghost Ranch retreat and education center and horseback ride some of the 21,000 acres (8498 hectares) of landscape inspiration.

Clockwise from top: candy-colored skies at White Sands National Park; Frank Lloyd Wright's desert laboratory, Taliesin West; the high road to Taos, New Mexico

Spend the night at the Mabel Dodge Luhan House (_mabeldodgeluhan.com_). In the early 1900s, this fascinating arts patron and connector flexed her esthetic and social impulses in Florence and New York City before falling in love with a Puebloan and settling in Taos, where she entertained famous photographers, writers, dancers, and artists like Georgia O'Keeffe, Ansel Adams, D.H. Lawrence, Aldous Huxley, and Martha Graham. Rooms are quaint and charming with quilted bedspreads and kiva fireplaces.

Spend the next morning with works from renowned Navajo painter and sculptor R.C. Gorman's namesake gallery. It's just a few minutes from painter (and Taos Society of Artist member) Ernest Blumenschein's home and museum.

Then drive down to **Albuquerque** to wander Old Town and Albuquerque Museum of Art and History (_cabq. gov/culturalservices/albuquerque-museum_). Spend an extremely relaxing evening at Los Poblanos (_lospoblanos. com_), an inn and organic farm with lavender fields. It was designed in the early 1930s by the "Father of Santa Fe Style," New Mexico visionary architect and preservationist John Gaw Meem, who championed Regionalism over Modernism.

Something like 10 percent of all hot air balloons in the US are registered in Albuquerque, which has generally windless mornings. A soar would be an epic way to get your fill of fresh air before the flight home or to clear your head for the next leg of the trip.

Where art and architecture obsessives should go from here:

Make your way from Albuquerque to Flagstaff, Arizona, stopping in **Gallup**, gateway to the Navajo and Zuni trading posts, galleries, and historic districts. **Flagstaff** is a neat little mountain town with high altitude and a laidback attitude. Go forest bathing among the ponderosa pines, use it as a base to explore the Grand Canyon (choose Route 180 and be sure to pit stop at the Chapel of the Holy Dove), or work whatever connections you have to James Turrell, whose impossibly large Roden Crater installation has yet to open to the public.

Check out Arcosanti (_arcosanti. org_), an ambitious and radical urban development where architecture meets environmentalism. It's one of the modern world's first attempts at creating a densely integrated, environmentally conscious, vertical urban living experience. Join an architecture tour or lecture and stop for lunch in the distinctive cafe.

Head down to the Valley of the Sun, **Phoenix-Scottsdale**, for a full-throttle dose of Frank Lloyd Wright (_franklloydwright.org_). Start with his remarkable home and avant-garde architecture school, Taliesin West. Then tour the Arizona Biltmore Hotel and Gammage Auditorium before sneaking peeks at a number of private homes. Absolutely carve out time for The Heard Museum (_heard.org_), which has been advancing the wide-ranging work of Native American artists and tribal communities for ninety years.

From top: Georgia O'Keeffe's historic house museum in Abiquiú; El Santuario de Chimayó in the foothills of the Sangre de Cristo Mountains

Make your way to **Tucson**, stopping in at the Center for Creative Photography (_ccp.arizona.edu/home_), lined with work from Adams to Zuzunaga; and the Arizona-Sonora Desert Museum (_desertmuseum.org_), a botanical garden, art gallery, natural history installation, and all-around ecological marvel.

Opposite, clockwise from top left: The Pearl hotel's black-and-white beach umbrella setup; skimming Grayton Beach Lake; a snow cone at Airstream Row; Grayton's white sands; a cruiser in Alys Beach; Seaside roofscapes

Florida's Emerald Coast for Families

A whisper network of hidden charms (with a Southern accent) throughout the Panhandle.

The 100-mile-long (161-kilometer-long) Emerald Coast got its name from the jewel-like color of the Gulf waters, and the warm temperatures and gentle waves draw families (and dolphins) in droves. First-time visitors to the Panhandle will quickly realize that the Gulf Coast of Florida has a distinctly different feel than the more popular tourist destinations to the south. The Emerald Coast is closer to Atlanta, Birmingham, Memphis, Nashville, and New Orleans than to Miami, and you can tell: this is a place where sugar-sand beaches and fun shopping meet old-fashioned Southern hospitality (and po' boys).

Most families rent cottages and condos along the waterfront, and the area is a real hodgepodge of design and, well, non-design. Zero in on South Walton, an upscale region of thirty small, idealistic planned beach communities unique in look and feel, from the all-white stucco homes of Alys Beach to the pan-Caribbean vibes of Rosemary Beach to *The Truman Show* stand-in, Seaside (it really was the setting for the film). All are popular (though not too popular) for their safe bike paths and easy walks to the towns. Each neighborhood has its own vibe, daily activities, and destinations, like Airstream Row, where a half-dozen vintage trailers sell everything from organic juices to gourmet doughnuts and grilled cheese melts.

One of the area's few boutique hotels, The Pearl (*thepearlrb.com*), has distinctive turrets and black-and-white striped awnings and a shock of green lawn that leads to a private beach. Just off scenic highway 30A are state parks like Topsail Hill Preserve State Park and Grayton Beach State Park, which have public beaches and nice bathrooms. The 15,000-acre (6070-hectare) Point Washington State Forest is home to campgrounds, diverse wildlife, and hundreds of miles of hiking, fishing, and biking trails that you may not even think to look for during a beach vacation.

Baja Peninsula for Epicureans

Captivating landscapes and unforgettable flavors that surprise and delight.

One of the world's most enchanting wine regions is a two-hour drive south of San Diego, California. Mexico's Valle de Guadalupe is really something special: a beautiful valley of rocks and wildflowers and Pacific Ocean breezes with a mix of century-old wineries and cool newcomers off the main road on bumpy dirt paths. There's very little of this wine distributed outside Mexico, so you'll be tasting things you can't get anywhere else.

Driving across the US border is easy – the scenic route from San Diego is I5 to CA905 to Tecate (don't forget your passport and be prepared to wait). Drop your bags at a cliffside modern steel-and-glass cabin at Encuentro Guadalupe (*grupoencuentro.com.mx*), or one of six cozy bedrooms at the small, art-filled luxury inn La Villa del Valle (*contryretreat.lavilladelvalle.com*). The options on Airbnb are lacking, but there are plenty of beautiful guesthouses at reasonable prices – see Finca La Divina (*fincaladivina.com*), a "culinary house" run by a local chef with nearby restaurant Finca Altozano (*fincaltozano.com*), or the wild and futuristic Campera bubbles (*camperahotel. com*), literally an inflatable clear sphere encasing a bedroom and bathroom for a camping-like experience under the stars.

Make your plan of attack: you can probably visit three to five wineries a day, many of which are by appointment only, so do research and get in touch with the wineries ahead of time (many restaurants and wineries are only open Thursday–Sunday). Don't miss Monte Xanic, Vena Cava, Tres Mujeres, Pijoan, and Casa de Piedra. Also of note are the natural and biodynamic wines produced at Bichi by Noel Téllez and his chef brother, Jair, whose locavore dining spot Laja (*facebook.com/LajaMexico*), in Ensenada, is destination dining par excellence.

The food and Mexican bubbly at outdoor dining room Conchas de Piedra (*facebook.com/Conchasdepiedra*) is terrific. On weekends, grab an outdoor seat at Adobe Food Truck (*facebook.com/foodtruckadobe*) before heading to the unique tasting room made from recycled materials like upside-down boats. Deckman's (*deckmans. com*) serves beautiful (flower-strewn!) options for all kinds of eaters on an outdoor, wood-fired hearth. A husband-and-wife team sling scrambled eggs, fresh tortillas, and stovetop espresso at their road spot on Route 3, Tortilla Flats Café. The food is amazing and the cafe is charming: a round brick structure that looks like a gigantic wine barrel.

Opposite: the outdoor bar at Vena Cava

From top: country chic Eastwind bar; a woodsy waterfall walk in Catskill, New York

New York's Hudson River Valley for Serial Weekenders

All the urban creature comforts – now, with fewer distractions! And much more space.

The 150 miles (240 kilometers) or so that fan out north of Manhattan and climb up either side of the Hudson River provide a true break from the pace and scene of the energized NYC metropolis. The National Heritage Area, with its dense forests of changing colors, rolling farmlands, and sophisticated villages, makes for incredibly scenic drives and stopovers anytime you need to shake off the city. It's remarkable to think that just 90 miles (145 kilometers) away, Ulster County is home to 250,000 "forever-wild" acres (101,171 hectares) for kayaking, hiking, and biking, and that the country's oldest wine-producing areas are in Dutchess County.

The Culinary Institute of America (*ciachef.edu*) and the impressive farm laboratory and restaurant Blue Hill at Stone Barns (*bluehillfarm.com*) are here. As are the former homes of Franklin Delano Roosevelt and various Vanderbilts. The farmers' markets are stocked. The art, design, fashion, and maker scene is thriving, thanks to the Manhattan and Brooklyn diaspora. It's incredible to see what creative people can do when given some space. Take, for instance, Dia Beacon's expansive art exhibitions (*diaart. org*) and Storm King Art Center's (*stormking.org*) dramatic outdoor setting for works of contemporary sculpture.

Further north, the town of Kingston, at the base of the Catskill Mountains, has a vibrant art community and cool shops, taverns, restaurants, galleries, and bars. Guests can stay at the well-appointed Hotel Kinsley (*hotelkinsley.com*), indulge in cultural pursuits at Rough Draft (*roughdraftny.com*), eat an unforgettable scone at Outdated Cafe (*outdatedcafe.com*), salvage excellent records at Rocket Number Nine (*facebook. com/rocketnumberninerecords*), or go deep into history at the A.J. Williams-Myers African Roots Library (*africanrootslibrary.org*). And there will still be time to tromp through one of the many protected forests, rivers, and reservoirs of the Catskills and Minnewaska State Park Preserve on the same day.

To make any weekend a very special occasion, book an impeccable room at The Villa at Saugerties (_thevillaatsaugerties.com_), where the owners will make you a fab breakfast and stoke the living room fire for a cozy afternoon with wine and handsome furnishings. The town of Saugerties is possibly the cutest, tiniest one around, with nearby destinations like the uber photogenic Saugerties Lighthouse and the bizarrely stark and beautiful Opus 40 (_opus40.org_), a hand-excavated, hand-sculpted bluestone earthwork built by one man on 6.5 acres (2.6 hectares) over forty years.

You're not far from the vestiges of Woodstock and Phoenicia, old and new – cozy mom-and-pops, herb shops, farmers' markets, festival grounds, funky diners, and adorable stays that cater to lots of moods. Want curated yet outdoorsy? Try Eastwind (_eastwindny.com_) or The Arnold House (_thearnoldhouse.com_). For curated yet outdoorsy with a dose of camp, try Urban Cowboy Lodge (_urbancowboy.com/catskills_). For straight-up camp with your camp, it's all about Kate's Lazy Meadow (_lazymeadow.com_).

Further north, the town of Hudson has been called Brooklyn-lite for a self-contained coolness that includes industrial buildings repurposed for the arts like Basilica Hudson (_basilicahudson.org_), meticulously curated antique shops, locavore dining, a lively bar and music scene, and great-looking boutique stays, like The Maker (_themaker. com_), where every detail, from the light fixtures to the textiles to the antiques, is an aesthete's dream. There's farm life, fly fishing, ski cultures, spiritual retreat outposts, and hints of the anti-establishment, too. The well runs deep in these parts. No wonder tri-state area folks head back to fill their buckets again and again.

Clockwise from top: throwback dining room at The Maker; prime leaf peeping; handsome Hotel Kinsley bedroom; an epic tub scenario at Urban Cowboy; the hand-hewn stone sculpture installation known as Opus 40

CALIFORNIA'S PACIFIC COAST FOR HEDONISTS

Where California myth and legend come to life.

Clockwise from top: sunset perch in San Diego; surfer heading for the break in Encinitas; Butterfly Beach at sunset

Rugged beauty, strong waves crashing into vast shores, jagged cliffs, and dense forests for miles on end – let's agree that it's no great mystery why the Pacific Coast Highway is one of the finest drives in North America and a strong symbol of the free-wheeling, fun-loving, beach-living, midnight-toking, love-making vibe that makes California the myth-meets-reality playground it is.

Start in the south in San Diego, pretty much where Highway 101 begins its 790-mile (1270-kilometer) journey to the Oregon border. Your first stop is the La Jolla tide pools to explore the flora and fauna that live in the nooks and crannies along the shore. The two daily low tides are the best times to spot marine life – gooseneck barnacles, sea slugs, surf grass, and, if you're lucky, a rare abalone.

A few miles north of the tide pools, the sand is black and the people are naked at Black's Beach in Torrey Pines, one of the few clothing-optional beaches in California. If you'd rather take the high road in nature, hike one of the half dozen winding trails in the cliffs of Torrey Pines State Natural Reserve for sweeping views of the beach below.

The next stop is **Encinitas**, the hippie-meets-high-class beach town that's all about catching rays, fish tacos, and om'ing your way to enlightenment. Imagine summertime all the time: that's why you come to Encinitas. A pleasing combination of rolling hills and Pacific coastline, the palm-tree-lined neighborhoods are a mix of old-school bungalows with overgrown bougainvillea and modern structures with tasteful, drought-resistant landscaping. (Stay in a local Airbnb to see for yourself.) The sporting equipment around here – surfboards, paddleboards, bikes, and other sand and stay-fit gear – almost outnumbers the locals. The iconic local landmark is Self-Realization Fellowship (*encinitastemple.org*), an Indian temple and meditation learning center where devoted monks in orange robes mingle with fit California girls and boys amid beautiful gardens overlooking one of the hottest surf spots on the West Coast, which really is called Swami's Beach (and was name-checked in the Beach Boys' "Surfin' USA"). People swear this area is a fantastic energy vortex, and you'll find scores of vegan and organic eateries along the beach to nourish that clean living. If you don't want to leave without trying yoga, find the class that's right for you: Ashtanga Yoga Center (*ashtangayogacenter.com*) leads workshops, Yoga Tropics (*yogatropics.com*) does hot yoga, The Soul of Yoga (*soulofyoga.com*) offers different styles, and Gather Encinitas (*gatherencinitas.com*) is small and special. Your third eye never looked brighter.

If you're here in the springtime, stop in **Carlsbad** to see what a 50-acre (20-hectare) blanket of ranunculus blossoms look like at The Flower Fields at Carlsbad Ranch (*theflowerfields.com*). Now take a two-hour detour inland to check out that other geological wonder in Southern California: the desert. With no traffic lights or restaurant chains, **Borrego Springs** is the quintessential balm for the soul, a surreal alternative to its bourgeois neighbor, Palm Springs. Entirely surrounded by Anza-Borrego Desert State Park (at 600,000 acres/242,811 hectares, it's the largest park of the lower forty-eight United States),

From left: Old Mission Santa Barbara, a.k.a. "Queen of the Missions"; kayaking in Santa Barbara

Opposite, clockwise from top: mirrored perspective in Palm Springs; groovy Parker Palm Springs; San Ysidro Ranch entrance in bloom; sunset at Post Ranch Inn; ingredients foraged from the Big Sur coastline at once-in-a-lifetime restaurant Sierra Mar

Borrego Springs also has one of the blackest night skies in the USA California's only Dark Sky Community, this town is Disneyland for stargazers. If you're spending the night, do so at The Palms at Indian Head (*thepalmsatindianhead. com*), the swinging 1950s hangout for Hollywood jetsetters like Clark Gable and Marilyn Monroe that's now a practical, clean bungalow with the great mid-century bones the area is famous for. Spanning hundreds of acres in both directions off Borrego Springs Road, Galleta Meadows Estate is a mini Marfa and an urban safari rolled into one. The road is lined with 130 playful – and totally unexpected – steel animal sculptures by Ricardo Breceda: lions and zebras and eagles (oh my!), as well as mythical dragons and sea serpents. If you can time it right (and if you're in a 4x4), hit Font's Point in Anza-Borrego at sunset. There's a reason they call what you're seeing California's Grand Canyon. If your car isn't up to it, Carrizo Badlands Overlook is an excellent substitute.

Palm Springs is the ring-a-ding-ding stop where mid-century chic meets the festival-going lifestyle. Palm Springs Art Museum (*psmuseum.org*) needed three locations to showcase its impressive collection of contemporary art, though not as contemporary as the site-specific biennial installations at Desert X (*desertx. org*) and the self-guided Coachella Walls murals tour in Coachella. Sunnylands (*sunnylands.org*) is Southern California's bipartisan Davos. When golden hour strikes, decamp to the mountains on the Palm Springs Aerial Tramway (*pstramway.com*), a rotating cable car that scales the cliffs of Chino Canyon up to Mount San Jacinto State Park, offering stellar views. Many of the iconic mid-century modern homes around here are privately owned, but if you come during the annual Modernism Week, you can get a rare peek inside. The hotels we love in town are The Saguaro (*thesaguaro.com*), The Parker Palm Springs (*parkerpalmsprings.com*), and Colony Palms Hotel (*colonypalmshotel.com*).

You've made it all the way out here, so you have to go to Joshua Tree. For a sound bath at the too woo-woo for school Integratron (*integratron.com*). For the wacky extraterrestrial trees and wildlife that form where

the distinct Mojave and Colorado desert ecosystems collide in Joshua Tree National Park. For the live blues at Joshua Tree Saloon (*joshuatreesaloon.com*). For the hedgehog cactus, beavertail cactus, and teddy bear cholla that fill the Cholla Cactus Garden. For the hospitality at 29 Palms Inn (*29palmsinn.com*) and the carousing at The Palms Restaurant and Bar, (*palmswondervalley. com*) both in the cute town of Twentynine Palms. For the vintage finds on the weekends at Sky Village Market Place (*skyvillageswapmeet.com*) in Yucca Valley.

Right about now, you're missing the ocean, so let's get back to the coast. It's a straight shot west on Highway 10 to Los Angeles, where we're not stopping on this trip, to get back to the 101. If you're hungry, stop in **Venice Beach** for snacks for the road at everyone's favorite all-day eateries Gjusta (*gjusta.com*) and Erewhon (*erewhonmarket.com*), the iconic 1970s health food shop that the resident celebrities and hipsters absolutely adore. If all this modernity has you craving some time with the ancients, make a leisurely pit stop at The Getty Villa (*getty.edu*) in Pacific Palisades to see exquisite Greek and Etruscan antiquities in a structure that J.P. Getty commissioned based on a 1st-century A.D. Roman villa.

If your back is starting to get cramped from all that driving, make your way to **Ojai** for moments of extreme beauty and a massage at Ojai Valley Inn & Spa (*ojaivalleyinn.com*), which has everything you need to emerge refreshed – pool, healthy eatery, gym, and artist cottage. Stop at Bart's Books (*bartsbooksojai.com*), the world's largest outdoor bookstore, to pick up a novel in a charming setting without a roof. An hour up the coast is **Santa Barbara**, the Euro-minded town that calls itself the American Riviera and still bears traces of its 1600s Spanish settlers, notably at Old Mission Santa Barbara (*santabarbaramission.org*), overlooking the Pacific. Downtown is a mix of social classes and interests, where high-ticket restaurants and boutiques sit alongside mom-and-pop shops. If you need a break from all this perfectly curated consumerism, visit the flock of sheep at Elings Park. If you want to stay the night, Hotel Californian (*hotelcalifornian.com*) has a cool Moroccan vibe and seaside views. But if you want a totally-worth-it splurge, make your way to **Montecito**, where history, old Hollywood, and extreme hospitality meet at San Ysidro Ranch (*sanysidroranch.com*), a citrus farm-turned-luxury hideaway in the foothills of the Santa Ynez Mountains. A sanctuary for Franciscan monks in the 1700s and a winter respite for Winston Churchill before World War I, the forty-one cottages along San Ysidro Creek offer an outstanding experience – a twelve on a scale of one to ten – for a long weekend, a honeymoon, a mellow family vacation, or all of the above.

Opposite, clockwise from top: art and nature in situ at 29 Palms; arcaded silhouettes and spindled window grills at Hotel Californian; the ancient Roman country house–inspired interiors of Getty Villa; manicured gardens and lily pond at San Ysidro Ranch; the bold beauty of a lobby at Hotel Californian; sunlight and a breeze by an Ojai Valley Inn pool daybed

Clockwise from left: still lake at Calistoga Ranch; Big Sur's Bixby Bridge; water lilies ready for their close-up at San Ysidro Ranch

The low-key and lovely **Central Coast** is being hailed as the new Napa for its undulating hills and vineyards, proximity to the ocean, and stunning scenery (see: the spectacular rocky beach at Morro Bay) – though it won't stay undiscovered for much longer. In Paso Robles in San Luis Obispo County, the midway point between San Francisco and Los Angeles, the prices are lower and the vibe is more laidback and authentic, a mix of farm workers and fancy types, gay and straight, making everything feel inclusive and interesting. You won't be able to visit all of the area's few hundred wineries, but a great route from town along Adelaida Road would get you to Daou (_daouvineyards. com_), Adelaida (_adelaida.com_), Kukkula (_kukkulawine. com_) on Chimney Rock Road, then south to Halter Ranch (_halterranch.com_) and Epoch Estate (_epochwines.com_) on Highway 46 West. You'll reach Highway 1 and the San Luis Obispo Coast in about fifteen minutes, where you'll stop to see enormous elephant seals stage epic battles while their young pups bob in the surf at Hearst San Simeon State Park. Right up the road is another legendary tycoon's European-inspired folly, Hearst Castle (_hearstcastle. org_), where William Randolph Hearst spent the Roaring '20s entertaining his mistress, actress Marion Davies, and the A-List of the day – Charlie Chaplin, Cary Grant, Greta Garbo, Jean Harlow, Charles Lindbergh, and P.G. Wodehouse – in its dazzling 165 rooms, endless gardens, and shimmering swimming pools.

Continue on the twisty way to **Big Sur**, the wild and breathtaking stretch of land that's been inspiring travelers, artists, musicians, and literary greats like Henry Miller and Jack Kerouac for a little over a century. The rocky coastline is isolated and rugged, the beauty is magical and staggering, and the cell phone service is blessedly nonexistent. It's a slice of a Golden State long gone, a largely undeveloped, slightly off-kilter spot with wood-paneled buildings, indoor-outdoor living, and a certain relaxed, groovy vibe. A window, if you will, onto a time when people came west to reinvent themselves – not through apps and equity grants but with open spaces and free thinking. You're here to mellow out, so let's keep the checklist easy: Big Sur Roadhouse (*glenoaksbigsur.com/big-sur-roadhouse*) has the best breakfast game in town; lunch should be perched above the ocean at Nepenthe (*nepenthe.com*). If you're blowing the bank on an overnight at the epic Post Ranch Inn (*postranchinn.com*) (one of the best hotels not only in California and North America but also the world), you can have dinner at the hotel restaurant, Sierra Mar. If you didn't rob a bank before your trip but still want stylish, neo-retro accommodations, check into a cabin in the redwoods at Glen Oaks Big Sur (*glenoaksbigsur.com*). The essential thing to see at Julia Pfeiffer Burns State Park is McWay Falls, one of the few waterfalls in the world that empties into an ocean. Take a few hours for a lively tour of the 128-year-old lighthouse on a 362-foot-tall (110-meter-tall) volcanic rock at Point Sur State Historic Park and Lighthouse. Finally, do whatever you can to get a reservation for a midnight bath overlooking the Pacific at Esalen (*esalen.org*), whose cliffside hot springs here have been in use for over 6000 years, making it Big Sur's first tourist destination.

On your way up to Carmel, you'll drive across Bixby Bridge. You've seen it in commercials and the opening credits of *Big Little Lies*, but that doesn't make it any less spectacular. Before you get to the Monterey Peninsula, stop at Point Lobos State Marine Reserve to follow one of the woodsy trails out to the ocean. (No, there's no such thing as too many catch-your-breath views of the Pacific on this trip.) If you haven't had your fill of wildlife yet, book a tour with Monterey Bay Kayaks (*montereybaykayaks.com*) and spend a few incredible hours kayaking into animal habitats to see otters grooming their babies and sea lions doing back flips. They'll be here for a long time, as the animals and the area are heavily protected.

Palms flank the vines at Round Pond in Napa

Carmel by the Sea is exactly what you'd expect of a town that once made Clint Eastwood its mayor: understated and timelessly cool with no-nonsense style and very expensive tastes. The grounds at Carmel Mission (*carmelmission.org*) are yet another reminder that, though those evangelizing Catholic priests swore vows of poverty, they sure had an eye for priceless real estate. Finally, we challenge anyone who has never picked up a nine-iron not to wish they played the sport of kings after cruising 17-Mile Drive around the golf course at Pebble Beach (*pebblebeach. com*). There aren't many scenic roads you have to pay to access, but this one is worth every cent.

Sprint past San Francisco along the east side of the Bay to get to **Napa Valley**. If you have food on the brain (always), sign up for a cooking class at CIA at Copia (*ciaatcopia.com*), the Culinary Institute of America's Napa campus, test kitchen, exhibition center, and shop. If you've ever wondered what 4000 jelly molds, butcher's knives, and duck presses look like when arranged like Faberge eggs, don't miss the Chuck Williams Culinary Arts Museum on the top floor. Next door is Oxbow Public Market (*oxbowpublicmarket.com*), a one-stop shop for the area's best eateries and foodstuffs (namely English muffins from Model Bakery and charcuterie from Fatted Calf).

Route 29 is the main thoroughfare through Napa Valley, which is, yes, touristy and expensive and not at all unknown, but nonetheless beautiful. You won't get a table at The French Laundry (*thomaskeller.com*) in Yountville, but you can eat at any of a number of Thomas Keller's other restaurants in town, like Ad Hoc. If it feels like every other building is a winery or a tasting room, that's because it is. Even Oakville Grocery (*oakvillegrocery.com*), home of the best sandwiches in the valley, has a picturesque tasting room next door. Among the more memorable and/or exclusive wineries are Promontory (*promontory.wine*), by appointment only, and Round Pond (*roundpond.com*), which also has an olive oil and vinegar tasting room, and Hall (*hallwines.com*), where the modern art collection rivals the wines. The collection at Inglenook (*inglenook.com*) in Rutherford details the history of California winemaking – in photos, paraphernalia, and artifacts – as only owner Francis Ford Coppola could. Napa's most notable (and pricey) hotels include Meadowood (*meadowood.com*), the award-winning hotel, restaurant, spa resort in the woods; the fabulously eco-minded Bardessono (*bardessono.com*) in Yountville; and Calistoga Ranch (*aubergeresorts.com/calistogaranch*), the luxurious escape in the Calistoga hills where individual cabins overlooking the woods lead uphill to a cozy lakefront restaurant, and any soreness built up while hiking the property's trails can be relieved at the indoor-outdoor spa.

Yountville may hog the spotlight, but **St. Helena** is the most charming of Napa's towns. Main Street is lined with a cute used bookstore, Main Street Bookmine (*napabookmine. com*), an arch interior design shop Martin Design (*erinmartin. com*), and a knife store that lets you try your hand at axe throwing, New West Knifeworks (*newwestknifeworks.com*). Las Alcobas Napa Valley (*lasalcobas.com*) is a refined (but not stuffy) hotel where the rooms have firepits and balconies overlooking vineyards, and an incredible spa and knockout restaurant round out the amenities.

Your final stop is at the north end of the valley in **Calistoga**, a little town that still maintains its Gold-Rush-era charm. If the budget doesn't permit checking into Calistoga Ranch, Calistoga Motor Lodge and Spa (*calistogamotorlodgeandspa.com*) is an affordable refurbished motel at the end of the Silverado Trail with playful decor and an impressive spa with terrific outdoor facilities for use in nice weather.

You've had a long journey of hiking and drinking and being at one with nature, and you need a little me time. You need to sink into a low-fi and totally restorative volcanic ash mud bath at Indian Springs Calistoga (*indianspringscalistoga. com*). Thermal geysers have been bubbling up here for eons, and into the Olympic pool since 1910. Relax and float a while.

Opposite: pure floral joy in Carlsbad

This page, from top: the famous baths at Esalen in Big Sur; vineyards in Santa Barbara

Pit stop for: fruit stands – artfully wrapped sage leaves – bottles of cabernet – roadside tacos – good vibes – wicked surf breaks – saltwater taffy on the boardwalk – In-N-Out burgers

Tasty fact: California's winemaking tradition traces its roots back to the Spanish missionary priests, who planted the vines for communion wines. Three centuries later, California is the world's fourth biggest wine producer, after France, Italy, and Spain.

THE LOCALS TO KNOW

Make the most of your stop-offs by linking up with tour guides passionate about their place and people and dedicated to responsible storytelling and adventuring.

Clarksdale, Mississippi, USA If you want to know what it feels like when time slows to a crawl, get to know the "Voice of the Lower Mississippi River," an eclectic newsletter dispatch of musings, poetry, and artwork from the Quapaw Canoe Company (*island63.com*). Quapaw offers real-deal floating wilderness expeditions on the backwaters of the Lower Mississippi River. Voyageur John Ruskey may lead you, in a dugout canoe, on an overnight or multiday trip to teach you about the nature spirits, the snow moon, the trees, and local lore as well as river survival skills.

Charleston, South Carolina, USA Olivia Williams is a historical interpreter at McLeod Plantation, a carefully preserved 37-acre (15-hectare) Gullah/Geechee heritage site. But rather than focus on the grand home and legacy of the white family who once lived there, Williams zeroes in on the living quarters of the enslaved people and, in particular, the unspeakable hardships of enslaved women.

Mexico City, Mexico Chefs and hosts-with-the-mosts Beto Estúa and Jorge Fitz are just the kind of friends you want to make when hanging out in Mexico. The pair lead market tours and cooking classes in their gorgeous home through Casa Jacaranda (*casajacaranda.mx*).

Squamish, British Columbia, Canada First-Nations-owned company Talaysay Tours (*talaysay.com*) leads Aboriginal cultural and sustainable experiences in and around Vancouver and the Sunshine Coast. Guides are delightful storytellers, crafters, and naturalists who share old legends and contemporary tales of living in the area.

From top: on a Civil Bikes city history tour in Atlanta; cooking up something delicious at Casa Jacaranda, Mexico City

Opposite, from top: Mexican hospitality starts with tequila cocktails; a scene in Queens, New York; foraged lunch over an open fire in Newfoundland

Atlanta, Georgia, USA Civil Bikes (_civilbikes.com_) is a historic cycling tour that spotlights the stories of the area that have been egregiously left out of the history books – neighborhood history, moments in Civil Rights history, communities that impact Atlanta – to build awareness, sensitivity, and hope for the future.

Everglades, Florida, USA Few people know that the marshy swampland in the subtropical wilderness of Florida is home to Native American tribes. Today, a handful of reservations exist in the area, and Buffalo Tiger Airboat Tours (_buffalotigerairboattours.com_), founded by Miccosukee Tribe of Indians chief and elected chairman William Buffalo Tiger, takes groups around to highlight the history of the people and the ancestral tribal lands.

Queens, New York, USA Fun, eccentric food obsessives deliver edible crash courses on the global food scene that's thriving in New York's most diverse borough. A Culinary Backstreets (_culinarybackstreets.com_) tour is more like a neighborly stroll where you and your guide chat with and sample from street food vendors, small restaurateurs, and local mongers, learning the history, hardships, and meaning behind each dish along the way. (They also host cool eating tours in Mexico City and Oaxaca.)

Newfoundland, Canada Lori McCarthy founded Cod Sounds (_codsounds.ca_) to share her love of her terroir and stories of hunting, fishing, trapping, and gathering in Newfoundland. She leads gastro-minded outdoor adventures on day hikes and workshops through the woods and beaches, foraging as she goes and stopping to make lunch over an open fire (an impromptu cooking class), always imparting her passion for local history and the art of bushcraft wilderness survival.

Kailua-Kona, Hawaii, USA One of the most incredible brushes with nature is interacting with the majestic, enormous, ghost-like manta rays that glide through the waters on the western edge of the Big Island. Through Hawaiian-led Anelakai Adventures (_anelakaiadventures.com_), travelers keep in line with the Pono Pledge (to rightfully and righteously care for the land and sea) by ditching the motorboat (and its noise and oil pollution) for a double-hulled canoe rigged with night lights, setting out at sundown to snorkel with the serene creatures. (Manta rays are attracted to the plankton are attracted by the lights under the canoes.)

THE MOTEL REFURB

Motor lodges across the continent are getting the updated vintage makeover they deserve. Repurposing roadside locales with outside doors and pull-up parking is smart, relevant, and sustainable.

Brentwood Hotel, Saratoga Springs, New York, USA
Three hours up the Hudson River from NYC, just across the road from the Saratoga Race Track paddock, is a refurbished twelve-room motel that has been beautifully retrofitted with brass fixtures, custom-crafted beds, French linens, and classy (not kitschy) equestrian design details. There's a fireside lounge, a black-walled bar, and Linus bicycles. But the best feature of all? Terrific views of the track from every guest room. *brentwood-hotel.com*

Skyview Los Alamos, Santa Barbara, California, USA
A Central California thirty-three-room motel pays homage to its mid-century and Western roots without falling into twee territory – no mean feat! – using cowhide rugs, Pendleton blankets, crisp white shiplap walls, and cedar outdoor showers. A Tivoli speaker, tiny tube of Marvis toothpaste, and booklet titled "How To Skyview, And Other Stuff" – a small yet remarkably informative guide to the area – are just a few of the thoughtful, elevated touches. *skyviewlosalamos.com*

Drake Motor Inn, Prince Edward County, Canada
Playful accommodations for Torontonians on the run nod toward nostalgic fun (Polaroid cameras, vending machines) and an upgraded design sensibility (modern Scandinavian furnishings, colorful artwork) on a small island that is hip and historic (and not Prince Edward Island, some 800 miles/1300 kilometers east). It's just down the road from big sister hotel Drake Devonshire (thedrake.ca/drakedevonshire), which is beautiful and cool and has yoga and a lakeside restaurant and several cute dining and drinking establishments orbiting around the place. *thedrake.ca/drakemotorinn*

Opposite: welcoming vibes at The Drake Motor Inn in Prince Edward County

This page, from left: the Drake Motor Inn's mod interiors and bar from which to contemplate bold design decisions

Skyview Los Alamos evokes the California way at the retro pool under the marquee and on the patio

Opposite: the entrance at Skyview Los Alamos

The Drifter, New Orleans, Louisiana, USA
A restored neon roadside sign beckons travelers away from the French Quarter fray and the recently developed hotel row in the Warehouse District to the less-trodden path (for tourists, anyway) to Mid-City. The low-slung 1950s building has been jazzed up with new finishes and furnishings that give it a stylish Cuban vibe; the on-site, on-trend food trucks serve Mexican, Cuban, and Caribbean foods to be paired with frozen cocktails at the bar. _thedrifterhotel.com_

Ojai Rancho Inn, Ojai, California, USA
This quirky log-cabin-style lodge with a lot of heart in a former '50s roadside motel has been a mainstay in the super groovy town of Ojai. Rooms are simple with kitchenettes and king-size beds (and sometimes retro hot tubs). There's a fire pit for gathering around with drinks from the tiny, adorable bar on site. _ojairanchoinn.com_

Anvil, Jackson, Wyoming, USA

A down-and-out motel with a 21st-century conversion equals a cozy, streamlined, and well-appointed but unfussy gathering spot for out-of-towners looking to stay on the doorstep of Yellowstone and the Tetons. Shaker-inspired design (wainscotting, iron bed frames) is given the mountain treatment. The reincarnated restaurant focuses on wood-fired Italian cooking, and a dark wood general store called Mercantile functions as a gathering place for locals and travelers in need of a nice cup of coffee, maps, WiFi, woolen caps, or leather bolo ties. *anvilhotel.com*

The Verb, Boston, Massachusetts, USA

A Fenway Park refurbishment pays homage to the misbehaving musicians who used the place as a crash pad back in the day with a rock'n'roll design theme – vintage speakers, music memorabilia, '70s-era telephones – and regular live music programming. The Mondrian-like stained-glass floor-to-ceiling windows surround a sundeck and heated saltwater pool that stays open all year long. *theverbhotel.com*

The Sandman, Santa Rosa, California, USA

Studio Tack, the NYC-based firm that designed Coachman Hotel (coachmantahoe.com) in Lake Tahoe, is behind another cute refurbished California motel off US-101 (among many other roadside delights) full of fun and quirky touches: an outdoor pool and hot tub, a lively pool house and bar, a bocce ball court, bamboo lounge areas, and tastefully minimalist rooms that accommodate families and pets. *sandmansantarosa.com*

Nobu Ryokan, Malibu, California, USA

The ultimate upcycle of a '50s-era inn may be Nobu Matsuhisa and billionaire Larry Ellison's contemporary take on a Japanese inn above Carbon Beach and just steps from the celeb-magnet sushi restaurant. The Eastern version of the Western roadside motel includes tatami mats, teak wood soaking tubs, shoji screens, and bronze finishings. Garden rooms have private green space; second-floor ocean rooms have crazy coastline views. _malibu.nobuhotels.com_

Amigo Motor Lodge, Salida, Colorado, USA

A scrappy couple of dreamers purchased a seventy-year-old high-desert stopover in Central Colorado and turned it into a chill, laidback, sixteen-room oasis. An old carport is now a sunroom filled with leafy plants. A few Airstreams and a tall teepee serve as funky guest room alternatives. Through some smart and efficient design decisions, the motel has eased its use of valuable resources like water, electricity, and gas (which the local national parks are thankful for) and donates a portion of its revenue to Salida-area organizations. Keep the retro theme going with a visit to the nearby drive-in cinema. _stayamigo.com_

Austin Motel, Austin, Texas, USA

This motel's motto says it all: "So close, yet so far out." Vibrant colors and attention-grabbing wallpaper adorn all forty-one guest rooms in a style as unapologetically playful as it is effortlessly cool, while the kidney-shaped pool in the center of the property and surrounding lido deck are Instagram heaven. The original 1930s sign at the entrance, still standing, is the inspiration behind the vintage aesthetic. _austinmotel.com_

The Wayfinder, Newport, Rhode Island, USA

Nostalgia for mid-century Americana has made its way to Newport's yacht-filled harbor. There's nothing cliché about the seaside decor in this hotel, which is relaxed and stylish with cool tones and vintage elements sourced from antique markets and local artists. The lobby and its sunshine-yellow floating fireplace give off retro vibes and have plenty of seating for cocktails and conversation. Rhode Island food trucks park near the outdoor pool and raw bar – pure summer fun. Sustainability is top of mind, too: take note of the electric car charging stations, news of regular beach cleanups, and the absence of single-use plastics. _thewayfinderhotel.com_

Opposite, clockwise from top left: the Wayfinder in Newport's envy-inducing indoor fireplace lounge, cute kiosk setup, and eclectic preppy charm; groovy red leather at Austin Motel; mercantile and general store entrance at Anvil in Jackson; welcoming neon rainbow carport at Austin Motel

CHAPTER 9

EXPAND YOUR MIND

As we are all well aware by now, the tidy narrative that the United States and its neighboring countries are havens of religious and spiritual tolerance is more myth than reality. For privileged people who have been sheltered from this legacy, reckoning with that history has been awkward, embarrassing, and, at times, violent. We have a lot of work to do! At the same time, it's incredible (and maybe even staggering) to realize that the land that attracted the foreign, the heretic, the heathen, the dissident, and the unbeliever has also nurtured the freethinker, the individual, the peacenik, and the magnanimous. How's that for unexplained phenomena?

Previous page: dreamcatchers in the wind

This page: inside the multi-wave sound chamber known as The Integratron in California

Opposite: The Integratron has been a desert destination since the 1950s

Across North America you will find a whole host of contradictory, transcendent, bizarre, and sometimes head-scratching experiences: supernatural ideas, superstitions, omnipresent forces, spirit-inhabited lands, shaman ceremonies, occult rituals – and, further into the fringe, alien invasion lore – and the people who wholeheartedly believe in it all. It can be thrilling, fun, and downright cuckoo (hopefully in a good, eye-opening way) to encounter or seek out these kinds of obscura and curiosities on the road. For one thing, it gets the traveler out of their comfort zone. For another, such explorations can crack a community wide open, giving the visitor a better understanding of how, why, and in what way a place functioned in the past and present. Wonder is good for us.

Current vibes are dovetailing with the self-care trend in the form of rituals, retreats, intentional communities, and personal experiences that tap into energies and frequencies that haven't been explored with such gusto since the free-spirited '60s and '70s.

In other words: It's all woo-woo from here on out.

CULT CLASSICS

Familiarize yourself with the mystical, magical, and otherworldly hotbeds of spiritual activity for all your pseudoscientific inclinations. Consider this a hitchhiker's guide to the cosmos.

Science Meets Art and Magic: The Integratron, Landers, California, USA

This man-made phenomenon was originally designed to house powers of rejuvenation, human-life extension, and anti-gravity time travel in the heart of California's Mojave Desert. It was built in the 1950s by aeronautical engineer and UFOlogist George Van Tassel – under instruction from an alien from Venus that he encountered during a space trip. (Hey, that's the story!) The structure, made of wood, fiberglass, and concrete, was sadly never put to the test as a vehicle for time travel (Van Tassel died in 1978). But you can step inside for meditative sonic-healing sound bath sessions, where participants lie down in the main chamber and immerse themselves in harmonic sounds produced by quartz crystal bowls. In the supposedly perfect wooden geometric structure, the experience is so soothing you'll feel like you're actually bathing in sound. Sound baths happen bi-monthly and are on a first-come-first-serve basis. Private sessions and group rates are available, too. (*integratron.com*)

Good to Know: Colony Palms Hotel (*colonypalmshotel.com*), a palm-dotted oasis in the California desert with casita-style suites and outdoor soaking tubs, is about an hour's drive from The Integratron. With a backyard of 2 million acres (809,371 hectares) of open land in the California High Desert, 29 Palms Inn (*29palmsinn.com*) is sprinkled with adobe bungalows and wood-framed cabins. If house rentals are more your thing, The Joshua Tree House (*thejoshuatreehouse.com*) is a two-bed, two-bath 1949 hacienda located ten minutes from the west entrance of Joshua Tree National Park.

Grounding Rituals in the Grand Canyon of the East: Linville Gorge Wilderness, Marion, North Carolina, USA

This pure, virgin forest within the Pisgah National Forest is said to have natural healing energy and is considered to be the state's best-kept secret. Steep, rugged cliffs carved over millennia by the Linville River protect the oldest trees in the forest – a natural shield from loggers. The earth here has long been considered sacred; the Cherokee performed ceremonies on Table Rock Mountain, which they called "Attacoa" – "mystic altar." Today, hikers often remove their shoes for grounding rituals and to embrace the natural healing energy of the gorge. A free camping permit is needed on weekends and holidays from May through October.

Good to Know: The other must-sees while visiting the gorge are Linville Caverns (*linvillecaverns. com*), North Carolina's only cave system; the hidden treasures inside Humpback Mountain; and more than 150 miles (240 kilometers) of beautiful shoreline at Lake James. Closest lodging in the national park is at the Linville Falls Campground (*linvillefalls.com/cabin-rentals*) with cabins available to rent. (There are also cute, affordable Airbnbs nearby.)

A Sacred Site for Vision Quests: Devils Tower, Crook County, Wyoming, USA

It's quite a sight to see rising out of the Black Hills prairie: a stunning volcanic butte as tall as four football fields, shaped by a millennium of erosion. It was the first site declared a US National Monument by President Theodore Roosevelt in 1906, but had been regarded for thousands of years before that as sacred by dozens of Northern Plains tribes, who told tales that the deep crevices along the rock face were scratchings made by a giant grizzly in battle. (What an excellent legend.) Devils Tower, which is also known as Bear Lodge, remains a spiritual place for ceremonial vision quests, sun dance rituals, and indigenous blessings.

Good to Know: The small, colored bundles of cloth around the base of Devils Tower are sacred offerings left by Native Americans. If you want to see the top of the tower, the only way to do so is by climbing. Two local cowboys were the first to ascend the tower with a handmade ladder system, remnants of which are still at the top, and it remains a favorite of crack climbers. June typically has a voluntary climbing closure, as that's when Native Americans partake in ceremonies for the summer solstice.

Opposite, from left: summit of Hawksbill Mountain in the Linville Gorge Wilderness in North Carolina; channeling higher dimensions at Mount Shasta, California

This page: the imposing Devil's Tower in Wyoming

An Alpine Energy Vortex Where Heaven and Earth Meet: Mount Shasta, California, USA

This 14,180-foot (4322-meter) ice-covered dormant volcano in Northern California is highly praised by spiritual seekers as one of the most powerful energy vortexes in North America. With thousands of visitors each year (some become full-time residents), the peak's high-vibrational energy has led to many shamanic awakenings, spiritual growth pursuits, emotional restorations, and good old a-ha moments. The Shasta worshippers are often compared to Ancient Greeks who were obsessed with Olympus and to Moses and his Sinai. Legend has it that inside the peak is a hidden city inhabited by higher-dimensional beings from the lost continent of Lemuria, and that the saucer-shaped clouds that often gather at the summit are engineered for the disguise of alien-aircraft arrivals. Talk about far out.

Good to Know: Guided meditations, vision quests, and hiking excursions are available through Shasta Vortex Adventures (_shastavortex.com_). The Trinity Divide trails are especially breathtaking, with no expert hiking experience required. The 3-mile (5-kilometer) Heart Lake Trail takes hikers up to Castle Peak with stunning views of Mount Shasta's reflection over the small and serene lake. The best time to visit is the late spring, when temperatures are in the low 60s (around 15°C), cooler than the average 75°F (24°C) during peak tourist season in the summer. Nestled at the foot of Mount Shasta, McCloud Hotel (_mccloudhotel.com_) is an ideal location for guests hoping to take advantage of the surrounding river and its three waterfalls. The quirkiest accommodations are the refurbished vintage Cotton Belt train cabooses on 50 beautiful acres (20 hectares) of private property at Railroad Park Resort (_rrpark.com_).

Navajo Sacred Land of the Creator: Monument Valley, Arizona–Utah Border, USA

Famously known as the backdrop to America's 1930s Westerns by John Ford and John Wayne, Monument Valley remains what many imagine to be the true snapshot of the American West. Visitors come to drive the 17-mile (27-kilometer) scenic loop, admire the majestic, free-standing sandstone buttes, and imagine themselves embracing a kind of let-their-hair-down freedom, a la *Thelma & Louise* (but with a happier ending). This sprawling valley is home to the Navajo Nation and remains tribal-owned sacred land dedicated to their Creator. In addition to the loop drive, visitors can experience this ever-changing natural beauty by hiking the eleven trails and lookouts in the park. A famous spot is John Ford Point, where visitors can re-create the iconic image of a lone horseback rider overlooking the high plateau at the edge of the desert.

Good to Know: Peak season is from May through September; off-season is October through April. The View Hotel (*monumentvalleyview.com*) is located in Monument Valley Park and offers guests unsurpassed vistas from charming cabins with private porches, perfect for sipping coffee before a morning hike.

Communing with the Spirits: Janitzio Island, Lake Pátzcuaro, Michoacán, Mexico

Día de Muertos is famously celebrated throughout Mexico from October 31 until November 2. The Day of the Dead tradition, a mash-up of the Christian feast days All Saints' Day and All Souls' Day and the Aztec festival honoring the goddess of the underworld Mictēcacihuātl, ranks as a UNESCO Intangible Cultural Heritage of Humanity. People paint skeletons on their faces, visit cemeteries, and build beautiful altars overflowing with offerings – fruits and photos and flowers – to honor loved ones who have died. The locals on this tiny fishing island, one of five on Lake Pátzcuaro, celebrate with particular gusto, beginning with a duck hunt on October 31. After sunset on November 1, the fishermen take their flower-filled boats and butterfly-shaped nets onto the lake for a dramatic candlelit procession. The festivities last until dawn.

Good to Know: Nearby Pátzcuaro is a 14th-century town with a beautifully preserved colonial charm. Villa Victoria (*villavictoriapatzcuaro.com*) is an exquisite bed and breakfast with rustic details and charming, old-fashioned rooms that lead onto a lush hidden courtyard.

Opposite, from left: Mother Nature's sculpture at Monument Valley Navajo Tribal Park; the candlelit beauty of Hotel St. Francis in New Mexico

This page: the library of Rosewood Inn of the Anasazi in Santa Fe

The Shaman's Path to Big Blue: Crater Lake, Klamath County, Oregon, USA

Formed 7700 years ago by the volcanic explosion of Mount Mazama, the 6-mile-wide (10-kilometer-wide), 1943-foot-deep (592-meter-deep) Crater Lake is the deepest in the US, and is famous for its crystal-clear blue water, which comes entirely from rain or snow. No other sources stream in or out, making it also one of the cleanest lakes in the world. The Klamath people worshipped the water and, for centuries, the tribe's shaman was the only one allowed to visit the lake, as many feared that looking into its depths for too long would invite lifelong sorrow or death. Mystical sites within abound. The Old Man of the Lake is a hemlock tree that's been floating for 100 years. Wizard Island, so named for its resemblance to a sorcerer's hat, is the top of a cinder-cone volcano now covered with 800-year-old trees. Phantom Ship Island is formed by lava that's 400,000 years old. Don't forget to look up or you'll miss Pumice Castle, the orange-colored rock formation that looks like, yes, a castle.

Good to Know: Crater Lake Park is snow-covered from October through June. Peak season is between June and August. Crater Lake Lodge (_travelcraterlake.com_) overlooking the lake is a great place to unwind after a full day of swimming, hiking, fishing, and touring.

The Teeniest-Tiniest, Holiest Church: El Santuario de Chimayó, Chimayó, New Mexico, USA

This 19th-century adobe-style church (_holychimayo.us_) is a historical landmark in the foothills of the Sangre de Cristo Mountains in northern New Mexico, which are famous for what many believe to be holy and healing dirt. A sort of American Lourdes, it's one of the most important Catholic pilgrimage centers in the USA, drawing more than 300,000 visitors a year who come seeking deep healing of the mind, body, and spirit. During the Christian Holy Week, pilgrims make the 30-mile (48-kilometer) trek from Santa Fe, and the 90-mile (145-kilometer) journey from Albuquerque, sometimes on their knees. Returning pilgrims leave behind testimonials of the healing power of the dirt, which is dug out of a tiny well named El Pocito Sagrado. Handouts suggest silent prayers to say while rubbing it on the body parts that need it most.

Good to Know: The landmark is an easy drive from Rosewood Inn of the Anasazi (_rosewoodhotels. com_) a warm, cozy spot nestled in the heart of Santa Fe, with Navajo rugs, hand-carved doors, beamed ceilings, and sandstone walls. The city's oldest hotel, Hotel St. Francis (_hotelstfrancis.com_), is beautiful and simple.

Psychic Capital of the World: Cassadaga Spiritualise Camp, Volusia County, Florida, USA

A small community between Daytona and Orlando is home to an unusually large number of psychics and mediums (there's a reason they call this the Psychic Capital of the World) and is heavily infiltrated by paranormal-seeking tourists. (Because, you know, Florida isn't kooky enough.) This spiritualist camp was founded in 1875 by George P. Colby, a trance medium who traveled the country giving readings and séances and was led to the area by his Native American spirit guide, Seneca. Today, the residents practice the religion of Spiritualism, based on the guiding principle of one continuous life.

Good to Know: Cassadaga Spiritualist Camp (_cassadaga. org_) offers guided tours, weekly seminars, tarot card readings, and animal spirit meditations. Cassadaga Hotel (_hotelcassadaga.com_) has a 1920s speakeasy vibe and "friendly" spirits that guests are warned about on the hotel website. Fun fact: The camp is where Bright Eyes wrote the album _Cassadaga_ and what Tom Petty alludes to in his song "Casa Dega."

A Cathedral Without Walls: Red Rock Vortexes, Sedona, Arizona, USA

Known for its ethereal red mountains, towering sandstone buttes, and legendary energy cyclones with intense healing powers, Sedona has long been regarded as one of the most sacred and powerful geographies in the USA. Cathedral Rock, Airport Mesa, Bell Rock, and Boynton Canyon are the four most powerful vortexes, each categorized as having energy that is either "feminine" (energy entering the earth) or "masculine" (energy leaving the earth). Masculine energy is said to strengthen self-confidence and motivation, while feminine energy fosters goodness, patience, and compassion. Some sites are off the beaten path and require a moderate half-day hike that leads to rewarding panoramas of the red rock formations and Native American ruins and cave paintings.

Good to Know: The Chapel of the Holy Cross (_chapeloftheholycross. com_), sitting high atop the red rocks in Sedona, was inspired and commissioned by local rancher and sculptor Marguerite Brunswig Staude after she saw the Empire State Building in 1932. Staude initially attempted to build this in Budapest, Hungary, with the help of Lloyd Wright, son of architect Frank Lloyd Wright. When World War II broke out, she decided to construct the church in her native land instead, protruding from the red cliffs of Sedona in the heart of vortex country. Plan your visit right before it closes (5pm), when the sunset radiates from the red rock's vortex energy and shines through the cross's stained-glass windows. You'll get the best photos and perhaps stumble across an intimate music performance in the tiny chapel.

Center for the New Age (_sedonanewagestore.com_) offers celestial tours at sunset, past life readings, aura photography, and chakra balancing workshops. For an extra dose of good juju, pick up a sage bundle that you can use to clear blocked energy wherever you go. For the para-curious, Sedona UFO Tours (_sedonaufovortexfoodtours.com_) begins with a two-hour meditation walk through the vortexes after sunset, providing special night-vision goggles for a closer look at weird, unexplained activity in the sky.

Opposite: Chapel of the Holy Cross sits atop Sedona's red rocks

This page: feathers and totems from Crystal Magic in Sedona, Arizona

Spiritual Trips in the Wirikuta Desert: Real de Catorce, Mexico

Once a thriving 18th-century silver mining town, Real de Catorce in the desert expanses of San Luis Potosí is one of eleven pueblos mágicos in Mexico, a designation bestowed on towns considered to be extra interesting and, well, magical. The village has attracted pilgrims for centuries, but today it's especially popular with the trippy set who come to try peyote, the backpacker's favorite hallucinogen. Blame Carlos Castaneda's 1968 book *The Teachings of Don Juan*, which told the story of a graduate student who experimented with hallucinogens under the supervision of a Yaqui Indian shaman. Whether it was memoir or fiction remains a mystery, but travelers since have flocked here in search of a life-changing trip from the psychedelic buttons that form on the slow-growing Lophophora williamsii cactus, which is now endangered due to illegal foraging by tourists. The Indigenous Wixárika people believe peyote grants them wisdom and the ability to communicate with the gods, and for more than 6000 years made pilgrimages across thousands of miles from Nayarit, Durango, Jalisco, and Zacatecas to reach the valley of Catorce and leave offerings to Cerro Quemado, the sacred mountain where the cactus grows.

One Man's Painted Heaven: Salvation Mountain, Niland, California, USA

Leonard Knight's self-built 50-foot (15-meter) clay mountain is inscribed with religious passages that focus on a simple message: God is Love. Knight began his sculptural tribute after a hot air balloon journey failed in this patch of the desert near the Salton Sea. He planned to stay for a week, but the project took thirty years to complete and has since become an ever-growing community art collaboration, as Knight encouraged visitors to bring paint and supplies for their own contributions. It is estimated that the mountain has been covered by over 100,000 gallons (370,000 liters) of paint and thousands of hay bales (the basis of the sculpture).

Good to Know: Harvesting peyote is illegal for everyone except the Wixáritari. But Real de Catorce will get you high in other ways through charming architecture, cobblestone streets, roofless mansions, and horseback riding in the high plain deserts.

Good to Know: Rent a desert cruiser bike and head to the Korakia Pensione *(korakia.com)*, a pretty little Mediterranean oasis where you can relax on daybeds by the pool and play bocce in the courtyard.

Devotion rendered in design at Prabhupada's Palace of Gold in West Virginia

Opposite: looking down at Our Lady of the Rockies in Montana

A 10,000-Year-Old Astrology App: Big Horn Medicine Wheel, Lovell, Wyoming, USA

Situated in a forest dating back 10,000 years, this phenomenal large stone structure made from local limestone is a sacred landmark used to predict astrological events. Built by the Plains Native Americans perhaps as long as 800 years ago, it is now protected by the Crow Tribe. The wheel is located at the summit of Medicine Mountain and is said to be a locus point for the balancing energies of the earth, the sun, and the moon. At the center of the wheel is a donut-shaped pile of twenty-eight limestone rocks – twenty-eight being a sacred number associated with the lunar cycle. Today, the Wheel continues to help the Crow predict the summer solstice and represents the beauty of changing seasons and new life.

Good to Know: The site is accessible to visitors only during the summer months. Native Americans have placed prayer flags and other sacred symbolic items around a circular fence that protects the sculpture. It is expected that tourists respect these items and do not disturb.

Sisters of the US: Our Lady of The Rockies, Butte, Montana, USA

A 90-foot (27-meter) statue of the Virgin Mary sits atop the Continental Divide overlooking the city of Butte and 100 miles (161 kilometers) of Montana's peaks and valleys. She's the second-tallest statue in the United States after the Statue of Liberty, and is dedicated to all women, regardless of religion. A secret entrance inside the statue leads to walls covered in letters and mementos left by visitors in memory of their loved ones, along with a memorial wall commemorating thousands of women who have died throughout the world.

Good to Know: The road to the statue crosses private land and is only accessible by bus tour from June to October. A round trip from Butte takes about two-and-a-half hours.

Site of the Sacred and Superstitious: Marie Laveau's Tomb, New Orleans, Louisiana, USA

Of the fifteen "voodoo queens" who reigned in 19th-century New Orleans, Marie Laveau was the most famous priestess of all. A hairdresser by trade, Laveau practiced voodoo – a popular religion based on the melting-pot practices of Catholic, African, and Native American religions in the 18th and 19th centuries – which also involved reading fortunes and selling charms and pouches of gris gris (a mix of herbs, oils, stones, bones, hair, and dirt) for good luck and protection from evil spirits. It was said that politicians, lawyers, businessmen, and wealthy planters all consulted Laveau before making important financial or business-related decisions, and that many runaway enslaved people credited their successful escapes to Laveau's powerful charms. She passed in 1881, and since then believers have paid homage by visiting her grave and scribbling Xs on her mausoleum to pray to her spirit in hopes of having their wishes granted.

Good to Know: Racontours (*racontoursinnola.com*) leads a three-hour New Orleans voodoo tour through the French Quarter, with stops that include the New Orleans Historic Voodoo Museum (*voodoomuseum.com*) and Marie Laveau's final resting place in the St. Louis Cemetery No. 1, the city's oldest. At the Voodoo Authentica cultural center (*voodooshop.com*), you can learn about the history and practice of voodoo, purchase dolls, and have your fortunes told by Laveau's disciples.

SPIRITUAL FOLKWAYS

You probably know about voodoo dolls and the consequences of a single pin poked into one, but beneath this cartoon cultural runoff, voodoo is a complex diasporic religion practiced by enslaved West Africans brought to the Caribbean and Southern United States, blending over time with the beliefs and traditions of French and Spanish Catholics, and, in some cases, incorporating witchcraft. Physical charms, herbs, amulets or gris gris imbued with spiritual powers protect their owner or harm their enemies. Because it was born from the brutality of colonialism and the slave trade, voodoo culture and religion centers around death — and the influence the dead have on the living.

A symbol for the ages in Joshua Tree, California

Opposite: a renegade rock on Racetrack Playa, California

Like a Rolling Stone: Racetrack Playa, Death Valley National Park, California, USA

Racetrack Playa continually bewilders wanderers of California's Death Valley with its mysterious "sailing stones." Due to erosion forces, hundreds of heavy rocks tumble from the surrounding mountains, some weighing hundreds of pounds, rolling and zig-zagging and leaving trails in their wake. The curious phenomenon occurs every few years during rare periods of heavy rain and strong winds, when water washes down from the surrounding mountains and drains into the playa, creating a shallow, short-lived lake that evaporates in the hot desert sun.

Good to Know: The racetrack is located in a remote area of the park and road conditions are iffy, requiring off-roading vehicles and heavy-duty tires. Do not attempt a trip without plenty of fuel and water. You will not want to get stranded, as there is no cell phone service in the area.

Spangled Spirituality: Prabhupada's Palace of Gold, Moundsville, West Virginia, USA

Perched on a hilltop in middle-of-nowhere West Virginia, this glittering, golden Hare Krishna palace (_palaceofgold.com_) appears like a mirage of Indian marigolds. In 1973, devotees of the International Society for Krishna Consciousness, more commonly known as the Hare Krishna movement, planned to build a home for their leader, Srila Prabhupada. But when Prabhupada died unexpectedly in 1977, the disciples' course of construction changed, and, in promise to their leader, they built the elaborate Palace of Gold, which has marble floors, crystal chandeliers, stained-glass windows, wood-carved furniture, and walls covered in 22-karat gold. The young devotees built the palace without blueprints, architects, or artisans, guided instead by a strong spiritual force as they chiseled, cemented, and polished. Wander the grounds to see the impressive rose garden, fountain, and lotus-filled lake.

Good to Know: The palace is open seven days a week from March to December and on weekends in January and February. A short drive takes you to Swan Lake, where you can pose for photos beside a pair of oversized statues of the gods Gaura and Nitai.

SPAS AND ESCAPES FOR BODY AND MIND

Transporting you to the next level.

Lake Austin Spa Resort, Austin, Texas, USA Texas Hill Country meets lakefront paradise with innovative therapies and practices like hydro bikes and water workouts. *lakeaustin.com*

Amangiri, Canyon Point, Utah, USA Mars for famous people. Prepare to empty out your pockets for otherworldly treatments of sage smudging ceremonies, ending with crystal sound baths and Navajo healing amid the wild west of Southern Utah. *aman.com/resorts/amangiri*

Two Bunch Palms, Palm Springs, California, USA An energy vortex where earthquake faults, natural hot springs, mountains, wind, and solar energies all converge. *twobunchpalms.com*

Mii Amo, Sedona Arizona, USA Drift from Chi Nei Tsang and Abhyanga Shirodhara to lymphatic drainage facials, vision board crafting, psychic massage, and Sedona clay wraps. *miiamo.com*

From top: Two Bunch Palms, Palm Springs; Mii Amo in the Sedona sunshine

Opposite, clockwise from top right: woodsy appeal at The Wickaninnish Inn in Tofino; exclusive and elusive Amangiri in Utah; hiking at Mountain Trek Fitness Retreat & Health Spa in British Columbia; the garden at Lake Austin Spa

Ancient Cedars Spa at The Wickaninnish Inn, Tofino, Canada Look out from the steam cave nestled into the rocks on the edge of the forest as Pacific waves lap the shoreline. *wickinn.com*

Miraval, Tucson, Arizona, USA
Transformational healing treatments offer deep cleansing of the physical and spiritual realms. *miravalarizona.com*

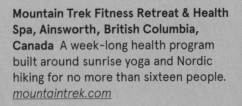

Mountain Trek Fitness Retreat & Health Spa, Ainsworth, British Columbia, Canada A week-long health program built around sunrise yoga and Nordic hiking for no more than sixteen people. *mountaintrek.com*

San Ysidro Ranch, Montecito, California, USA Get massages and treatments on the porch of your casita, surrounded by flowers, sweet scents, and mountain views. *sanysidroranch.com*

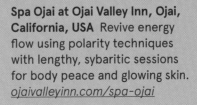

Calistoga Ranch, Calistoga, California, USA A wooded canyon where you'd expect forest nymphs to usher you from mineral hot springs to your treatment room for magic potions made with local mud and sage to detoxify and purify. *aubergeresorts.com/calistogaranch*

Spa Ojai at Ojai Valley Inn, Ojai, California, USA Revive energy flow using polarity techniques with lengthy, sybaritic sessions for body peace and glowing skin. *ojaivalleyinn.com/spa-ojai*

Clockwise, from left: Botánico pool at Dorado Beach, a Ritz-Carlton Reserve; an aerial view of Dorado beach; firepit scene at Two Bunch Palms in Desert Hot Springs, California

Opposite: Two Bunch Palms grotto

Spa Botánico, Dorado Beach, A Ritz-Carlton Reserve, Puerto Rico A twisted 100-year-old ficus tree, canopy of leaves, azure sky, as well as tons of dried herbs and flowers (gardenias, eucalyptus, lavender, sage) perfume your treehouse treatment room. *doradobeach.com*

Ten Thousand Waves, Santa Fe, New Mexico, USA Inspired by Japanese mountain hot spring resorts, with traditional gardens and woodwork in the tranquil foothills of the mysterious Sangre de Cristo Mountains. *tenthousandwaves.com*

4UR Ranch, Creede, Colorado, USA If nature is your therapy, this no-frills dude ranch offers hiking, horseback riding, and hot springs in sublime mountain air. *4urranch.com*

Rancho La Puerta, Tecate, Mexico One of the original destination spas in North America, offering and pioneering the latest in wellness since 1940. *rancholapuerta.com*

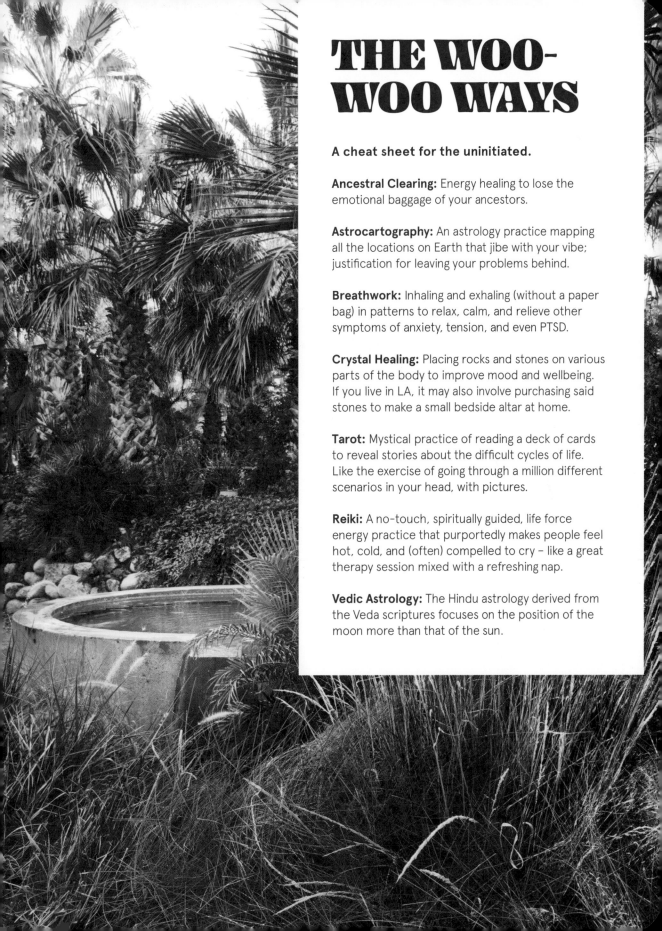

THE WOO-WOO WAYS

A cheat sheet for the uninitiated.

Ancestral Clearing: Energy healing to lose the emotional baggage of your ancestors.

Astrocartography: An astrology practice mapping all the locations on Earth that jibe with your vibe; justification for leaving your problems behind.

Breathwork: Inhaling and exhaling (without a paper bag) in patterns to relax, calm, and relieve other symptoms of anxiety, tension, and even PTSD.

Crystal Healing: Placing rocks and stones on various parts of the body to improve mood and wellbeing. If you live in LA, it may also involve purchasing said stones to make a small bedside altar at home.

Tarot: Mystical practice of reading a deck of cards to reveal stories about the difficult cycles of life. Like the exercise of going through a million different scenarios in your head, with pictures.

Reiki: A no-touch, spiritually guided, life force energy practice that purportedly makes people feel hot, cold, and (often) compelled to cry – like a great therapy session mixed with a refreshing nap.

Vedic Astrology: The Hindu astrology derived from the Veda scriptures focuses on the position of the moon more than that of the sun.

RETREATS FOR SELF-CARE

Ready to go deeper but hoping for a little expert guidance? Start at these centers dedicated to helping you along your inner journey.

Prayer flags at the Shambhala Mountain Center, Colorado

Shambhala Mountain Center, Red Feathers Lake, Colorado, USA

This Tibetan meditation retreat, set high in the Rocky Mountains since 1971 and surrounded by majestic pine and shimmering aspen forests, offers 100 programs a year, from two-day introductions to meditation to week-long deep dives into Indigenous mindfulness practices, love and compassion workshops, and silent retreats. Accommodations vary from sophisticated lodge rooms to shared dormitories and tent-style lodging. The site is also home to the 108-foot-tall (33-meter-tall) Great Stupa of Dharmakaya, one of the largest Buddhist shrines in North America. _shambhalamountain.org_

Spirit Rock Meditation Center, Woodacre, California, USA

Of the many reasons to attend a meditation retreat, the top one might be to chill the heck out. The frazzled should find their way to the woods an hour north of San Francisco, where the programs are based on Buddhist teachings (dharma), insight meditation (vipassana), and loving kindness meditation (metta). Everyone is welcome, as evidenced by programs as brief as two hours and as long as two months. Those who get *really* good at sitting quietly stay more than a year. *spiritrock.org*

Menla, Phoenicia, New York, USA

Surrounded by thousands of acres of Catskills Forest Preserve, this modern Tibetan mountain oasis is the Dalai Lama's cultural center in North America and a wellspring of spiritual offerings. Dewa Spa promises bliss through a full spectrum of Eastern and Western services, from Ayurvedic treatments to herbal baths and massages, and is one of the few places in the West that does Tibetan KuNye massage. Workshops are hosted by renowned Buddhist teachers and healers who guide participants in tantric study, mindful leadership, memoir writing, psychedelic integration, and a no-nonsense exploration of life after death. *menla.org*

From left: meditation circle and Dewa Spa exterior at Menla in New York

A reflecting pool and a Zen pergola at Golden Door in Escondido, California

Ann Wigmore Natural Wellness Institute, Aguada, Puerto Rico

A pioneer of the plant-based diet, Ann Wigmore introduced the world to wheatgrass and organic foods before any millennial walked into Whole Foods. Her method is simple: eat living foods – uncooked, raw, sourced from nature – to nourish and ultimately heal the body. Her Caribbean retreat, established in 1990, takes a deep dive into her nutritional approach with minimal yet comfortable accommodations in a relaxed, tropical setting on a quiet beach on the wild western shores of Puerto Rico. If buzzwords like "night shades," "fermented sprouts," and "bean diets" excite you, you'll love the one-week intensive and two-week immersive retreats that include a total body cleanup with customizable treatment plans of colonics, lymphatic massages, and, of course, a menu chock-full of living foods. At Ann's tropical paradise, the (wheat)grass is truly greener. *annwigmore.org*

Golden Door, Escondido, San Diego, California, USA

California's original destination spa retreat two hours south of LA. Celebrities have loved it since 1958 for the anonymity, but anyone can drop into a personal bubble of privacy in the meditative Zen gardens and escape to next-level nirvana. Days are filled with challenging fitness warm-ups, diving deep into the soul with shamanic healings, Japanese bathhouse sessions, nutrition education classes, and meditative walks through the extensive vegetable gardens. Visits are usually a full, week-long program, with each daily routine mapped out on a paper fan. The activities are optional, yet few skip out on the daily in-room massage. *goldendoor.com*

Shou Sugi Ban House, Water Mill, New York, USA

Shou Sugi Ban House is a comprehensive wellness program with a wabi-sabi design sensibility in the tony Hamptons enclave of Long Island, New York. Inspired by Japanese principles, the space is a mix of lovingly weathered and lived-in environments that are tranquil, minimal, and transcendent. Conditions are perfect for an escape here, as the grounds are open and airy with beautiful landscaping, outdoor spa pools, and a focus on centering and self care. Guests book custom stays and curate a personal itinerary with wellness and fitness activities, advanced skincare treatments, tea ceremonies, heart-stirring sound baths, expert-led workshops, and beautifully prepared organic meals tailored to guests' needs. _shousugibanhouse.com_

Arcosanti, Arizona, USA

If you could design a perfect eco-friendly city from scratch, what would it look like? That's exactly what architect Paolo Soleri set out to do in 1970, creating an experimental micro city in the high desert and basing it on the principles of living in harmony with the natural world, rather than against it. "Urban implosion, rather than explosion" is how he referred to this blending of architecture and ecology to nurture those who live and work there. The resulting solar-powered structures, many of which were built from the roof down, blend with the Sonoran background – and look more than a little like a sci-fi movie set. The city's most striking feature is the apse of the ceramics foundry (an arching semicircle resembling the hollows of Romanesque cathedrals). Since its founding, more than 8000 volunteers have helped contribute to the project – building a futuristic utopia without roads, eating food from adobe greenhouses – and many more have come to Arcosanti's education center for workshops, classes, and to lend a hand on unfinished construction projects. _arcosanti.org_

High desert harmony at Arcosanti in Arizona

Opposite, clockwise from top left: a jungle room at Kalanimua in Hawaii; a teepee at Feathered Pipe Institute in Montana; contemplative morning canoe; a mindful message at Blue Cliff Monastery in the Catskills

Feathered Pipe Institute, Helena, Montana, USA

One of the oldest centers for yoga in the United States is where you'd least expect it: nestled in the heart of the Montana Rockies. This peaceful mountain sanctuary is surrounded by 1 million acres (404,686 hectares) of mountainous wilderness in Helena National Forest, providing more than enough wildlife, fresh air, and vistas to awaken the soul. Guests choose from teepees, glass-domed yurts, tents, and luxurious chalet-style rooms before running from hot tub to sauna or ceremonial lodge by the spring-fed lake. Workshops are held morning and afternoon with ample time built in for hiking, swimming, and wandering through the wildflower meadow. Personal reflection may come naturally near the on-site stupa, a ceremonial Buddhist temple made from dirt, stone, and peaceful offerings, protected by prayer flags. *featheredpipe.com*

Kalanimua Oceanside Retreat, Big Island, Hawaii, USA

Set in the wild jungle of the island's hippie capital, Pahoa, this nonprofit retreat promotes a lifestyle dedicated to nature and wellness – a holistic alternative to traditional pre-packaged beachside resorts. You'll want to stay a while in the secluded cottages and bungalows, surrounded by native plants, organic edible gardens, and colorful original artwork, with frequent trips to the ceremonial lodge. There are no TVs or air conditioning, and the open-air restaurant incorporates fresh, local ingredients into every meal. Classes are centered on Hawaiian culture, with daily activities like lauhala weaving, hula, and dancing. *kalani.com*

Sivananda Ashram, Nassau, Bahamas

The mission and practice at this yoga center are as traditional as can be, based on Swami Vishnudevananda's Five Points of Yoga: proper exercise, breathing, relaxation, diet, and thinking and meditation. What comes as a special bonus is the heavenly Paradise Island location, accessible only by boat. Tucked within dense tropical gardens, with lizards and hermit crabs roaming the tourist-free, white-sand beaches, it's easy to feel as though all of life's problems can be cured by a single tree pose. Which doesn't mean the living is lazy here. The Yoga Vacation Program is full-on, starting at 6am with two hours of silent meditation, chanting, a spiritual talk, and prayers, followed by two hours of yoga and yogic breathing. After brunch, guests can take workshops and classes – or just chill on the beach. At 4pm, the program picks back up with yoga, dinner, and evening meditation. Accommodations are designed to fit all budgets, from self-pitched tents to ocean suites, and month-long teacher training programs are also available. *sivanandabahamas.org*

Blue Cliff Monastery, Catskills, New York, USA
This mindfulness practice and monastic training center was founded by author, peace activist, and Vietnamese Zen Buddhist monk Thich Nhat Hanh. Thay, as he is known to his millions of followers, is praised for his teachings of mindfulness and living happily in the present. The tranquil sanctuary is nestled on 80 acres (32 hectares) of land with pure mountain air and pathways of meandering streams and trails in the Catskills region two hours from New York City. *bluecliffmonastery.org*

THIS SHIT IS BANANAS

Get up to speed on weird stuff happening on the continent.

Area 51: E.T. phones home to the US Air Force base in Nevada that's tied to countless instances of unexplained activity and guarded by extremely high security. The closest you can get is Little A'Le'Inn, a UFO-themed restaurant and bar located in a tiny desert settlement off Nevada State Route 375, a.k.a. the Extraterrestrial Highway.

Bermuda Triangle: An area of the Atlantic Ocean roughly bounded by Miami, Bermuda, and Puerto Rico where ships, planes, and people mysteriously disappear. Navigating these waters can be tricky, as compasses can point to true north instead of magnetic north, potentially disorienting travelers.

Bradshaw Ranch: Visitors equipped with night-vision glasses, binoculars, and telescopes report a staggering number of sightings – orbs, portals, aliens, and even Bigfoot – in the high desert of Sedona, Arizona.

The Crooked Bush: It's a botanical brainteaser why a grove of twisted aspen trees grows over and around each other instead of straight up like every other aspen in the world. Local Saskatchewan legend blames evil waters or other spooky forces, though the truth is closer to a genetic mutation.

Marfa Lights: Glowing orbs hover, twinkle, float, and dart unexpectedly, mystifying viewers of the night sky in West Texas.

Roswell: The heart of the UFO scene since July 1947 when alien conspiracy theorists claimed that remains of a flying saucer, along with dead aliens, crashed on Earth and were taken into storage in New Mexico.

From top: Marfa Lights; the seemingly bottomless Thor's Well in Oregon

Opposite, clockwise from top: Florida's Swamp Rainbow; flying into the Bermuda Triangle; the mobile life in Taos; Area 51

St. Louis Ghost Train: Phantom headlights appear nightly on an abandoned rail line in Saskatchewan. Legend has it the source is the ghost of the conductor, who roams the rails at nightfall with his lantern.

Swamp Rainbow: A psychedelic happening best seen in Florida in February and March, when sunlight breaks through the trees and hits the oils from decomposing leaves at just the right angle.

The Taos Hum: Some folks in the small city in New Mexico are puzzled (and annoyed!) by a faint low-frequency whir in the desert air. No one has yet been able to locate the sound's origin.

Thor's Well: A powerful geyser rages off the coast of Cape Perpetua in Oregon's Siuslaw National Forest, the result of a whirlpool of sea water rushing into a deep sinkhole then violently erupting onto the shore. No one knows exactly what caused this phenomenon. Is it simply a collapsed sea cave ... or a gateway to the underworld?

Tremble Island: A tiny sailor's refuge on the northern tip of Vancouver Island, where strong storms and high tides can cause the entire island to shake violently. Hundreds of signs (some dating back 100 years) hanging from trees recount tales of seamen's haunted nights spent clinging to small bushes to avoid being thrown into the ocean.

CHAPTER 10

TAKE CARE

A pause, by definition, is a break from routine, an interruption of our usual ways of behaving and being. It's fifteen minutes of meditation to start the day, a few deep breaths before making a presentation, counting to ten before telling someone what you *really* think about what they just did.

Previous page: nirvana at
Rockhouse in Jamaica

This page: serenity in bloom in
Sonoma County

The coronavirus pandemic was the pause that nobody wanted – and its ripple effects will be felt for generations to come. We'll talk about this period in history the way we do the World Wars, the Great Depression, and, to cite the most obvious reference, the Spanish Influenza of 1918.

One of the things we were able to do during this unwanted pause is imagine how things could be if we start over.

Imagine what the world would look like if things went right. If we protect the environment and are thoughtful stewards of our natural resources. Connect with and focus on the people we care about. Channel our money and time to the causes and ideas we believe in. Demand that powerful forces (politicians, corporations, special interests) be accountable for inequality and injustice. Realize that more doesn't mean better, that commodities like fast fashion and behaviors like over-tourism extract far too great a cost – and refuse to be part of those patterns and problems. Slow down. Find joy in small pleasures and details that we were too frenzied to notice before.

We will always return to travel. Being forced to stay home only reinforced our desire to go exploring. At the same time, we've never been more aware of how interconnected we all are globally. These are really comforting thoughts in times of uncertainty. We probably won't ever travel again in the same way, but that's no bad thing, since we had been on a path that was a little too fast and furious and careless.

So now we want to wave our magic wand and wish for a new way of thinking and being.

A Manifesto of Hope for the World (and how we move in it):

01

That we travel the world with care, minimizing any unnecessary and harmful impact we may have. We're reminded of that great nature motto: Leave only footprints; take only memories.

02

That we actively play a role in not only minimizing damage but generating growth – engaging in preservation, contributing to local economies, and building cultural connections.

03

That we treat the people we encounter everywhere we go with respect.

04

That we go to fewer places but stay longer, with more focus and intention.

05

That we value experiences over objects.

06

That we leverage our individual power as consumers to make purchasing decisions that make things better, not worse.

07

That we recognize that being able to travel is a great privilege, not a right, and behave accordingly.

08

That when we travel to a place we consider who was here before us, who made it possible for us to enjoy it, and what we can do to support its most marginalized communities.

09

That we do our research in order to challenge stereotypes and leave our colonialist tendencies at home.

10

That we do not forget our connections. And that we share our findings with others.

Do we sound a little too kumbaya, pie-in-the-sky idealistic? We'll cop to the charge. (We're feeling hopeful!) We want the smog to clear forever in Los Angeles, for there to be fewer cars on the road, period, and for our cities (and ourselves) to get a little taste of rewilding. We want everyone to be able to spend quality vacations with loved ones in a beautiful setting, enjoying simple pleasures, like a game of cards and roasting s'mores and telling stories around a fire – things that can't happen if everyone is staring into their devices.

And, perhaps above all else, we want you to go out and explore different places and people and ideas, with an open heart and an open mind and a sense of wonder and joy that lets you step away from your day to day, pause your routine – and do, see, feel something unexpected, wonderful, and new.

Essential Travel Tips and Hacks

The secrets that only travel pros know turn out to be a clever mix of common sense, organization, ingenuity, and small changes. And now you know them, too.

Keep Your Passport Updated.
Check with the country that issued yours for more details. As a general rule, US passports need to show at least six months of validity for international travel. If yours is set to expire before six months, renew it before you leave the country.

Find Out Country Requirements for Entry.
Visit state department or government website of the places you're gong to make sure your visas and vaccines are up to date and that you know of any other regulations that could impact your arrival.

Keep Travel Essentials in One Place at Home.
If you keep the things you always need for a trip (like foreign currency, immunization records, travel blankets, and electrical adapters) in one drawer, you'll never have that "Where's my passport?!" pre-flight panic again.

Invest in a Good Suitcase.
Preferably something with spinner wheels. You want to glide, not lug, your stuff.

Be Easy to Find.
Look into the US Department of State's Smart Traveler Enrollment Program (STEP) or your country's equivalent so your embassy or nearest consulate can contact you in an emergency.

Plan Ahead to Skip the Lines.
For domestic travel within the US, enroll in TSA Pre-Check to make going through security quick and painless. If you travel internationally with regularity, enroll in Global Entry to sail through US Customs. Even better, download the Mobile Passport app and skip the kiosk line, too.

Check Your Data Plan Before Leaving.
Many cell phone companies offer options for staying connected while traveling abroad. Give them a call to find out your options.

Know Your Insurances.
Be clear about the insurance your credit card does and doesn't cover before you leave home or get to the car rental counter. If you travel often, an annual travel insurance policy is an inexpensive investment. If you're going to a potentially dangerous destination, medical evacuation insurance is a really good idea.

Ready to roll

Crowd-Source Travel Advice.
Ask your network – friends, family, Instagram, Facebook – for tips on destinations.

Map In Advance.
On Google Maps, star all the places you want to visit on your trip. Download the map on your phone for easy, offline access.

Read a Novel Set in the Destination You're Visiting.
Immerse yourself in a book about a place while you're there to get a whole new understanding of a foreign culture.

Get Your Emergency Contacts in Order.
Before a trip, make hard copies of your passport, itinerary, prescriptions, and important phone numbers. Keep a set at home and take a set with you. Make digital copies of the same documents: email a set to your parents/BFF/boss and upload them to the cloud.

Update Your App Arsenal.
Think: meditation, workout, map, weather, currency converter.

Make the Most of Your Credit Card.
Get a no-fee version for international charges or an airline-specific card to earn points.

Invest in a Reusable Water Bottle.
There's enough plastic in the ocean.

Stay Charged.
Invest in a portable battery for your mobile phone. And carry it all the time, because phones have a way of dying at the worst possible moment.

Get Electronics for Two.
You'll be everyone's best friend at the lone outlet if you carry an outlet expander. And you and your pal can enjoy the same movie if you have a headphone splitter.

Make Your Luggage Stand Out.
Put tag and/or ribbon on your suitcase to easily identify yours in a sea of black suitcases.

Travel with a Deck of Cards.
Leave it inside your suitcase so you don't have to remember to pack it.

Pack Light.
Plan the clothes you want to take, then only pack half of that. You won't wear it all anyway.

Pack a Go Kit.
What would make your flight or ride more comfortable? Think headphones, ibuprofen, tissues, lip balm, eye drops, a pen, tea bags, gum, hand sanitizer, lotion – and put it all in a small bag for easy access.

Organize with Small Bags.
Pack your things in pouches – shoes, dirty laundry, wet bathing suits, electronics, underwear, and socks – to keep things tidy and easily accessible. Bring an extra tote or zippered bag for souvenirs and in case your suitcase is overcrowded.

Pack Breakables in the Center of Your Suitcase.
Wrap wine bottles in ziplock plastic bags before burying them among your socks and sweaters.

Pack the Dopp Kit Once.
Keep your flight-friendly bag of 3-ounce (100-milliliter) toiletries (toothbrush, toothpaste, shampoo, face wash, deodorant) packed at all times. If you vary your arsenal, keep a master checklist of the products you like to travel with, and you'll never forget anything.

Pack a Scarf.
It does triple duty as a blanket, sun shield, or windbreaker, and it takes up barely any space.

Pack a First Aid Kit.
Bandages for cuts and blisters, melatonin for crossing time zones, antacid for heartburn.

Bring Extra Meds.
If you take prescription drugs, bring more than you need in case your trip is delayed or you get stuck in a destination. And always carry them in your hand luggage.

Download Your Entertainment.
Load shows, songs, and books on your iPad or other devices the day before you travel.

Write Things Down on Paper.
In case your phone battery betrays you, jot down the address and phone number of the place where you are staying.

Divide Your Cash and Cards and Pack a Dummy Wallet.
Keep your money, credit cards, and other important items split between bags and pockets. If you're traveling to a risky destination, carry a fake-out wallet (with a few bills and old cards) that will be easy to give up should a dangerous situation arise.

A good book is essential (the library at Hotel Esencia in Mexico has so many)

Avoid Lost Luggage Panic.
Stash an extra set of underwear, socks, and toiletries, along with a small wad of cash, in your carry-on in case your checked baggage gets lost.

Look Nice When You Travel.
Wear something comfortable but not schleppy to the airport. Shoes that are easy to slip on and off, a few layers and accessories. You do not want to spend ten minutes undressing/dressing at security, and you want to look nice enough to be upgraded.

Get In the Time Zone.
As soon as you get on the plane, set your watch to local time at your destination.

Catch Shut-Eye On the Plane.
For the closest thing to a good night's sleep, wear ear plugs and an eye mask. A neck pillow will save your life on long-haul flights.

Stretch on the Airplane.
Get up and loosen up. When it's time to disembark, limber joints will help you hit the ground running.

Keep Your Phone Tracker On.
For when you lose it.

Have a Plan B With Your Travel Companions.
Talk about scenarios for dealing with emergencies and disasters and determine meeting places and backup plans ahead of time.

Carry Small Change For Tips.
And break big bills as soon as you can.

Walk. Then Walk Some More.
The best way to get to know a new city is by walking through it. See something interesting? Pop your head in, say hello, and start a conversation.

Utilize Public Spaces.
If you want to use a clean bathroom or rest your feet, hotel lobbies can be welcoming and anonymous places. In case of an emergency, front desks are most likely to have English-speaking staff that's well informed. Public libraries are a nice place to take a quick snooze, use free internet, or source information.

Wear Good Walking Shoes.
Vacation is not the time to break in a new pair of shoes.

Save Your Battery.
Set your phone to "low power mode" even if you have 100 percent battery to make it last longer.

Take Pictures. Then Put Down the Camera.
Photos are fun. But some of the best memories are made hands-free.

Make Friends Wherever You Go.
Then you'll always have people to visit, couches to sleep on, dinner tables to sit at, postcards to send, and stories to tell.

Index

1 Hotels 148
4UR Ranch, Creede, CO, USA 260
10th Mountain Division Hut Association, Aspen, CO, USA 169

A Room at the Beach, Bridgehampton, NY, USA 22
Acapulco, Guerrero, Mexico 142
adventure touring supporting local artisans 35
Agua Azul, Palenque Chiapas, Mexico 65
Aguada, Puerto Rico 264
Ainsworth, BC, Canada 259
Alabama, USA 44, 151
Alaskan walruses 97
Albuquerque, NM, USA 218–19
Alida, The, Savannah, GA, USA 131
Allerton Garden, Kauai, HI, USA 27
Almont, CO, USA 165
Amangiri, Canyon Point, UT, USA 258
Amenia, NY, USA 179
Amigo Motor Lodge, Salida, CO, USA 242
Anacostia Park, Washington, DC, USA 159
ancestral clearing 261
Ancient Cedars Spa at The Wickaninnish Inn, Tofino, BC, Canada 258
animal migrations 94–7
Ann Wigmore Natural Wellness Institute, Aguada, Puerto Rico 264
Antelope Canyon, Navajo Nation, AZ, USA 54
Antelope Valley California Reserve State Nature Reserve, CA, USA 79
Anvil, Jackson, WY, USA 241
Anza-Borrego Desert State Park, CA, USA 80
Apostle Islands, The, WI, USA 45
Apostle Islands National Lakeshore, WI, USA 89
Appalachian Trail, USA 18
archaeological sites 68–71, 73
Arches National Park, UT, USA 65, 72
Arcosanti, Arizona, USA 265
Area 51, NV 268
Armstrong Redwoods State Natural Reserve, Sonoma County, CA, USA 66
Arrive Hotels 148
art, American Southwest 214–19
artists' residencies, USA 31, 34, 39
Asbury, The, Asbury Park, NJ, USA 144
Asbury Park, NJ, USA 144
Aspen, CO, USA 169
Assateague Island, MD, USA 96
astronomical events 84, 87, 88
Athabasca University Geophysical Observatory, Edmonton, AB, Canada 89
Atlanta, GA, USA 151, 237
Auberge du Vieux-Port, Montréal, QC, Canada 141
aurora borealis 87, 88–9
Austin, TX, USA 120, 137, 146, 242, 258
autumn activities 86–7
autumn foliage 87
Avella, PA, USA 69
Azulik, Tulum, Mexico 91

Badlands National Park, SD, USA 72
Bahama House, Dunmore Town, Bahamas 22
Baie des Flamands, St. Barts 177
Baja Peninsula, Mexico 95, 223
Baker's Cay Resort, Key Largo, FL, USA 21
Banff, AB, Canada 201, 202, 203, 204
Banff National Park, AB, Canada 19, 66, 205
Barbados for beach babes (mini road trip) 210–11
Barnard, VT, USA 13
Basecamp Hotel, Boulder, CO, USA 180
beach locations 20–5, 210–11
being better travelers 32
Berkerley, CA, USA 157
Bermuda Triangle 268
berry u-picks 83
Betsy, The, Miami, FL 130
Big Bend National Park (Chihuahuan Desert), TX, USA 81
Big Horn Medicine Wheel: A 10,000-Year-Old Astrology App, Lovell, WY, USA 255
Big Island, HI, USA 31, 40, 237, 266
Big Pine Key, FL, USA 21
Big Sur, CA, USA 180, 233
Big Thicket National Preserve, TX, USA 159
Biscayne National Park, FL, USA 158
Blackberry Mountain, Walland, TN, USA 166
Blue Cliff Monastery, Catskills, NY, USA 267
Bluffton, SC, USA 39
BodyHoliday, Cariblue Beach, St. Lucia 179
Boise, ID, USA 15
Boon Hotel + Spa, Guerneville, CA, USA 146
Borrego Springs, CA, USA 227–8
Boston, MA, USA 150, 241
botanical landscapes 26–7
Boulder, CO, USA 180
Bradshaw Ranch, Sedona, AZ, USA 268
Breakers, The, Newport, RI, USA 150
Breakers, The, Palm Beach, FL, USA 43
breathwork (relaxation) 261
Brentwood Hotel, Saratoga Springs, NY, USA 239
breweries 111, 213
Bristol Bay, AK, USA 96
Broad, The, Los Angeles, CA, USA 150
Bryce Canyon National Park, UT, USA 60, 158
Butte, MT, USA 255

cabane à sucre (sugar shack), Eastern Canada 79
Cahokia Mounds, Collinsville, IL, USA 73
Caldera House, Teton Village, WY, USA 166
California Mission Walkers, CA, USA 17
California Missions Trail, CA, USA 17
California wilderness, CA, USA 17
Calistoga, CA, USA 235, 259
Calistoga Ranch, Calistoga, CA, USA 259
Cambria, CA, USA 174
Cambria Beach Lodge, Cambria, CA, USA 174
Canadian Museum for Human Rights, Winnipeg, MB, Canada 151

Canadian Rocky Mountains, Canada 19, 200–5
Candlewood Cabins, Richland Center, WI, USA 15
Cannon Beach, OR, USA 66
Canyon Point, UT, USA 258
Canyonlands National Park, UT, USA 72
Cape Elizabeth, ME, USA 40
Cape Perpetua, OR, USA 269
Cariblue Beach, St. Lucia 179
Carlsbad, CA, USA 227
Carmel by the Sea, CA, USA 234
Casa Faena, Miami, FL, USA 130
Casa Vitrales, Old Havana, Cuba 174
Cascade Range, USA 19
Cassadaga Spiritualist Camp: Psychic Capital of the World, Volusia County, FL, USA 252
Catskill Mountains, NY, USA 12
Catskills, NY, USA 267
Cavallo Point Lodge, San Francisco, CA, USA 128
Cave Hill Farm, McGaheysville, VA, USA 180
Cenotes, Yucatán Peninsula, Mexico 60
Central Coast, CA, USA 232
Central Platte River Valley, NE, USA 96
Chablé Yucatán, Chocholá, Mexico 181
Chaco Canyon, Nageezi, NM, USA 70
Chalk Hill Artist Residency, Healdsburg, CA, USA 34
Channel Islands State Park, CA, USA 158
Charleston, SC, USA 136, 159, 236
Charlie, The, Los Angeles, CA, USA 128
chefs 154–5
Chicago, IL, USA 118, 132, 145
Chicago Athletic Association, Chicago, IL, USA 132
children, traveling with 171
Chimayó, NM, USA 251
Chincoteague Island, MD, USA 96
Chocholá, Mexico 181
Chugach State Park, AK, USA 89
Churchill, MB, Canada 95
cities 116–27
city hotels
    Canada 140–1
    Mexico 142–3
    USA 128–39, 144–7
Claiborne County, MS, USA 153
Clarksdale, MS, USA 236
Clayoquot Wilderness Lodge, Tofino, BC, Canada 176
Cleveland, OH, USA 159
Cloister, The, Sea Island, GA, USA 24
Closson Chase, Hillier, ON, Canada 86
Cobá, Yucatán Peninsula, Mexico 73
Collinsville, IL, USA 73
Congaree National Park, SC, USA 159
conservation project volunteers 33, 36, 38
coral reef health and marine life monitoring 36, 38
Cordova, NM, USA 217
Cosmopolitan, The, Las Vegas, NV, USA 134

Cosmos Saint Lucia, St. Lucia 43
crafts
    Cuba 35
    Mexico 35, 113, 206–9
    see also art
cranberries 87
Crater Lake: The Shaman's Path to Big Blue,
    Klamath County, OR, USA 251
Crater Lake National Park, OR, USA 72
Crawford Hotel, The, Denver, CO 129
Crawford Path, NH, USA 18
Creede, CO, USA 260
Crested Butte, CO, USA 83
Crook County, WY, USA 248
Crooked Bush (aspen trees), The, SK,
    Canada 268
crystal healing 261
Cuixmala, Jalisco, Mexico 167
cult classics 247–55
cultural institutions 150–1
Cumberland Island, GA, USA 45
Cuyahoga Valley National Park, OH, USA 159

Dallas, TX, USA 137
Dean, The, Providence, RI, USA 144
Death Valley, CA, USA 88
Death Valley National Park, CA, USA 72, 257
Denali National Park and Preserve, AK,
    USA 72
Denver, CO, USA 110–11, 129, 158
Detroit, MI, USA 134, 153
Devils Tower: A Sacred Site for Vision Quests,
    Crook County, WY, USA 248
Dinosaur Park, Laurel, MD, USA 56
Dinosaur Provincial Park, AB, Canada 57
donations and giving 46
Dorado Beach, A Ritz-Carlton Reserve,
    Puerto Rico 260
Drake Hotel, The, Toronto, ON, Canada 140
Drake Motor Inn, Prince Edward County,
    Canada 239
Dreamcatcher, The, San Juan,
    Puerto Rico 145
Drift San Jose, San José del Cabo, Baja
    California Sur, Mexico 142
Drifter, The, New Orleans, LA, USA 240
Dropbox 189
Dunmore Town, Bahamas 22
Dunton Hot Springs, CO, USA 93

early human settlements 68–71, 73
Earthship Biotecture, Taos, New Mexico,
    USA. 90
East Hampton, NY, USA 22, 26
Eastwind, Upstate New York, NY, USA 12
eating/meals 154–7
Edmonton, AB, Canada 106
El Santuario de Chimayó: The Teeniest-
    Tiniest, Holiest Church, Chimayó,
    NM, USA 251
El Yunque National Forest, Puerto Rico 65
elders, traveling with 170–1
Eleuthera, Bahamas 22, 173
Emerald Coast, FL, USA 220–1
Encanto Acapulco, Acapulco, Guerrero,
    Mexico 142
Encinitas, CA, USA 227

English in Mind Institute, Port-au-Prince,
    Haiti 36
English language skills development,
    Haiti 36
Esalen Institute, Big Sur, CA, USA 180
Escondido, San Diego County, CA USA 264
Everglades, FL, USA 237

Fairbanks, AK, USA 88–9
fall foliage season, WI, USA 87
farm stays, US Virgin Islands 36
Farmer's Daughter, Los Angeles, CA, USA 147
Feathered Pipe Institute, Helena, MT,
    USA 266
Fiestas de la Vendimia, Valle de Guadalupe
    region, Mexico 84
fireflies 82, 97
Flagstaff, NM, USA 219
Flat Creek Ranch, Jackson Hole, WY,
    USA 39
Flathead National Forest, MT, USA 83
Florida Keys, The, FL, USA 21
Fogo Island Inn, NS, Canada 92
Forestiere Underground Gardens, Fresno,
    CA, USA 27
fossils 53–7, 63
Franconia Ridge, NH, USA 18
Fresno, CA, USA 27

G Adventures (small group tours) 35
Gallup, NM, USA 219
gardens of contemplation 26–7
Geminid meteor shower 88
Generator (hotels) 148
geological wonders 50–63, 65–6
Germain Hotels 148
Ghost Ranch, NM, USA 54
Glacier National Park, MT, USA 72, 83
glamping 183
Glen Canyon National Recreation Area,
    AZ/ UT, USA 72
Golden Door, Escondido, CA, USA 264
Golden Isles, The, GA, USA 24
GoldenEye, Oracabessa, Jamaica 165
Google Docs 189
Graduate Hotels 148
Grand Canyon, AZ, USA 58–9
Grande-Terre, Guadeloupe 17
Great Divide Trail, The, Canada 19
Great Northern Peninsula, NL, Canada 73
Great Sand Dunes National Park and
    Preserve, CO, USA 158
Great White Heron Refuge, Big Pine Key, FL,
    USA 21
green travel 30–47
Greenwich Hotel, The, New York City, NY,
    USA 135
group travel
    planning 184–9
    stuff to bring 186
    tools of the trade 189
    see also trips with friends
Grupo Habita (hotels) 148
Guadalajara, Jalisco, Mexico 143, 154
Guadeloupe Islands 17
Guanajuato, Mexico 113
Guerneville, CA, USA 146

Habitas Tulum, Tulum, Mexico 25
Haleakala volcano, Maui, HI, USA 15
HALL Arts Hotel, Dallas, TX, USA 137
Hampton beaches, Long Island, NY, USA 22
Hanakāpīʻai Beach, Kauai, HI, USA 18
Harbour Island, Bahamas 22
Hasbrouck House, Hudson Valley, NY, USA 172
Hatch chiles, NM, USA 84
Havana, Cuba 153
Hawaiian Legacy Reforestation Initiative,
    HI, USA 31
Hawaiian Volcanoes National Park,
    Big Island, HI, USA 40
Headlands Dark Sky Park, MI, USA 87
Helena, MT, USA 266
Hermosa Inn, Scottsdale, AZ, USA 128
Hierve el Agua, Oaxaca, Mexico 66
Highway 101, CA, USA 17
Hix Island House, Vieques, Puerto Rico 40
hobbies in the wild 67
Honolulu, HI, USA 131
Hot Springs National Park, TN, USA 159
Hotel Alessandra, Houston, TX, USA 137
Hotel Amparo, San Miguel de Allende,
    Guanajuato, Mexico 142
Hotel Carpenter, The, Austin, TX, USA 137
Hotel de la Parra, Oaxaca, Oaxaca de Juárez,
    Mexico 143
Hotel Demetria, Guadalajara, Jalisco,
    Mexico 143
Hotel El Ganzo, Los Cabos, Mexico 42
Hotel Eleven, Austin, TX, USA 146
Hotel Esencia, Riviera Maya, Mexico 174
Hôtel Gault, Montréal, QC, Canada 141
Hotel June 148
Hotel Le St-James, Montréal, QC,
    Canada 141
Hotel Normandie, Los Angeles, CA,
    USA 147
Hôtel Peter & Paul, New Orleans, LA,
    USA 133
Hotel St. Francis, Santa Fe, NM, USA 134
Hotel San José, Austin, TX, USA 146
Hotel Sorrento, Seattle, WA, USA 138
Hotel Valley Ho, Scottsdale, AZ, USA 147
hotels
    city hotels 128–47
    small hotel groups 148–9
houseboats 183
Houston, TX, USA 115, 137, 159
Hoxton, The (hotels) 149
huckleberries 83
Hudson River Valley, NY, USA 172, 224–5
Hump Mountain, TN, USA 18
Hunte's Gardens, St. Joseph Parish,
    Barbados 26

ice caves/ice sculptures 88, 89
Iceberg Alley, NL, Canada 65
Indianapolis, IN, USA 107
Inn by the Sea, Cape Elizabeth, ME,
    USA 40
Integratron: Science Meets Art and Magic,
    The, Landers, CA, USA 247
Isabella Stewart Gardner Museum, Boston,
    MA, USA 150
Islands of Lake Champlain, VT, USA 45

Jackson, WY, USA 241
Jackson Hole, WY, USA 39, 153
Janitzio Island: Communing with the Spirits, Lake Pátzcuaro, Michoacán, Mexico 250
Jardin Escultórico Edward James (a.k.a. Las Pozas), Xilitla, Mexico 26
Jashita Hotel, Tulum, Mexico 25
Jasper, AB, Canada 201, 203, 204
Jasper National Park, AB, Canada 19
Jazzland, New Orleans, LA, USA 153
Jekyll Island, GA, USA 24
Joggins Fossil Cliffs, NS, Canada 53
John Pennekamp Coral Reef State Park, Florida Keys, FL, USA 21
Judd Lake, AK, USA 173
Juluchuca, Mexico 38
Jungle Bay, Soufrière, Dominica 92

Kailua-Kona, Big Island, HI, USA 237
Kalalau, Kauai, HI, USA 18
Kalalau Trail, HI, USA 18
Kalanimua Oceanside Retreat, Big Island, HI, USA 266
Kauai, HI, USA 18, 27, 61, 65
Kauai's Na Pali Coast, HI, USA 18
Keahiakawelo, Lanai, HI, USA 65
Ke'e Beach, Kauai, HI, USA 18
Keint-He Winery, Wellington, ON, Canada 86
Kennett Square, PA, USA 27
Key Largo, FL, USA 21
Klamath County, OR, USA 251
Klemtu, BC, Canada 42
Kootenai National Forest, MT, USA 83
Kootenay National Park, BC, Canada 19

La Bohemia, Todos Santos, Baja California Sur, Mexico 142
La Bohemia Baja Hotel Pequeño, Todos Santos, Mexico 165
La Brea Tar Pits, Los Angeles, CA, USA 63
La Guarida Restaurant, Havana, Cuba 153
Laguna Beach, CA, USA 147
Lake Abraham, AB, Canada 89
Lake Austin Spa Resort, Austin, TX, USA 258
Lake of the Clouds Hut, Mount Washington, NH, USA 18
Lake Pátzcuaro, Michoacán, Mexico 250
Lanai, HI, USA 65
Landers, CA, USA 247
L'Anse aux Meadows, Great Northern Peninsula, NL, Canada 73
Las Alcobas, Mexico City, Mexico 143
Las Pozas, Xilitla, Mexico 26
Las Trampas, NM, USA 217
Las Vegas, NV, USA 134, 158
Lassen Volcanic National Park, CA, USA 158
Laurel, MD, USA 56
leaf-peeping season, Upper Peninsula, MI, USA 87
Legacy Museum, The, Montgomery, AL, USA 151
Lenox, MA, USA 172
Life House Hotels 149
lighthouses (as accommodation) 182
Line, The (hotels) 149

Linville Gorge Wilderness: Grounding Rituals in the Grand Canyon of the East, Marion, NC, USA 248
Little Nell, The, Aspen, CO, USA 129
Little Palm Island, Little Torch Key, FL, USA 21
Little St. Simons Island, GA, USA 24
Little Torch Key, FL, USA 21
Lo Sereno Casa de Playa, Troncones, Mexico 21
locals tours 236-7
Lodge, The, St. Simons Island, GA, USA 24
Lodge at Blue Sky, The, Park City, UT, USA 93
Long Island, NY, USA 22
LongHouse Reserve, East Hampton, NY, USA 26
Longman & Eagle, Chicago, IL, USA 132
Longwood Gardens, Kennett Square, PA, USA 27
Loot, Zihuatanejo, Mexico 21
Los Angeles, CA, USA 63, 119, 128, 147, 150, 157, 158
Los Cabos, Mexico 42
Lovell, WY, USA 255
Lowell, The, New York, NY, USA 177
Lumeria, Maui, Hawaii, USA 15

McAfee Knob, VA, USA 18
McGaheysville, VA, USA 180
Magdalena Bay, Mexico 95
Maidstone, The, East Hampton, NY, USA 22
Maine, USA 18, 40, 44, 102-3
Mainland Ice Caves, Apostle Islands National Lakeshore, WI, USA 89
Maison de la Luz, New Orleans, LA, USA 133
Makauwahi Cave Reserve, Kauai, HI, USA 62
Makeready Hotels 149
Malibu, CA, USA 181, 242
Mammoth Cave, KY, USA 61
Mammoth Cave National Park, Mammoth Cave, KY, USA 61
mangoes, St. Lucia 82
maple syrup 79
Marathon, FL, USA 21
Marfa, TX, USA 214-15, 268
Marfa's Lights, TX, USA 268
Marie Laveau's Tomb: Site of the Sacred and Superstitious, New Orleans, LA, USA 256
Marion, NC, USA 248
Mark, The, New York City, NY, USA 135
Marlton Hotel, The, New York City, NY, USA 144
Mary's Point, NB, Canada 97
Massacre Rim International Dark Sky Sanctuary, NV, USA 84
Maui, HI, USA 15
Meadowcroft Rockshelter and Historic Village, Avella, PA, USA 69
Meadowood Napa Valley, St. Helena, CA, USA 164
Meadows of Dan, VA, USA 90
Mémorial ACTe Museum, Pointe-à-Pitre, Guadeloupe 151
Memphis, TN, USA 124, 159
Mendocino, CA, USA 39
Menla, Phoenicia, NY, USA 263
Meteor Crater, Winslow, AZ, USA 63
meteor showers 84, 88

methane bubbles, Lake Abraham, AB, Canada 89
Mexico City, Mexico 27, 117, 143, 150, 236
Mexico for hungry, crafty creatives (mini road trip) 206-9
Miami, FL, USA 116, 130, 150, 156, 158
Michigan Central Station, Detroit, MI, USA 153
Mii Amo, Sedona, AZ, USA 258
mind and body 244-6
    cult classics 247-55
    retreats for self-care 262-7
    spas and escapes 258-63
    spiritual folkways 256-7
    terminology 261
Minneapolis, MN, USA 154
Minnesota's North Shore for naturalist beer drinkers (mini road trip), MN, USA 213
Miraval, Tucson, AZ, USA 259
mobile homes 182
Mohave Desert, CA, USA 79
Mohonk Mountain House, New Paltz, NY, USA 169
monarch butterflies 95
Montage Palmetto Bluff, Bluffton, SC, USA 39
Montana, USA 44, 72, 83, 255, 266
Montecito, CA, USA 231, 259
Montgomery, AL, USA 151
Montréal, QC, Canada 141
Monument Rocks and Castle Rock, Gove County, KS, USA 56
Monument Valley: Navajo Sacred Land of the Creator, Arizona–Utah Border, USA 250
Morgan Library, The, New York City, NY, USA 150
Mormon Row, Jackson Hole, WY, USA 153
motor lodges (motels) 238-43
Moundsville, WV, USA 257
Mount Katahdin, ME, USA 18
Mount Shasta, CA, USA 249
Mount Shasta: An Alpine Energy Vortex Where Heaven and Earth Meet, Mount Shasta, CA, USA 249
Mount Washington, NH, USA 18
Mountain Trek Fitness Retreat & Health Spa, Ainsworth, BC, Canada 259
Moxy (hotels) 149
Multnomah Falls, OR, USA 88
Murray Springs Clovis Site, Sierra Vista, AZ, USA 69
Museo Dolores Olmedo, Mexico City, Mexico 27
Museum of Anthropology at the University of British Columbia, Vancouver, BC, Canada 151
museums 150-1
Mustang Monument, NV, USA. 91

Na Pali Coast, Kauai, Hawaii, USA 65
Nageezi, NM, USA 70
Napa Valley, CA, USA 164, 234-5
Nashville, TN, USA 112
Nassau, Bahamas 266
National Center for Civil and Human Rights, Atlanta, GA, USA 151
National Museum of African-American History and Culture, Washington, DC, USA 151

national parks
    art residencies, USA 31
    on the big screen 72
    Canada 19, 66
    USA 40, 53, 60–1, 62, 65, 66, 72,
        80, 81, 83, 97, 158–9, 257
nature 65–7, 76–7
    by the seasons 78–87
    near American cities 158–9
    painters and sculptors of 64
    staying close to 90–3
Navajo Nation, AZ, USA 54, 250
Negril, Jamaica 41
New England autumn foliage, USA 87
New Hampshire's White Mountains, NH,
    USA 18
New Orleans, LA, USA 104, 133, 153, 157, 240
New Paltz, NY, USA 169
New York City, NY, USA 126, 135, 144, 150,
    177, 237
Newfoundland, Canada 65, 73, 237
Newport, RI, USA 242
Niland, CA, USA 254
Nimmo Bay Wilderness Resort, BC,
    Canada 90
Nobu Ryokan, Malibu, CA, USA 242
NoMad Hotels 149
Norman Hardie Winery, Wellington, ON,
    Canada 86
North Adams, MA, USA 167
North Cascades National Park, WA, USA 159
Northern Lights 87, 88–9
Nova Scotia for lobster lovers (mini road
    trip), NS, Canada 194

Oahu, HI, USA 31
Oakes Gulf, Mount Washington, NH, USA 18
Oaxaca, Oaxaca de Juárez, Mexico 66,
    143, 206–9
ocean protection and monitoring 33, 36, 38
Ojai, CA, USA 231, 259
Olas, Tulum, Mexico 25
Old Havana, Cuba 174
Old Mesilla, NM, USA 216
Oracabessa, Jamaica 165
Orcas Island, WA, USA 45
Other Side, The, Eleuthera, Bahamas 173
Our Lady of The Rockies: Sisters of the US,
    Butte, MT, USA 255

Pacific Coast, CA, USA 226–35
Pacific Crest Trail, Mexico to Canada 19
Pacific Edge Hotel, Laguna Beach, CA,
    USA 147
Pacific grey whales 95
Palenque Chiapas, Mexico 65
Palisociety (hotels) 149
Palm Beach, FL, USA 43
Palm Springs, CA, USA 228, 258
PAMM | Pérez Art Museum Miami, Miami, FL,
    USA 150
Pando Aspen Grove, Richfield, UT, USA 65
Papahānaumokuākea Marine National
    Monument, HI, USA 33
Paradise Beach Nevis, Nevis 167
Park City, UT, USA 93
Peñasco, NM, USA 217

Pendry (hotels) 149
Perseids meteor shower 84
persimmon harvest, IN, USA 87
Petit Ermitage, Los Angeles, CA, USA 128
Philadelphia, PA, USA 155, 156
Phoenicia, NY, USA 263
Phoenix, AZ, USA 219
Pictured Rocks National Lakeshore, MI, USA 66
Pink Sands, Harbour Island, Bahamas 22
Piton Mountains, The, St. Lucia 66
Playa Viva, Juluchuca, Mexico 38
Point Resort, The, Saranac Lake, NY, USA. 91
Pointe-à- Pitre, Guadeloupe 151
Pointe des Châteaux Trail, Guadeloupe 17
polar bears 95
Portland, ME, USA 102–3
Portland, OR, USA 136
Prabhupada's Palace of Gold: Spangled
    Spirituality, Moundsville, WV, USA 257
Presidential Traverse, NS, USA 18
Primland, Meadows of Dan, VA, USA. 90
Prince Edward County, Canada 239
Providence, RI, USA 144

Queens, New York City, NY, USA 237
Queen's Bath, Eleuthera, Bahamas 22
Quinta Real Zacatecas, Zacatecas, Mexico 176
Quirk Hotel, Richmond, VA, USA 138
Quonochontaug Pond, Westerly, RI, USA 14

Racetrack Playa: Like a Rolling Stone, Death
    Valley National Park, CA, USA 257
rail bike contraption, Catskill Mountains, NY,
    USA 12
Ranch, The, Malibu, CA, USA 181
Rancho La Puerta, Tecate, Mexico 260
Real de Catorce, Mexico 254
Real de Catorce: Spiritual Trips in the
    Wirikuta Desert, Real de Catorce,
    Mexico 254
Red Feathers Lake, CO, USA 262
Red Rock Vortexes: A Cathedral Without
    Walls, Sedona, AZ, USA 253
Redwood National Park and State Parks, CA,
    USA 72
reiki 261
responsible giving 46
restaurants 154–7
Restoration, The, Charleston, SC, USA 136
retreats for self-care 262–7
Richfield, UT, USA 65
Richland Center, WI, USA 15
Richmond, VA, USA 138
Ridge to Reef, Saint Croix, US Virgin
    Islands 36
Riviera Maya, Mexico 168, 174
road trips 190–3
    American Southwest for art
        pilgrims 214–17
    Baja Peninsula for epicureans 223
    California's Pacific Coast for
        hedonists 226–35
    Canadian Rockies for chionophiles 200–5
    Florida's Emerald Coast for families
        220–1
    mini trip itineraries 194–99, 206–13
    New York's Hudson River Valley for

    serial weekenders 224–5
Robey, The, Chicago, IL, USA 145
Rockhouse, Negril, Jamaica 41
romantic interludes 172–7
Room at the Beach, A, Bridgehampton, NY,
    USA 22
Rosewood Mayakoba, Riviera Maya,
    Mexico 168
Ryo Kan, Mexico City, Mexico 143

Saguaro National Park, AZ, USA 80
Saguenay Fjord, QC, Canada 17
Saguenay Fjord Trail, QC, Canada 17
St. Helena, CA, USA 164, 235
St. Joseph Parish, Barbados 26
St. Louis Ghost Train, SK, Canada 269
St. Lucia 43, 66, 82
St. Simons Island, GA, USA 24
Salida, CO, USA 242
Salt Hotels 149
Salt Lake City, UT, USA 158
Salvation Mountain: One Man's Painted
    Heaven, Niland, CA, USA 254
San Diego, CA, USA 226
San Francisco, CA, USA 125, 128, 158
San Ignacio Lagoon, Mexico 95
San José del Cabo, Baja California Sur,
    Mexico 142
San Juan, Puerto Rico 145
San Miguel de Allende, Guanajuato,
    Mexico 113, 142
San Ysidro Ranch, Montecito, CA, USA 259
Sandbanks Provincial Park, Picton, ON,
    Canada 86
sandhill cranes 96
Sandman, The, Santa Rosa, CA, USA 241
Santa Barbara, CA, USA 231, 239
Santa Fe, NM, USA 134, 216–17, 260
Santa Rosa, CA, USA 241
Santuario de la Mariposa Monarca el Rosario,
    Michoacán, Mexico 95
Saranac Lake, NY, USA. 91
Saratoga Springs, NY, USA 239
Savannah, GA, USA 121, 131
scallop collecting, FL, USA 83
Scammon Lagoon, Mexico 95
Scottsdale, AZ, USA 128, 147, 219
Sea Island, GA, USA 24
Sea Ranch, The, Sonoma County, CA, USA 14
Sea Ranch Chapel, Sonoma County, CA,
    USA 14
seasons, for mingling with nature 78–87
Seattle, WA, USA 108, 138, 159
Sedona, AZ, USA 253, 258, 268
Shambhala Mountain Center, Red Feathers
    Lake, CO, USA 262
Shinola Hotel, Detroit, MI, USA 134
shorebirds, Mary's Point, NB, Canada 97
Shou Sugi Ban House, Water Mill, NY,
    USA 265
Sian Ka'an Biosphere Reserve, Tulum,
    Mexico 25
Sierra Club (environmental organization),
    USA 33
Sierra Nevada's, CA, USA 19
Sierra Vista, AZ, USA 69
Sip Sip, Harbour Island, Bahamas 22

Sister City (hotels) 149
Sisters, OR, USA 168
sitting still 12–15
Sivananda Ashram, Nassau, Bahamas 266
Skwachàys Lodge Hotel & Gallery, Vancouver, BC, Canada 140
Skyride, Catskill Mountains, NY, USA 12
Skyview Los Alamos, Santa Barbara, CA, USA 239
small hotel groups 148–9
social media hashtags 189
solo travel 178–81
Sonoma County, CA, USA 14, 66
Soufrière, Dominica 92
South Dakota, USA 44, 72
Spa Botánico, Dorado Beach, A Ritz-Carlton Reserve, Puerto Rico 260
Spa Ojai at Ojai Valley Inn, Ojai, CA, USA 259
spas and escapes for body and mind 258–63
Spirit Bear Lodge, Klemtu, BC, Canada 42
Spirit Rock Meditation Center, Woodacre, CA, USA 263
spring activities 78–81
Springer Mountain, GA, USA 18
Squamish, BC, Canada 236
Stanford Inn, Mendocino, CA, USA 39
Staten Island, NY, USA 153
Staten Island Boat Graveyard, Staten Island, NY, USA 153
summer activities 82–4
sustainability 38–43, 47
Suttle Lodge, Sisters, OR, USA 168
Swamp Rainbow, FL, USA 269

Tabard Inn, Washington, DC, USA 138
take care 270–3
Taos, NM, USA 90, 217–18
Taos Hum, The, NM, USA 269
tarot 261
Taylor River Lodge, Almont, CO, USA 165
Tecate, Mexico 260
tents (glamping) 183
Teotihuacán, Teotihuacán, Mexico 70
Teton Village, WY, USA 166
Texas Hill Country for Retrophiles (mini road trip), TX, USA 197
Texas Hill Country Wildflower Trail, TX, USA 81
The Alida, Savannah, GA, USA 131
The Apostle Islands, WI, USA 45
The Asbury, Asbury Park, NJ, USA 144
The Betsy, Miami, FL 130
The Breakers, Newport, RI, USA 150
The Breakers, Palm Beach, FL, USA 43
The Broad, Los Angeles, CA, USA 150
The Charlie, Los Angeles, CA, USA 128
The Cloister, Sea Island, GA, USA 24
The Cosmopolitan, Las Vegas, NV, USA 134
The Crawford Hotel, Denver, CO 129
The Crooked Bush (aspen trees), SK, Canada 268
The Dean, Providence, RI, USA 144
The Drake Hotel, Toronto, ON, Canada 140
The Dreamcatcher, San Juan, Puerto Rico 145
The Drifter, New Orleans, LA, USA 240
The Florida Keys, FL, USA 21
The Golden Isles, GA, USA 24

The Great Divide Trail, Canada 19
The Greenwich Hotel, New York City, NY, USA 135
The Hamptons, NT, USA 22
The Hotel Carpenter, Austin, TX, USA 137
The Hoxton (hotels) 149
The Integratron: Science Meets Art and Magic, Landers, CA, USA 247
The Landing, Harbour Island, Bahamas 22
The Legacy Museum, Montgomery, AL, USA 151
The Line (hotels) 149
The Little Nell, Aspen, CO, USA 129
The Lodge, St. Simons Island, GA, USA 24
The Lodge at Blue Sky, Park City, UT, USA 93
The Lowell, New York, NY, USA 177
The Maidstone, East Hampton, NY, USA 22
The Mark, New York City, NY, USA 135
The Marlton Hotel, New York City, NY, USA 144
The Morgan Library, New York City, NY, USA 150
The Other Side, Eleuthera, Bahamas 173
The Piton Mountains, St. Lucia 66
The Point Resort, Saranac Lake, NY, USA. 91
The Ranch, Malibu, CA, USA 181
The Restoration, Charleston, SC, USA 136
The Robey, Chicago, IL, USA 145
The Sandman, Santa Rosa, CA, USA 241
The Sea Ranch, Sonoma County, CA, USA 14
The Surfjack Hotel + Swim Club, Honolulu, HI, USA 131
The Taos Hum, NM, USA 269
The Verb, Boston, MA, USA 241
The Wayfinder, Newport, RI, USA 242
Thompson Zihuatanejo, Zihuatanejo, Mexico 21
Thor's Well, Cape Perpetua, OR, USA 269
Tlaxcala, Mexico 82
Todos Santos, Baja California Sur, Mexico 142, 167
Tofino, BC, Canada 176, 258
Tordrillo Mountain Lodge, Judd Lake, AK, USA 173
Toronto, ON, Canada 140
Tourists, North Adams, MA, USA 167
trains 183
travel tips and hacks 274–5
Tremble Island, Vancouver Island, BC, Canada 269
trips with friends 164–9
    see also group travel
Troncones, Mexico 21
tropical forest health 31
Troutbeck, Amenia, NY, USA 179
Truchas, NM, USA 217
Tucson, AZ, USA 123, 219, 259
Tulum, Mexico 25, 91
Turtle Hospital, Marathon, FL, USA 21
TWA Hotel, Jamaica, New York City, NY, USA 135
Twin Farms, Barnard, VT, USA 13
Two Bunch Palms, Palm Springs, CA, USA 258

unconventional accommodation 182–3
under-touristed spots 44–5
Underwater Coral Reefs, Bonaire 66

Upper Peninsula, MI, USA 87
urban areas 102–15
Urban Cowboy (hotels) 149
urban ruins 153

Valle de Guadalupe region, Mexico 84, 223
Valley of Fire State Park, NV, USA 158
Vancouver, BC, Canada 122, 140, 151
Vancouver Island, BC, Canada 269
Vedic astrology 261
Venice Beach, CA, USA 231
Venmo 189
Verana's, Yelapa, Mexico 13
Verb, The, Boston, MA, USA 241
Vermont for Yankee enthusiasts (mini road trip), VT, USA 198
Vieques, Puerto Rico 40
Volcano House Cabins and Campsites, Big Island, HI, USA 40
volunteering, conservation projects 33, 36, 38
Volusia County, FL, USA 252

walking trails 16–19
Wallace, LA, USA 151
Walland, TN, USA 166
Washington, DC, USA 138, 151, 155, 159
Water Mill, NY, USA 265
waterfalls 58, 65, 88, 201, 205, 233, 249
Waterton Lakes National Park of Canada, AB, Canada 19
Wayfinder, The, Newport, RI, USA 242
Weekapaug Inn, Westerly, RI, USA 14
weird phenomena 268
Westerly, RI, USA 14
Whatsapp 189
Wheatleigh, Lenox, MA, USA 172
Whitney Plantation, Wallace, LA, USA 151
wild horses 96
wildflowers 79–81, 83
Windsor Ruins, Claiborne County, MS, USA 153
wineries/wine festivals 84, 86, 223
Winnipeg, MB, Canada 151
Winslow, AZ, USA 63
winter activities 88–9
Woodacre, CA, USA 263
Woodlark, Portland, OR, USA 136
Wrangell-St. Elias, AK, USA 66

Xilitla, Mexico 26

Yelapa, Mexico 13
Yellowstone Caldera, Yellowstone National Park, WY, USA 62
Yellowstone National Park, WY, USA 62
Yoho National Park, BC, Canada 19
Yucatán Peninsula, Mexico 60, 73

Zacatecas, Mexico 176
Zihuatanejo, Mexico 21
Zion National Park, UT, USA 53, 72

Acknowledgments

We wrote this book in the throes of a global pandemic, when the word "unprecedented" was tossed around to describe the day's news – every day. Throughout, we remained focused on the horizon, on the long term. We hope we can help guide the way to a hopeful and happy future.

This book – and indeed the whole Fathom project since its inception more than a decade ago – is bound by a shared sense of adventure, discovery, and generosity. It's one thing to find something amazing – a grandma-run restaurant, a heart-pumping surf break, a moving sculpture in a city park. It's another thing to want to share it with the world. Fathom is for, by, and about collective sharing.

Our award-winning website is as strong and beloved as it is because of contributions from a world of interesting and engaging travelers. Their discoveries helped inspire and inform this book. Thank you Sarah Abell, Andrea Bartz, Linda Cabasin, Jessica Cantlin, Malika Dalamal, Jillian Dara, Tiffany Davis, Kate Donnelly, Christina Ohly Evans, Meghana Gandhi, Maria Olson Goins, Adam Graham, Natasha Hecher, Sally Horchow, Elizabeth Johnson, Lanee Lee, Christine Lennon, Jamie Lewis, Crystal Meers, Carrie Molay, Celeste Moure, Emily Nathan, Ruby Nichols, Jesse Oxfeld, Anna Petrow, Abigail Radnor, Manon Reuter, Jessica Ritz, Becs Sanders, Antonio Sersale, Sally Spaulding, Jeffrey Sulman, Jean Tang, Heather Taylor, Stephanie Vermillion, and Suzanne Weinert.

We're especially thrilled that this book includes contributions from the Team Fathom diaspora: Becky Cheang, Delfina Forstmann, Rachel Kurlander, Tess Falotico LaFaye, Helena Madrid, Karsten McVay, and Kim VanderVoort.

We are particularly grateful for the work of Fathom editors Berit Baugher and Daniel Schwartz, whose years of personal journeys, connections, and shared stories strengthened the backbone of this company.

California Chaney made incredible contributions to the writing and production of this book – and is an invaluable part of the team. (And yes, she radiates as much sunshine as her name suggests.)

Fathom as a company wouldn't be possible without the ongoing support and counsel of John D'Aquila, Juliana Jaoudi, Stephanie March, Kenneth McVay, Maciej Pelc, Bob Pittman, Mayo Stunz, and Elliot Wadsworth.

Thank you to the Hardie Grant team across the globe. We can't wait to land in Australia to shower champagne all over Jane Grant, Melissa Kayser, Megan Cuthbert, Rosanna Dutson, Stephanie Moon, and Grace Jensen. We'll stop en route in Edmonton to pick up our editor, Allison Hiew, to join the party.

As for our next adventures, we look forward to taking them with the people we most want next to us on the journey: our family. Thank you for everything Justin, Gemma, Roman, and Navy Carter; Jennifer Slepin; the Gerbas; and Ben Schott. Giacomo Rosati, we will drink the best bottle of wine in your memory.

Finally, we save our most special thanks to our readers for exploring the world with us. We want to know what you're up to, so please find us on Instagram @FathomWaytoGo and tag your adventures #TravelwithFathom.

About the authors

Pavia Rosati

Pavia took her first plane journey at nine months old when her Italian mother took her to meet her grandparents at their villa outside Venice, a trip she repeated every year until college. As a result, her American classmates thought she was too Italian ("Where did you get those shoes?") and her Italian aunts thought she was too American ("You're so bold!"). Other early, formative trips took her to pre-Perestroika Russia, where she learned to travel light, and post–Berlin Wall Prague, where she learned to travel without a guidebook.

A voracious and tireless explorer, she has spent her career covering culture, entertainment, food, and travel, taking special pride in seeing it all to report on the things worth knowing. Old homes and kitchens hold a keen interest to her, because how we live the day-to-day speaks volumes about who we are and where we came from. She's happiest sitting around a dining room table in animated conversation with new and old friends.

Jeralyn Gerba

Part pragmatist, part nostalgist, and wholehearted enthusiast of the irreverent, Jeralyn grew up in a house filled with books – history, fiction, science, reference – that stoked her curiosity for people, places, and things. She started traveling when she finally made enough money from summer jobs to do so, and, while based in New York City for university, she also studied art history in Italy, politics and society in South Africa, and food culture in Louisiana, among other things. She started writing about art, culture, nightlife, food, and items people make by hand, and figured out that she was happiest when comparing and collecting those observations with others.

She was hooked on visiting cities until she started hiking volcanoes, swimming in lagoons, and bicycle riding through rustic, unpaved lands. These days, her favorite destinations are places on the verge of change – probably because they are a visceral reminder that nothing is static, provide an opportunity to capture transformation in the making, and force her to embrace the unknown. For Jeralyn, travel feels the best when a challenge is met with a breakthrough and a homemade snack on the other side.

So far, Jeralyn and Pavia have visited three continents together and six separately. They have countless more journeys to log.

Published in 2021 by Hardie Grant Travel, a division of Hardie Grant Publishing

Hardie Grant Travel (Melbourne)
Building 1, 658 Church Street
Richmond, Victoria 3121

Hardie Grant Travel (Sydney)
Level 7, 45 Jones Street
Ultimo, NSW 2007

www.hardiegrant.com/au/travel

A catalogue record for this book is available from the National Library of Australia

Hardie Grant acknowledges the Traditional Owners of the country on which we work, the Wurundjeri people of the Kulin nation and the Gadigal people of the Eora nation, and recognises their continuing connection to the land, waters and culture. We pay our respects to their Elders past, present and emerging.

Travel North America (and Avoid Being a Tourist)
ISBN 9781741177497

10 9 8 7 6 5 4 3 2 1

Publisher Melissa Kayser
Project editor Megan Cuthbert
Editor Allison Hiew
Editorial assistance Rosanna Dutson
Proofreader Lyric Dodson
Design George Saad
Typesetting Hannah Schubert
Index Max McMaster

Colour reproduction by Hannah Schubert and Splitting Image Colour Studio

Printed and bound in China by LEO Paper Products LTD.

Photo credits Images are courtesy of the following photographers and businesses: (Letters indicate where multiple images appear on a page, from top to bottom, left to right)
Front cover: Monument Valley: Gerson Repreza/Unsplash
Back cover: Oahu: Josh Miller/Unsplash; Rocky Mountain National Park: Evan Wise/Unsplash; Chablé Yucatán: Chablé Hotels
Primland iv, 90b; Eleven Experience 4a, 167a,b; Davis Gerber 4b, 167a,b; Twin Farms 11a, 13a; Oliver Olsson 11b; Michael Greco 12a, 224a; Lawrence Braun 12b; Laura Austin 13b; Sonoma County Tourism 14; Peter Godshall 15a; Christina Hussey 15b; Guadeloupe Islands Tourism Board 16b; Jean Hodgens 20a; Natasha Lee 20b, 25a; Tanveer Badal 20c, 23, 25b, 170, 175, 275; Thompson Zihuatanejo 20d; Sea Island 24; Longwood Gardens 26a,b; Benjamin Curtis 27, 159; Visit Montana 30, 44a,b, 255; Spencer Spellman 32; Steven Veit 33a; Elana Dweck 33b, 81; G Adventures, Inc., 34(all), 35; Warnecke Ranch & Vineyard 37a,b; Andrew Kearns/Playa Viva 37c; Emily Winiker 37d; Kevin Steele/Playa Viva 38; Kayla Mendez/Playa Viva 39; Inn by the Sea, ME 40, 41a,b; Rockhouse 41c, 273; The Breakers

Palm Beach 42; John Czornobaj 43a; Jack Plant 43b; Spirit Bear Lodge 43c; Visit Montana 44a,b; Emily Hall Dorio 45a; South Dakota Department of Tourism 45b; Tom Till 52; Wally Haye/Tourism Nova Scotia 53; Patrick Rojo/Tourism Nova Scotia 55; James Orr/New Mexico TRUE 57; The Arizona Office of Tourism 61; Meteor Crater 63; Utah Office of Tourism 67, 72, 250a; Viktoria Wakefield/North Grove Creative 69a; Meadowcroft Rockshelter and Historic Village 69b; Dan Monaghan/New Mexico TRUE 71a, 216, 218a,b, 219a,b; Paul Evans/New Mexico TRUE 71b; Richard Schultz 74, 79, 85; Jeremy Koreski 77, 82, 89a, 90a, 94a,b; Travel Texas 78, 196d; Jeralyn Gerba 80a, 83b, 127d, 210a, 210b, 211a, 211b, 211c, 218c, 253, 274; The Point 83a, 91a,b; Angelo Mitchell/New Mexico TRUE 84; Destination Ontario 86a,b; Sam Featherstone 92a, 93b; Fogo Island Inn 92b; Dunton Destinations 92c, 93a,c; Stephen Kent Johnson 98, 132(all); Daniel Schwartz 100a, 103a,c, 106, 107c,d, 117b, 237b, 282; Aaron Cohen/Canadian Museum of Human Rights 100b; Frasca Food and Wine 100c; Provenance Hotels 100d; Irvin Serrano/Press Hotel 103b; Rush Jagoe 104; DKM Photography/Idaho Shakespeare Festival 105; Visit Indy 107a; Dauss Miller 107b; Nick Jurich 109a,d; The State Hotel 109b; Jessica Cantlin 109c,e; Jeff Wells/Visit Denver 110; Stephanie Grado 111a; Evan Semon/Visit Denver 111b; James Dewhirst/Clyfford Still Museum 111c; RebeccaTodd/Visit Denver 111d; The Neighborhood Dining Group 112a; Nashville Convention & Visitor Corp 112b; Casa Dragones Tequila 113; Ray Viator Photography 114a; Kuhl-Linscomb 114b; Visit Houston 114c; Menil Archives, The Menil Collection, Houston 114d; Grupo Contramar 117a; Bloom & Plume 119a; Adam Alexander Photography 119b; Douglas Friedman 120; Chia Chong 121a,b; Visit Tucson 123a,b; Allen Gillespie/Memphis Convention Visitors Bureau 124; Eric Wolfinger 125a; Dora Tsui 125b; Julia Gillard 127a; Pete Deevakul/Morgenstern's Finest Ice Cream 127b; The Odeon 127c; The Hermosa Inn 129a; Kodiak Greenwood/Cavallo Point Lodge 129b; Jeremy Swanson/The Little Nell 129c; The Betsy - South Beach 130a,b; Casa Faena 131a; Andrew Thomas Lee 131b; The Surfjack Hotel & Swim Club 131c; Thomas Hart Shelby 133a; Christian Harder 133b; Heritage Hotels & Resorts 134a; TAO Group Hospitality 134b; Nicole Franzen 135a, 171b, 225e; King and Partners 135b; David Mitchell/TWA Hotel 135c, 139e; Alex Lau 136a, 139c; Jeremy Fenske 136b; Provenance Hotels 137; Betty Clicker Photography 138; Alba Fuentes 139a; Hotel Sorrento 139b; Chris Dibble 139d; The Drake 140; Chloé Crane Leroux 141a; Hôtel Gault 141b,c; Christian Harder 144a; Nikolas Koenig 144b, 149a; Nesha Torres 145a,c; Adrian Gaut/GRUPO HABITA 145b,d; ; Hannah Koehler 146a,b; Kelly Puleio 146c,d; Hotel Valley Ho 147a,b; Michael Kleinberg 148a; The Ingalls 148b; Steve Freihon 149b; Graham S. Haber/© The Morgan Library & Museum 150; Pavia Rosati 152, 232a, 233, 271; Steve Legato 154, 156b; Jennifer Chase 155; Link Restaurant Group: Cochon 156a; Karla Garcia/Mandolin Aegean Bistro 156c; Gentl and Hyers 157a,c; Emma Poling 157b; ; Clayoquot Wilderness Lodge 160, 164a; Island Outpost 162, 179, 188; Brandon Cole/Tordrillo Mountain Lodge 164b, 177; Caldera House 166; Natalie Puls/The Suttle Lodge & Boathouse 168; Mohonk Mountain House 169; AJ Meeker/The Suttle Lodge & Boathouse 171a; Story & Gold Photography 172a; Clean Plate Pictures 172b; Wheatleigh 173; Cheval Blanc 176a,b, 186; Chablé Hotels 178a; BodyHoliday Saint Lucia 178b, 189; Ali Kaukas 180; Paul Barbera 181a,b; Paul Joyner 182a; Collective Retreats 182b; Rocky Mountaineer 183a; Bailey Made 183b; Nick Simonite 189, 243c,f; Cody Johnson/New Mexico TRUE 192; Tess Falotico LaFaye 195(all); Rancho Pillow 196a,b,c; Woodstock Inn & Resort 199a,b,c,f; Jodi Whalen 199d; California Chaney 200b, 201a,b, 202a, 205b,d; Viktoria North, North Grove Creative 200c; Fairmont Banff Springs 202b; Paul Zizka 203a; Fairmont Jasper Park Lodge 203b; VIA Rail Canada 204a; Noel Hendrickson/Banff & Lake Louise Tourism 205c; Eduardo Plaschinski Drijanski 206b; Undine Pröhl/GRUPO HABITA 207a,b, 209; Erick Romo Balconi 208a; Thad Hutton 208d; Donald Judd, 15 untitled works in concrete, 1980-1984. Permanent collection, the Chinati Foundation, Marfa, Texas. Photo by Florian Holzherr, courtesy of the Chinati Foundation. Donald Judd Art © 2020 Judd Foundation / Artists Rights Society (ARS), New York, 214; Tim Trumble 215; Visit South Walton 221(all); Alejandro Alarcón/La Villa del Valle 222; Francine Zaslow 225a; Kit Chaney 225b; Ben Fitchett 225d; Jay Sinclair/Visit Santa Barbara 226b, 227a, 235b; Juliana Jaoudi 226c, 229a; Aaron Echols/Santa Barbara Adventure Co. and Visit Santa Barbara 227b; Kodiak Greenwood/Post Ranch Inn 229b,d; Parker Palm Springs 229c; San Ysidro Ranch 229e, 230f, 232c; Paige Campbell 230a; Ojai Valley Inn 230b; Hotel Californian 230c,d; Schoenholz/© 2018 J. Paul Getty Trust 230e; Marcie Gonzalez 234; Angie Smith 235a; Vox Media LLC 236a; Anna Petrow 236b, 237a; Marsha Tulk 237c; Michael Graydon and Nikole Herriott 238, 239a,b; Skyview Los Alamos 240a,b, 241; Read McKendree 243a,b,d; Mikael Kennedy 243e; Rosie Serago 245; The Integratron 246; Carl Rice 247; Visit NC 248a; Jeff Caven/Heritage Hotels & Resorts 250b; Rosewood Inn of the Anasazi 251; Sedona Chamber of Commerce & Tourism Bureau 252; WV Tourism 254; Jessie Chaney 256; Dylan + Jeni 258a, 260c, 261; Mii Amo 258b; Michael Becker for Wickaninnish Inn 259a; Lake Austin Spa Resort 259b; Mountain Trek Fitness Retreat & Health Spa 259c; Aman 259d; Dorado Beach, a Ritz-Carlton Reserve 260a,b; Corey Ruffner 262; Nina Choi for Tibet House US | Menla Retreat 263a,b; Rhiannon Taylor 264a,b; Jessica Jameson/The Cosanti Foundation 265a,b,c; Angel Lemaster 267a; Zane Williams 267b,d; Phap Khong/Blue Cliff Monastery 267c.
From Unsplash: Josh Hild iii, 3; David Rupert 5; Thomas Kelley 6; Isaac Wendland 9; Alain Bonnardeaux 16a; Jason Flaherty 19a; Evelyn Mostrom 19b; Malte 19c; Evan Buchholz 28; Claudia Altamimi 47; USGS 49; Andy McCune 51a; Dino Reichmuth 51b; Evan Sanchez 58; Julie Froelich 64; Justin Campbell 80b; David Wirzba 88; Vincent Guth 89b; Alex Guillaume 96; Sarah Cottle 97; Marco Tjokro 122; Dan Larson 185; Sergio R 191; Dennis Buchner 193; Kevin Wiegand 199e; Bantersnaps 200a; Touann Gatouillat Vergos 206a; Christopher Czermak 206a; Lorraine Mojica 206a; T Bortolus 206c; Analuisa Gamboa 208b; Max Böhme 208c; Linda Holman 212; Samantha Gades 212a; Luke Wass 212c; Luke Tanis 212d; Martin Robles 217; Robert Bye 224b; Nevin Johnson 225c; Jared Murray 226a; George Cox 232b; Bryan Goff 248b; Jeff Finley 249; Urip Dunker 257; Leonardo Corral 268a; Eric Muhr 268b; Steven Ford 268a; Ramy Kabalan 269b; Dustin Belt 269c; Daniel Burka 269d.

MAP OF
NORTH AMERICA